all about fabrics

AN INTRODUCTION TO NEEDLECRAFT

GCSE edition

Stephanie K. Holland

Oxford University Press

OXFORD
UNIVERSITY PRESS

Great Clarendon Street, Oxford OX2 6DP

Oxford University Press is a department of the University of Oxford.
It furthers the University's objective of excellence in research,
scholarship, and education by publishing worldwide in

Oxford   New York

Auckland   Cape Town   Dar es Salaam   Hong Kong   Karachi
Kuala Lumpur   Madrid   Melbourne   Mexico City   Nairobi
New Delhi   Shanghai   Taipei   Toronto

With offices in

Argentina   Austria   Brazil   Chile   Czech Republic   France   Greece
Guatemala   Hungary   Italy   Japan   Poland   Portugal   Singapore
South Korea   Switzerland   Thailand   Turkey   Ukraine   Vietnam

Oxford is a registered trade mark of Oxford University Press
in the UK and in certain other countries

© Stephanie K. Holland 1985
GCSE edition 1987
ISBN 978 0 19 832755 4

30 29 28 27 26 25 24 23 22 21

Acknowledgements

Illustrations are by Sheelagh Bowie, Pat Capon, Jill Feld, Lynne Riding

The publishers would like to thank the following for permission to reproduce photographs.

p. 5 t. Chris Honeywell, Photographers' Workshop. b. Shirley Institute; p. 6 t. The John Hillelson Agency
Ltd.; b. The National Trust; p. 7 l. to r. Camera Press. Sally and Richard Greenhill, Camera Press; p. 12.
The Photo Source; p.13 James Mackie and Sons Ltd.; p. 14 Camera Press; p 18 l. to r. Rex Features, The
Photo Source, Camera Press; p. 19 Chris Honeywell, Photographers' Workshop; p. 22 Chris Honeywell,
Photographers' Workshop; p. 30 Sally and Richard Greenhill; p. 31 Victoria and Albert Museum; p. 43
Courtaulds Ltd.; p. 47 Joanne O'Brien/Format Photographers Ltd.; p. 49 International Wool Secretariat;
p. 54 Silk Association; p. 55 Silk Association; p. 57 Camera Press; p. 58 l. Rex Features, r. Alastair Black;
p. 64 t. The John Hillelson Agency Ltd.; b. Mary Evans Picture Library; p. 66 William Hollins and
Company Ltd.; p. 70 Courtaulds Ltd.; p. 77 Chris Honeywell, Photographers' Workshop; p. 78 Chris
Honeywell, Photographers' Workshop; p. 80 Shirley Institute; p. 81 Shirley Institute; p. 84 Fisons Scientific
Equipment; p. 93 Chris Honeywell, Photographers' Workshop; p. 91 International Wool Secretariat; p. 88
Lever Brothers Ltd.; p. 89 Lever Brothers Ltd.; p. 123 t Chris Honeywell, Photographers' Workshop; b.
Mary Evans Picture Library; p. 126 The Singer Company (UK) Ltd.; p. 127 l. Frister and Rossmann, r. The
Singer Company (UK) Ltd.; p. 129 Viking Husqvarna; p. 131 Frister and Rossmann; pp. 133, 136, 151, 164,
166, 173, 179, 180, 182, 183, 184, 186, 200 Chris Honeywell, Photographers' Workshop.

The publishers would like to thank the Clothing Workshop for their assistance.

The publishers would also like to thank the following examination boards for permission to include
questions from examination papers

Associated Examining Board (AEB)
Associated Lancashire Schools Examining Board (ALSEB)
East Anglian Examinations Board (EAEB)
East Midland Regional Examinations Board (EMREB)
North West Regional Examinations Board (NWREB)
Scottish Examination Board (SCE)
South-East Regional Examinations Board (SEREB)
Southern Universities Joint Board (SUJB)
University of Cambridge Local Examinations Syndicate (UCLES)
University of London University Entrance and School Examinations Council (London)
University of Oxford Delegacy of Local Examinations (OLE)
Welsh Joint Education Committee (WJEC)
Yorkshire and Humberside Regional Examinations Board (YHREB), formerly Yorkshire Regional
    Examinations Board and West Yorkshire and Lindsay Regional Examining Board.

The author would like to thank her father for all his hard work in typing the manuscript.

Phototypeset by Tradespools Limited, Frome, Somerset
Printed in Great Britain by Bell & Bain Ltd., Glasgow

Preface

All about fabrics is suitable for candidates working towards GCSE examinations in Home Economics: Textiles.

The book contains eight chapters, each of which is divided into a number of self-contained double-page units. Each unit deals with one particular topic in detail and ends with questions designed to reinforce understanding of the main teaching points. Notes made from answers to these questions can serve as a basis for future revision. Each chapter ends with a section of further work, including practice in answering examination questions.

Much of the text, particularly in the first few chapters, is of a simple experimental and practical nature. The symbol ▲ indicates a practical activity, observation exercise, or investigation, designed to increase the students' understanding of the topic. The students learn about the qualities which fibres possess, and those added during production and finishing, and they are then helped to match those qualities with what they want from a fabric when it is used for a particular purpose.

The first chapter examines some readily-available fibres and looks at how they are spun and woven into fabric. The second looks in more detail at weaving and knitting. In the third chapter each fibre is examined in detail and its properties are related to its uses. Tests for identifying fibres are included.

Chapter 4 discusses how to care for fabrics according to their properties and finishes and what to look for when choosing fabrics and clothes. Chapter 5 moves on to patterns and includes activities for experimenting with scale pattern pieces. Modern sewing equipment and repair aids are reviewed in Chapter 6, while the final two chapters cover in detail the various processes involved in the construction of clothing and household items.

The GCSE edition gives guidance on problem solving, design and evaluation, and on investigative procedures in textile work. These skills are developed further in the complementary book **All about creative textiles**.

All about fabrics combines the study of textiles with the practicalities of needlecraft and aims to help the student, through an understanding of the properties of fibres and fabrics, to make the right choices in evaluating and selecting fabrics, and constructing and caring for clothes.

Contents

Glossary

RS	right side of fabric
WS	wrong side of fabric
SG	straight grain
FL	fitting or seam line
CB	centre back
CF	centre front
NP	neck point
SP	shoulder point
r.h.	right hand
l.h.	left hand
▲	Activity

Chapter 1

From fabric to fibre

This wedding dress is made of silk.

What is fabric?

Fabric is a vital part of our world. Since early times people have used fabric for both clothing and shelter. The earliest fabrics were the furs or skins of animals. They were used for **warmth**, to cover the body or to lay on the floor of the cave for comfort in sleeping. For **shelter** skins were used as a roof-covering to keep out rain, or hung at the opening of the cave to keep out wind and cold.

Plants were used too. Grasses, straw, and reeds were woven into roofing to provide protection from the elements. This simple type of roof was the forerunner of the thatched roof still used today. Grass skirts, still seen in the Pacific Islands, were one of the earliest and simplest forms of dress. As civilization progressed, people discovered the natural fibres around them and learned to twist them into yarns and weave them into fabrics.

Gradually simple weaving techniques were discovered and applied to fibres. Interweaving reeds makes a good shelter; interweaving finer fibres makes fabric.

Simple pieces of flat fabric appeared and have been used in all cultures throughout history. Later, people learned to add shape to clothes, but flat pieces of fabric are still widely used: for example, for the baby's shawl, the sheet, the blanket, the simple cloak, the nun's coiffe, and the bridal veil.

The traditional Indian dress is called the **sari**. It is a simple length of fabric woven from the thread of the silkworm's cocoon. This silk, beautifully coloured with natural dyes, is wound around the body and draped in elegant folds.

As civilization progressed, people began to use fabrics as a decoration for their homes. Fabrics can teach us about the people and their lives. The ornate wall hangings from earlier centuries – a feature of many castles and stately homes today – were a symbol of wealth, and depicted the family's interests, their travels, and the battles they had fought in. The type of material people dressed in also showed their rank. Silks and fine fabrics were worn by the upper classes, but cheaper cottons and rough materials by the lower classes.

Fabric has always been used as a medium to convey messages about a person, their status in a tribe or family, their religious beliefs, their trade or profession, their age, their financial state, possibly even their political persuasion, their school, and their interests.

Can you think of more examples?

Fabric also indicates something about a person's character: whether they want to be noticed by choosing a vivid colour or pattern, or to remain in the background in a neutral or less noticeable colour. Nowadays people even put messages on their clothes expressing their attitude to life.

Questions

1 **Name four ways (other than those mentioned above) in which a flat piece of material is worn as an item of clothing (at any stage in life).**
2 **Give some examples of how a person's rank in their job or profession is shown by what they wear.**
3 **How is a person's age shown by their clothes? Does everyone always want to show their true age? Give some examples of how people might use clothes to give the wrong impression of their age.**
4 **How do people show their sporting or other interests by the way they dress?**
5 **White is the colour traditionally worn at weddings. On what other occasions are clothes of a particular colour used to reflect a particular mood or event?**

Working with fabrics

Fabrics are part of our world, our home, and our family life, but we do take them for granted.

▲ Do this simple exercise. Then look at the comments below.
1 List each garment you have on, or fabric item you have used today.
2 Why did you *choose* to wear or use it today?
3 What fabric is it made of?
4 What qualities has that fabric that makes it good to wear or use?
The first question is easy.

What were your answers for question 2? You were late and it was handy? You liked the colour? It's part of the uniform? Did you make a conscious decision at all?

Try looking at the label to answer question 3.

Did the qualities of your fabric match those that you expected from it? Did it have, for example, warmth, absorbency, safety, or wearability?

Getting dressed is the first simple problem of the day. We usually make a hurried decision, or don't even bother to think. Yet textiles are our barrier against the elements, and sometimes give protection in our work. They are very important for our health, safety, and personal comfort.

Choosing

▲ We consciously or subconsciously use what we wear to create an impression. Think about the impressions you like to create with your clothes. Here are some words: sporty, macho, casual, outrageous, individual, smart.

Do you like the same clothes, designs, and colours now that you did, say, three years ago? Have your views changed with age? Consult with the rest of the group. Did the boys make the same answers to question 2 as the girls? Do age and sex make any difference to people's views? If you like a garment and find it attractive to look at, the garment is said to have **aesthetic appeal**.

To solve a problem of choice easily:
1 Identify the individual **human needs** ⟶ Who uses the item, why, and how?
2 Match them with the **material factors** ⟶ What is the best size/fabric/design? Is it safe to use and make?

The first part of this book deals with the qualities that fibres possess. It then proceeds to match these qualities with human needs when choosing and buying.

In the second part you find the techniques used to make things from fabric. This section helps you to choose the most efficient process, i.e. the one that is within your capability, and gives the best result in the shortest time. Now let's look at how we might set about solving a problem.

Problem solving

Whenever you make an item in textile work you are solving a design problem. The table opposite shows you the steps you need to go through to understand the problem. The problem you are given is called your **brief**, for example, design a draught excluder.

You need to ask yourself the following questions when presented with a brief. The answers to these questions will help you to write a **design specification**.

Human needs	Affects of human needs	Examples of material factors
Who will wear it? use	Age – stage of growth changing tastes – aesthetics physical ability/ disability Sex –body shape interests	size and shape design of fabric fastenings (type and position) design features design and fabric
Why would they wear it? use	Function	design features – pockets fabric qualities – strength, warmth
Where would it be worn? used	Climate Effect of fabric on person	effect on fabric – fading in sun, rotting in damp absorbency, coolness or warmth
When will it be worn? used	wear and tear comfort storage	durability of fabric texture (avoid static cling) creasing, resistance to moths, damp
How will it be worn? used made	Pressure or strain on any part	close weave, warp grain for strength, stretch fabric if required, choice of seams and processes in using and making

Design specification

The material factors shown above specify exactly the requirements that the fabric and design must meet. The problem is beginning to look solvable!

When you have understood the problem the next steps to take are as follows:

1 **Research and investigation.** Use this book, your previous knowledge, and other sources to find possible fabrics, designs, and size.
2 **Experiment** with fabrics to check their suitability. Use the evidence to make a choice of design and fabric. Estimate quantities.
3 **Make a plan of action.** Consider the equipment available, the suitable processes, the fabric, your time, your ability. Plan the order of construction.
4 **Realization.** Make the item.
5 **Evaluation.** When you are designing and making your item keep checking that it meets the specification. When you have made the item write a report on it including your mistakes and what you have learned.

These stages come up again and again throughout textile work, so remember them! Now begin by experimenting with fabric.

Experimenting with fabric

A **sarong**, worn by men and women in Java and Malaya, is a length of fabric tucked around the waist or just below the arms. Can you think of any other examples of native or national dress that are composed of a simple length of fabric?

▲ You can make a very simple beach dress from a flat piece of fine material such as polycotton lawn, 1.4 metres long. Wrap it round your body just below the arms, bringing the top left corner to meet the top right corner at the back of the neck, tying them in a neat knot.
Adjust the length by tying a cord around the waist.
Now you see how easy it is to shape a beach dress, so turn the two raw edges in finely, machine them, and you have a useful addition to your wardrobe for the summer.
Can you think of any other use for a simple length of fabric in the house?

▲ Try doing the same thing with a large linen tablecloth, a cotton sheet, a blanket, or any other thicker, heavier fabric. You will find that the dress does not hang well.

Each fabric drapes differently. The weight of the fabric is one reason for this. But if you look closely at the fabric you will see threads are visible. They either criss-cross each other (**weaving**) or interlock with each other (**knitting**).

Fabrics hang differently depending on whether (and how) they are woven or knitted. The method of construction gives fabrics other qualities too, as we shall see in Chapter 2. But the thickness of the thread used to make the fabric, and how that thread is made up from the raw fibre, really begins the story of how fabric is made. A **fibre** is one of the thin strands of which animal and vegetable matter are made. By examining the threads in fabric more closely, we can find out about fibres.

Fabric to fibre

▲   Take some small scraps of wool, linen, and cotton fabrics. Use a magnifying glass or hand lens to look at them more closely.

1   Tease out a thread from a fabric with a pin.
> What do you notice about it? Does it appear twisted?

2   Untwist the thread gently.
> Is it made up of fine fibres?
> How many fibres make up the thread?
> How long is each fibre?

3   Look at your other scraps and tease out a thread from each fabric.
> Are the threads from each fabric made up of the same number of fibres?
> Are all the fibres the same length when teased out?

You will have found that a thread may be made up of any number of hair-like fibres which are twisted together. But why are fibres twisted together?
To find out:

4   Untwist the fibres which make up the thread of each fabric.
> Are the fibres twisted tightly or loosely? Compare them.

5   Pull the thread teased out from each fabric to try to break it.
> Are the tight twists stronger than the loosely twisted ones?

You will have found that the twisting of fibres gives them strength. The tighter the twist, the better the fibres hold together, and so the thread is stronger.

Wool fibres

In the last activity you used three different fibres. But the same fibre may be made into fabrics with quite different characteristics. Try comparing threads using scraps from three different fabrics all made from wool.

Worsted is used for men's trousers, ladies' skirts, and suits. It is a fine wool which presses well into smart clothes.

Tweed is a thicker material used for warm, more casual clothes.

Knitting wool is used for everything knitted, from soft babywear to thick sweaters, according to the thickness of the wool.

▲   From each of these fabrics tease out a thread and compare the tightness of the twist, the number of fibres, and the length of the fibres in each case.

Worsted is made of long fibres tightly twisted together. It makes a strong, fine fabric, for the tight twist gives the fibre strength.

Harris tweed is made of shorter fibres (known as **staple fibres**) and so does not have the fine smooth appearance of worsted, though the hairiness retains air, and thus it is a warmer fabric to wear.

Knitting wool is made of a number of fibres twisted into threads or yarns. Two, three, or four yarns are twisted together loosely to form a 2-, 3-, or 4-ply wool. Because the threads are twisted only loosely together, air is held between them, and this gives wool certain qualities such as the ability to hold in body warmth and the ability to hold water.

    From our study of wool fibre we therefore realize that it is the way in which a fibre is made into a yarn which gives it the qualities of strength, warmth, and absorbency, as well as the structure of the actual fibre itself, as we shall see later in Chapter 3.

Finding a fibre

Long ago, people learned to find the natural fibres around them and to weave them into fabrics. You can do this too. **Flax** and **wool** are both natural fibres.

Flax

Flax grows in the moist cool parts of Belgium, Central Europe, and Russia. It is cultivated to make **linen**. The flax plant grows to about one metre high and the stem is best used after the blue flowers have withered away. After harvesting the stems are 'retted' or soaked so that the outer part rots away, revealing the fibres inside.

Flax

In New Zealand flax grows wild. An old Maori craft still seen there today involves scraping the leaf of the flax plant with a mussel shell to reveal the fibres, dyeing some red and black, and then weaving them into traditional Maori garments.

▲ A type of flax plant is quite common in Britain. It grows wild. As it is quite an attractive bush it is often found in public parks, school grounds, and gardens. Get permission to pick a leaf. Don't take the stem as this would spoil the bush. However it is the **stem** that is actually used for linen production. Experiment by scraping the leaf with a knife or sharp shell, like the Maoris do, until a fibre appears.

Traditional Maori garments

You will notice that the fibres, being natural, are uneven, and this is a feature of linen cloth. Compare a piece of linen cloth with a piece of nylon – a man-made fibre.

What do you notice about the **texture** – is it even or uneven?

What do you notice about the **feel** – is it rough or smooth and slippery?

Because the linen fibres are rougher and more uneven they do not lie together so neatly when woven, and water can get between them. This is one reason why linen is absorbent and is used for tea-towels. Fine linen is also used for handkerchieves. Can you think why?

▲ Tease out a thread from a piece of linen material. Pull it.

Does it break? Does it stretch?

Soak the thread and pull it again.

Does it break? Does it stretch?

You will notice that linen is a strong fibre. It is even stronger when it is wet.

Wool

▲ Wool has always been a material readily available to man. On a moorland walk or in the countryside you may come across raw wool caught on a bush or wire fence against which a sheep has rubbed. Collect some and examine it closely. If you cannot find any, look at some cotton wool (a raw cotton fibre).

Notice the texture. Raw wool feels rather like greasy cotton wool. This is because **lanolin**, the natural oil from the animal's skin, is present. This gives the wool the waterproof quality that the animal needs for protection against the elements. It is removed by washing or scouring after shearing, and is used commercially to make ointments and cosmetics.

The raw wool you find will be rather matted, like cotton wool, but the fibre from either can be teased out by gentle brushing with a tooth-, nail- or hairbrush. This is a simple form of the **carding** process used commercially to make the mass of fibres run the same way.

Just as we brush our hair to remove tangles, condition it, and make it lie straight, so wool is carded or brushed. As we then comb it to give it a neater style, so the extra process of **combing** is done when the fibres are required to be straighter, more even, and have a better **lustre** (a smooth surface reflecting light). Wool is not generally combed because its characteristic hairy structure is pleasant and warm to the touch. However if it is used for finer or more expensive fabrics such as worsted, where the fibres are longer and must all be exactly parallel to give a compact even texture, it is combed. Sewing cotton of course has to be very even in thickness, and so that too is combed, as are the better qualities of fine cotton fabric.

Carding machine

Notice the parallel fibres that appear through gentle brushing. They are of different lengths, but are all relatively short. This is known as **staple fibre**. Staple fibre can be up to about 25 cm long. Wool, cotton, and linen, in fact all the natural fibres except silk, are staple fibres.

Questions

1 **Flax grows wild in Britain. Where is it cultivated for linen production?**
2 **What is lanolin? How is it useful (a) to the animal, (b) to people?**
3 **Fibres are usually carded. Why are fibres for worsted fabric combed too?**
4 **Why are fibres for sewing cotton combed?**

Spinning and weaving

Simple spinning

Twist some fibres together between your fingers and you will find that you are making a yarn. Staple fibres are held together by the twisting of the yarn.

If you twist from left to right it is known as an **S twist** – the way the letter S goes. If you twist from right to left it is known as a **Z twist** – the way that the letter Z is written.

Twisting the fibres not only binds them together but it gives strength. This is the process known as **spinning**. By twisting the fibres together you have spun a simple yarn. If yarns are twisted together, even more strength is given. This is called a **ply yarn**. The twisting together of the yarns should be done in the opposite way to the original fibre twist to avoid the yarn untwisting and knotting up.

This explains how knitting wool is produced and why it is called 2-ply, 3-ply, and 4-ply according to the number of yarns twisted together.

Fibres are twisted or spun in this way to make thread – the tighter the twist, the stronger the thread, and the finer it becomes. But if fibres are overtwisted, the yarn is weakened and may break. A loose twist will give a softer, thicker thread which is not so strong, for although the fibres do not break, they can slip apart when pulled. Spinning the fibres tightly binds them together better.

Weaving

weft

warp

The **warp** threads will run the length of the fabric when it is woven. A strong tight twist is spun for the warp threads, because they are exposed to pull in weaving. More loosely spun threads are suitable on the **weft** – that is those threads that will run across the warp. This gives the fabric a better feel. If a **nap** is to be brushed up, then the looser spun yarn in the weft can be used to raise the surface. A nap is a slight furriness on the surface.

▲ Tease out and compare the warp and weft threads of some cotton fabrics with nap, such as brushed denim or winceyette.
Look at them carefully with a magnifying glass or hand lens and untwist them. You should notice that the warp threads, those running parallel with the selvedge, are more tightly spun than the weft threads.

Identifying staple fibres

All natural fibres except silk are short staple fibres, though linen fibres are longer than wool and cotton. You can tell whether a fabric is made from staple fibre or not by holding it over your finger at eye level. If there are tiny hair-like fibres sticking up from the surface on either side, it has been made of staple fibre. At eye level you can also tell which is the right and wrong side of wool, cotton, or linen fabrics. Unless a nap surface has been deliberately raised on the right side, the side with the most fibres sticking up is the wrong side; the right side is the smoother side.

Continuous filament

Some fibres are not short staple fibres but are produced as a continuous filament, and therefore have a smooth surface. The silk worm, the larva of the silk moth, spins a cocoon by exuding (pushing out) a long filament and winding the thread around itself. It then pupates in the cocoon with the intention of hatching into a silk moth. But humans, prizing the silk, intervene, for the filament is a continuous fine thread of about a mile in length. It has been used since early times to weave into a fine fabric. During this century, synthetic fibres have been produced in a similar way by extruding nylon, polyester, or viscose from small holes in a spinneret (see p.70) and thus producing a continuous filament.

Making a continuous filament
▲ You can see the smooth nature of a synthetic by making a nylon thread.
1 Put some scraps of nylon, cut up very small, into a small metal tin.
2 Heat **gently** over a gas jet or a **firmly** held candle until the nylon melts. Put a lolly stick into the treacly liquid that forms and draw it away. You will find a nylon thread sticks to it which will set as it cools down with the air around it. Notice the feel of the thread. It is absolutely smooth.

Questions

1 **Why are fibres spun?**
2 **What is meant by a 'Z-twist' and an 'S-twist'?**
3 **What is the difference between 2-ply and 4-ply wool?**
4 **Which are the natural fibres?**
5 **Which of the natural fibres are staple fibres?**
6 **Which natural fibre is a continuous filament, and how is this different from a staple fibre?**

Finishes to yarns

Sometimes finishes are applied to yarns to give them a particular quality before they are woven or knitted into fabric.

Finishes to man-made fibres

The feel of a man-made fibre can be improved when continuous filament is cut into short lengths and made into staple fibre so that it becomes less regular. Synthetic fibres can be given bulk, which will enable them to stretch and recover well, and also make them warmer to handle. This can be done in several ways.

Twisting

▲ Wind a length of nylon thread around a knitting needle. Place it under a sheet of paper and iron with a hot iron (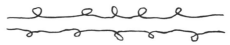), turning the needle to heat all the fibre right round it. Remove the thread from the needle. You will find that the thread has become twisted like a corkscrew. Now wash it. You will find that the thread remains twisted. This is the principle used when man-made fibres are twisted, heated, and cooled, and then made into fabrics such as Helanca and Courtolon. This makes them suitable for bathing suits, surgical stockings, and ski-pants, where elasticity is important.

Knit-de-knit

A similar process is used when a filament is knitted and heated and then unravelled. This is known as the knit-de-knit process. When it is knitted into fabric for outerwear the fibre has bulk and a crêpe-type finish, though it is not as elastic as the twisted fibre.

Crimping

The warm fibre is crimped by being bent over metal and then left in hot water. This makes it more stretchy when it is woven or knitted into fabric.

Looping

Another method, which does not use heat, is when a jet of compressed air makes some filaments loop and gives an uneven texture when the fabric is woven.

Mercerizing

This is a finish applied to natural fibres to make them smoother. Cotton and linen fibres are not smooth. In fact cotton fibres are twisted and they lack lustre. When raw yarn or fabric is put into a bath of caustic soda and stretched out, the fibres swell, untwist, and become smooth and round. As they swell they shrink lengthways. This treatment is called **mercerizing**. After rinsing, the tension is released and the yarn or fabric is stronger, smoother, has a lustre, is more absorbent, and takes dyes better.

Blending

Sometimes two fibres of different types are spun together into yarn so that the qualities of one can improve the other. This is called **blending**. Nylon and wool can be blended together to improve strength. Men's pure woollen socks are likely to wear into holes as the heel rubs against the shoe in wear, but nylon resists rubbing and so blended wool and nylon socks last far longer. (Wool gives warmth and absorbs sweat; nylon gives strength.)

Polyester and cotton can be spun together. Cotton absorbs moisture but polyester does not, so the blended fabric will dry much more quickly after washing than pure cotton would. The more polyester in the blend the quicker the fabric dries.

There are several other reasons for blending fibres into yarns:

1 A crimped appearance can be given when the fabric is finished if a mixture of acrylic staple fibres are spun together. (Some of these shrink easily at this stage in production and others don't.) In the hot finishing process those fibres capable of shrinking do so, causing the yarn or the fabric made from it to crimp. This gives warmth and bulk to the fabric.
2 All fibres do not take up dyes equally, so when two fibres are spun together and then dyed, an interesting effect is produced. This is known as **cross-dyeing**. What do you think happens?
3 As we saw by heating a synthetic fibre on a knitting needle, man-made fibres can be heat-set into creases. So a fabric of polyester and worsted or polyester and cotton can be set into pleats better than a natural fibre alone.

Unions

Blending is when two or more fibres or yarns are **spun** together.
Mixing is done during weaving. Sometimes one fibre is used for the warp, for example cotton, and another fibre for the weft, for example wool. This is called a **union** and is cheaper than a pure woollen fabric. Cross-dyeing gives a different effect.

Questions

1 **Why are finishes sometimes applied to yarns before weaving or knitting?**
2 **What does a continuous filament feel like to the touch?**
3 **What qualities might a man-made continuous filament lack?**
4 **What is the object of cutting continuous filament into short lengths to make staple fibre?**
5 **How can synthetic fibres be given bulk?**
6 **What is blending?**
7 **What are the reasons for blending fibres together?**
8 **What is a union, and how is it produced?**

Further work on Chapter 1

1 Look at some pictures of wall hangings, or better still, visit a castle and see the tapestries. What information do you get from them about their owners – their interests, battles, travels and so on?

2 Look in the library at illustrated books about life in other countries. What do the clothes tell you about the people, their way of life, status, religion? Do they tell you anything else?

3 Look in the history section of the library and find an illustrated book showing clothes through the ages. What do they tell you about the status and way of life of the people depicted?

4 Look at the clothes your family, your friends, and you yourself wear. What do they show you about each of these people – and about you?

▲ 5 Take a square of fabric. Use it as a headsquare and see how many different ways you can fold and tie it. Compare how it looks when you use a fine soft silky fabric and when you use a stiffer cotton material. For what purpose would each style be used?

6 Look at the labels on clothes and find some blends. Say why you think the two fibres have been put together.
Why do you think school clothes are often made of a blended fibre?

7 Explain the difference between staple fibre and continuous filament, stating the characteristics and giving examples of each.

8 Man-made fibres lack the feel and bulk of natural ones. How can the yarn be finished to give it the desirable qualities it lacks?

9 Give an example of how and why a natural fibre might be made smoother.

10 What is meant by the following terms: warp, weft, staple fibre?

11 Name some places that are likely to wear into holes on (a) school clothes and (b) men's clothes. What fibres can be blended together to strengthen them?

12 Labels tell you (a) that a fabric is 'mercerized' and (b) that a yarn is 'filament'. Explain fully what you understand by these terms.

13 Discuss the advantages to be gained from using fabrics made from mixed or blended fibres. (N.E.A.)

Chapter 2

Fabric construction and finishes

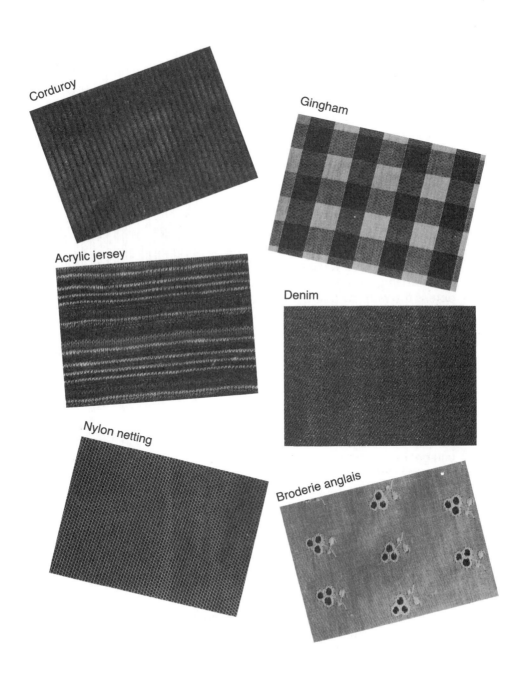

Corduroy

Gingham

Acrylic jersey

Denim

Nylon netting

Broderie anglais

Weaving

Weaving and **knitting** are the two main ways in which yarns are made into fabric.

▲ You can practise weaving by making a set of raffia table mats on a home-made bowed cardboard loom.

1 Take a narrow piece of cardboard 40 cm by 20 cm and stick elastoplast or masking tape along the narrow edges. Insert pins at 1 cm intervals along each edge exactly opposite one another.

2 Tie the end of the raffia to one pin and draw it round the pin exactly opposite bowing the cardboard evenly. Continue to wind it round the pins going from one end to the other until the diagonally opposite corner is reached.

3 Fasten off.
These threads will run the length of the mat and are called **warp** threads.

4 The **weft** threads are now woven across the warp by going over and under the warp threads alternately. To help you hold the yarn for weaving, make a cardboard shuttle as shown in the diagram and wind the raffia on to it. You will need about 12.5 m of raffia yarn.
Alternatively, you can wind the yarn round a ruler, but keep it flat so that it will go between the threads even when you get near the end.

5 In order to keep the weft thread straight, you need to push it down with a ruler edge. If you press the weft threads very close together you will have a close weave; if there is some space between you will have a loose weave.

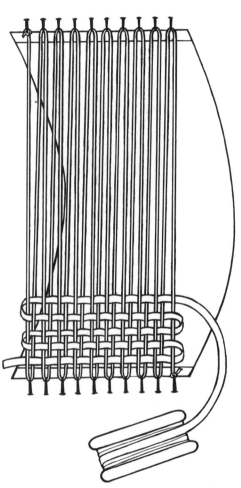

Commercial weaving

The facts you have learnt in weaving these mats are used in the weaving of cloth. Instead of having to lift each thread separately it would be much easier if you had something which would lift up all the alternate threads at once, whilst the shuttle is brought through, and would then pull the same threads down while the next weft thread is being brought across. Such an item is used in commercial weaving. It is called a **heddle**. Alternate warp threads pass through the holes. The others pass between the wires. The ones in the holes can be raised or lowered by the up-and-down movement of the heddle.

The space between the raised threads and the rest is called the **shed**. The shuttle is passed through it to make a weft thread. This is then 'beaten down' to keep it straight and firm. In a close-weave fabric this means that it is pushed up close to the last weft thread with a **reed**, a sort of comb. (You used your ruler for this.)

A loose-weave fabric is also straightened by the reed, but the weft threads are not pushed so closely together. This leaves air between the threads.

When the heddle is moved down the 'threads' running through the holes will be lower than the alternate ones. So a different shed is formed.

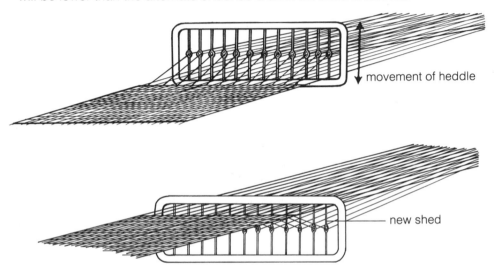

movement of heddle

new shed

The shuttle passes round the last thread at the edge and returns back through the new shed, passing **over** threads it went **under** the first time. This gives a weave like this:

selvedge

At each end the shuttle goes completely round the end thread and it**self** forms a neatened **edge**. This has come to be known as the **selvedge** ('self neatened edge').

On a commercial loom a bobbin of thread feeds each warp so that an endless length of fabric can be woven and rolled up.

A loom which has a weaving space 90 cm wide produces fabric which is 90 cm wide from selvedge to selvedge. Furnishing fabric needs to be considerably wider than this, so 115 cm or 140 cm widths are used. Woollens are often woven in widths of 150 cm.

Variations on a plain weave

The simple under-one over-one weave is known as **plain weave**. It may have a number of variations:

1 *Spacing*
Fabric can be closely or loosely woven. A close weave gives firmness and strength. A loose weave is weaker and forms fabrics which will pull out of shape easily. However, there is room for air between the threads and we shall see later that this is what makes a fabric retain the body's heat. Spacing can be wider between warp threads or weft threads or both, and this gives a different texture to the fabric in each case.

2 *Thickness of yarn*
The warp and weft threads may differ in thickness and number per centimetre. This causes the ribbed effect seen in poplin and grosgrain.

3 *Texture of yarn*
A textured yarn (see p.16) may be used. This gives a very different surface to the fabric.

Textured yarn

Bedford cord

Cotton poplin

All these variations can give a different appearance and different qualities to plain weaves. There are a number of other weaves besides the basic plain one.

Looking at weaves

▲ Find a number of scraps of different fabrics about 8 cm square. Look at them closely. You may find a number of weaves other than the plain one and probably some knits too.

Pay particular attention to the woven ones and see if you can find the warp threads. The sound made when you give a sharp tug along the warp is a 'snap'; when you do the same to the weft, you get a duller sound.

Now examine how the weft thread has been woven across the warp. To do this, tease out a weft thread with a pin. As you draw it out, count how many threads it goes over and under. Note this down by marking with a thick pen on the top line of a piece of graph paper. Then do the same with the next thread and the next. Gradually you will build up a pattern. The pattern depends on the sequence of how the weft threads were passed over the warp threads to form that particular weave.

Using patterns

▲ You can weave a raffia mat using different colours for the warp and weft threads. This design uses four different weaves. Have you found any of these on your fabric scraps? Look them up on the next page and identify them.

Weaving with wool

▲ You can weave squares of fabric to make small mats to go under drinks on a polished table, or a series of squares can be joined to make a cot blanket. Try out some of the different weaves in wool.

1 Cut a piece of thick card 8 cm by 8 cm.
2 Carefully pink the two ends.
3 Put a small loop around the top corner and wind the wool from end to end.
4 When you reach the diagonally opposite corner, use the wool as the weft thread and begin weaving using a darning needle. Finally sew the ends in.

weft rib over two warps

Z twill

hopsack

S twill

weft rib over two warps

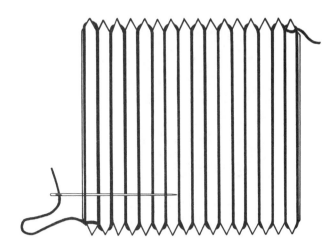

Questions

1 **What is a heddle and how is it used?**
2 **What is a 'shed' in weaving?**
3 **In weaving what is a 'reed' used for?**
4 **How is a selvedge formed?**
5 **What are the usual widths in which fabric is sold?**
6 **Many different fabrics have a plain weave. Account for any variations of texture and feel in a simple under-one over-one weave.**
7 **What are the advantages and disadvantages of loose weave material?**

Fabric weaves

Look out for these fabrics:

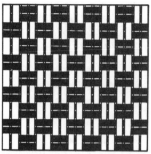

Hopsack

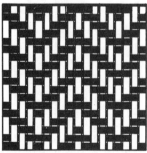

Twill

Herringbone

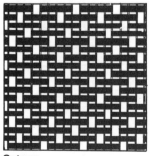

Sateen

Hopsack weave

Two weft threads go over two then under two, and vice versa on the return. There is a woollen fabric called **hopsack**. It is made from worsted (long, fine) yarn.

Twill

The weft goes over two warps again here, but do you notice the difference? If you half close your eyes the pattern looks diagonal. This is because the weft thread has altered one space only, yet it still goes over two, under two.

Strong close weaves are made in this way. You will find that woollen fabrics such as **serge** used for school skirts, and **gaberdine** for coats, suits, and skirts, have a twill weave. **Drill** used for aprons and overalls, and **denim** used for jeans are cotton twills. **Surah** is a firm, strong twill-weave silk. It is very expensive.

Herringbone

This is a twill weave which changes sequence regularly after a certain number of warp threads. Can you work out how many on this example? Woollen fabrics for coats, suits, and jackets often feature a herringbone weave.

Sateen

Filament threads give a smooth shiny fabric when woven in a sequence of five, going under one. Notice how the weft threads move along two warps at the end of each shed to achieve this result. Because there is more thread lying on the surface the fabric looks lustrous and glossy on the right side. But for the same reason these woven fabrics snag easily. Cotton is often used to produce the fabric **sateen**.

In **satin** the weft goes under several and over one. Silk is used. Nylon, acetates, and acrylics are also used to produce satin-type fabrics, because they are cheaper.

Jacquard weave

Other more complicated weaves may be made on a loom which can be set to weave in different sequences to produce patterns. These repeat after a set number of warp and weft threads. The type of loom on which this can be done is a Jacquard loom. The fabrics it produces are very good quality and quite expensive.

You may come across **damask**. This is a linen, woven into a pattern to be used for table-cloths and napkins. **Brocades** are woven from silk or nylon and used for heavy-quality furnishings, and evening and wedding dresses.

Terry

Towelling has loops on. These are woven by extra warp threads making the loops on a plain weave. These loops increase the surface area of the fabric and so make it able to absorb more water. Good quality 'Turkish' towels are thus thick with a good pile.

Velvet

Velvet also has a pile but this is cut. There are several ways of producing it but one is particularly interesting. Velvet is woven in two thicknesses facing each other and extra warp threads go alternately from one to the other. As the two thicknesses of fabric come off the loom, a knife cuts between the layers so that a cut pile is produced.

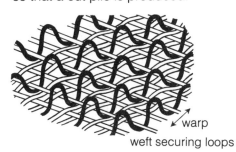

Terry towelling (magnified)

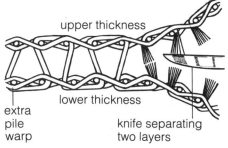

Cutting velvet (magnified)

Velveteen is a cotton material. The pile is an extra weft thread woven like a terry and cut after weaving.

After weaving, piles are sheared, brushed, and treated with steam to make the pile stand well. As all the pile goes one way, the fabric will look a slightly different colour if the light catches it upside down. For this reason cut pile fabrics are like those having a 'nap' – a brushed surface. The pile should stroke downwards only, and when working with velvet, extra allowance should be made for cutting out all the pattern pieces with the pile going from top to toe.

Questions

1 **Twill weaves make strong and serviceable fabrics. Give some examples of how twill fabrics are used and exposed to heavy wear.**
2 **Why do sateen fabrics snag easily?**
3 **We have seen that fibres have certain qualities and the way they are woven adds other features to them. Name qualities that are given to a fabric in weaving.**
4 **Why is a thick terry towel able to absorb more water?**
5 **Explain what special care is needed when cutting out velvet and why.**

Knits

▲ Look again at your scraps of fabric. You will see that not all your scraps are woven. Some are knitted. Examine the knits carefully.
Pull them. Do you notice that knits stretch more?
Crumple them up in your hand. Do they remain crumpled or do they spring back into shape?

Now think of what you are wearing and what you have at home which is knitted either by hand or machine. You will amass quite a lot of items.
For example:

Item	How knitted	Fabric
tights, stockings	machine	nylon
jumpers, cardigans	hand or machine	wool *or* acrylic
underwear: vests, slip, pants, bra	machine	cotton *or* synthetic *or* mixture
dress	machine	wool jersey *or* crimplene *or* other synthetic
ski pants	machine	stretchy synthetic
socks	hand or machine	wool *or* acrylic
scarf	hand or machine	wool *or* acrylic
hat	hand or machine	wool *or* acrylic
curtains	machine	acetate *or* nylon *or* acrylic

In fact all fibres and most types of clothing can be knitted.

▲ **Looking at knits**

Look closely at your scraps and examine the knitting. Try and pull out a thread. Is it easy to unravel or difficult?
You may notice that some knits are like hand knitting and unravel quickly. Others are very firm and it is difficult to pull out even one thread.
You may notice that some knits ladder, but others don't.
You will find that the smooth filament fibres ladder most easily.

Warp and weft knitting

There are two types of knitting. **Weft knitting** is done by knitting **across** the fabric. You will be able to pull a thread right across the weft easily. Because each stitch is looped over the one below it, it is quite likely to ladder. Tights ladder quickly because they are made of a smooth filament and they are stretched in wear. So the broken stitch shoots down the fabric to where it is less stretched. Weft knitting has great elasticity. Garments knitted by hand or machine are weft knitted.

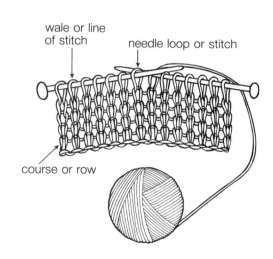

wale or line of stitch

needle loop or stitch

course or row

Warp-knitted fabric has a thread on each stitch and is knitted **vertically** as a number of chains of knitting. To connect these chains, the warp thread interlocks with its neighbouring stitches, so that the knitting is very firm and does not ladder. Warp knitting does not stretch as much as weft knitting. It is usually knitted as a fabric rather than as a garment.

Locknit, often used for underwear, blouse, skirt, and dress fabric, is a smooth warp knit. On fabrics such as crimplene, the knitting is more clearly visible on the wrong side.

Fashioning means shaping by increasing or decreasing the number of stitches. Fully fashioned stockings fit the shape of the leg. You can faintly see where any increases have been worked. Other stockings and tights are knitted as a tube. Their elasticity makes them take the shape of the leg.

Qualities of knitted yarn

By now you will have realized that knitting a yarn gives it different qualities from those given by weaving:

1 It will be more **elastic**. Fibres that have been crimped can be knitted into clothes which take up the body shape such as tights, ribbed sweaters, and swim-suits.
2 It will be more **resilient** – this means it will spring back into shape more easily. It can therefore be packed, used for full styles and furnishings, and it will need little pressing.
3 A warp-knitted fabric will not fray or ladder because the warp threads interlock with their neighbours firmly. Sewing construction processes can be modi-fied and speeded up. (A weft-knitted fabric would need extremely secure seam neatening as it would unravel easily. For this reason weft knitting is used for knitted garments where there are no cut seams.)
4 When knitted loosely, more air can be held between the threads, and so the knit tends to be warmer to wear. Weft or loose knits easily pull out of shape particularly when wet. Handle them very carefully when washing. Support the fabric in water, and dry them flat.
5 When sewing knitted fabrics, polyester or pure silk thread should be used. These have the same 'give' as the knit. Shoulder seams cut on the bias grain may stretch out of shape. The weight of the garment pulls them. Straight tape machined along the seam stops this.

Questions

1 **Why do tights ladder?**
2 **Why does hand knitting unravel quickly?**
3 **Why is a weft knit more elastic than a warp knit or a woven fabric?**
4 **In what way would a warp-knitted fabric be quicker and easier to use for dressmaking?**
5 **What special care does hand knitting require in washing?**
6 **Why should polyester or pure silk thread be used for sewing knitted fabrics?** (YREB)
7 **How are stretched shoulder seams prevented on a knitted fabric?** (SEREB)

How to knit

Hand knitting is a form of weft knitting.

loop over first finger

To cast on

1 Make a loop on the needle and hold it in the right hand, looping the wool from the ball around the first finger.
2 With the free end of the wool make a loop round the left thumb.
3 Put the needle point into the loop and bring the ball wool round to make a second loop on the needle.
4 Draw the thumb loop over the needle point to make a second stitch on the needle.
5 Repeat until the required number of stitches have been made.

free end long enough to make required number of stitches

Plain knitting

Hold the needle with stitches in the left hand and the other needle in the right hand. Loop the wool around the little finger and over the first finger of the right hand.

1 Put the r.h. needle point **into** the first stitch as shown.
2 Loop the wool **over** the r.h. needle.
3 Draw r.h. needle back **under** l.h. needle loop.
4 Slip the l.h. loop **off**.

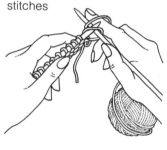

Purl knitting

1 With the wool at the front of the work put the r.h. needle **through** the first stitch.
2 With the r.h. forefinger pass the wool anti-clockwise **round** the r.h. needle.
3 Draw r.h. needle **through** the loop making the stitch form on the r.h. needle.
4 Slip the stitch **off** the l.h. needle.

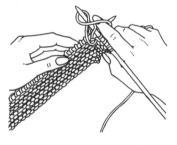

To cast off

1 Knit the first two stitches.
2 Pass the l.h. needle point through the first stitch as shown. Draw it over the second and off the r.h. needle.
3 Knit another stitch, and repeat until only one stitch remains.
4 Break off the wool and enlarge the stitch to draw the end through so that the last stitch disappears.

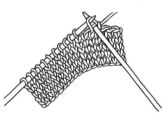

If you have mastered the four basic processes, knitting patterns offer immense scope for making plain, shaped, or patterned items. Shaping is usually done by knitting (or purling) two stitches together to decrease; and by making stitches to increase. Usually all the stitches on the right side are knitted with a plain stitch, and the stitches on the wrong side are worked in purl. This slips all the loops on to the wrong side.

A circular garment like a sock is knitted continuously on the right side using three double pointed needles to form the circle, and the fourth to knit each row in turn. All the loops therefore slip to the inside, if plain knitting is done.

Non-woven fabrics

You may have found some fabrics which are neither woven nor knitted.
Felt and **vilene** are two such materials. These are produced from a tangle of
fibres which are flattened and used as a fabric.

Felt is made in this way from woollen fibres. These matt together when
heated because the scales on them interlock. So a firm soft fabric is formed
which can be used to make toys, or steamed into a hat shape, which it will
retain permanently.

Other fibres can be laid at random or allowed to fall through a current of air
so that they form a web. They are then glued, bonded, or melted to join together.

Vilene, commonly used as a non-woven interlining, is made in this way.
You may have seen a variety of disposable clothes and furnishings which
resemble vilene of various weights – things like household cleaning cloths,
chairbacks on aeroplanes and coaches, aprons, tablecloths, hospital gowns,
sheets, and underwear too. Disposable underwear usually has holes between
the web of fibres to allow perspiration to escape.

The advantage of non-woven fabric is that it is easier to produce than
knits or weaves. It is economical to use because there is no warp and weft.
Where there is a warp and weft, the warp – the stronger thread – always runs
from top to toe in any item. Then the stronger thread takes the weight. Pattern
pieces are therefore positioned on fabric by means of a line marked to run
along the warp called the **straight grain line**. On a non-woven fabric there is
no need to use a straight grain line and so pattern pieces can be placed like
a jigsaw: nothing is wasted.

Bonding on woven material

Fabrics that will melt when heated can be bonded on to others. When they
cool they will set and stick permanently. Resin is also used to stick layers of
fabric together.

By doing this the qualities that each fabric has can be improved, or
increased, by the other. A loose weave will keep its shape if backed by a
closely constructed fabric. Plastic foam can be bonded inside thin cloth to
make it warmer. Thermoplastic fabric can be bonded inside cotton to stiffen
shirt cuffs and collars. This is one of the ways of **trubenizing** or permanently
stiffening fabric. (The other ways are given on p.38.)

A slight disadvantage of bonding is that, although it improves a fabric in
one way, it sometimes makes fabrics we do not wish to stiffen hang more stiffly.

Questions

1 **The turnings of felt toys are often oversewn on the outside. Why don't
  the turnings fray?**
2 **Why is non-woven fabric often used for disposable items?**
3 **Why are non-woven household cleaning cloths made with holes between
  the web of fibres?**
4 **How can one fabric be bonded with another?**
5 **Why is foam bonded inside other fabrics?**
6 **List the advantages of non-woven material.**

Colour

Much of the appeal of fabric comes from the colour. This is introduced by dyeing either the fibre, the yarn, or the fabric.

Synthetic fibres can be manufactured ready coloured. Dye is added to the liquid even before it is forced through tiny holes to come out as filaments of thread. Other synthetic and natural fibres can be dyed in a solution in large drums. Mixing the colours of woollen fibres gives very pleasantly shaded yarns for such fabrics as tweeds. Spun yarns can be dyed supported on hollow carriers in a dyeing machine which pumps liquid dye through them.

Dyeing the fibre or yarn means that patterns can be woven into the fabric, as you may have done on your table mats. Interesting woven or knitted effects are achieved by using different colours together.

Checks

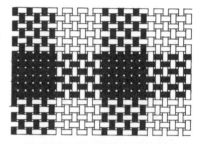

Gingham is a cotton fabric woven into checks by using a series of coloured and white threads alternately in both the warp and weft. The white weft crossing the white warp makes white squares. They contrast well with the bright colour of the red weft crossing the red warp. Where white threads cross red, or vice versa, a muted red is formed. The effect is a cheerful, serviceable fabric often used for children's clothes, aprons, and overalls.

A whole range of patterned checks can be made by using several coloured threads on the warp and weft. There are so many combinations making different patterns that every family, or clan, in Scotland has its own special design. This is called a **tartan**. Crofters used to take the wool from their sheep and weave the particular pattern of their clan to make it into the simple kilts and plaids that they wore.

▲ Examine a piece of denim. You will notice that it is a twill weave (see p.24). Tease out a warp and a weft thread. What do you notice about the colour? You will find that the warp is blue, and the weft white.

Dyeing woven fabric

It is cheaper to dye the fabric when it is already woven or knitted. Colours change with fashion, and a manufacturer can quickly dye stored, ready-woven natural-coloured cloth to the season's popular colour. This is done by vat dyeing, passing it through a dye or by pumping dye through the fabric

Dyes

Throughout the history of fabric production, natural dyes have been used. They came from plant and animal sources, usually relating to the area in which the fabric was produced. For example, lichens growing on cold damp Scottish stones produced the colours used for Harris tweeds.

The colours of Jacobean embroidery, traditionally done in muted browns, greens, purples, and blues, show clearly what dyes were available during that period in history. Berries, roots, leaves, tree bark, and wood were commonly used.

More expensive dyes came from abroad. Cochineal, the food colouring which comes from a Mexican insect, was used on wool and silk to produce scarlet, crimson and purple. This was done with the addition of **mordant**, a substance used to fix the dye to the fabric. The use of different mordants could produce different shades of red on the same type of fabric. Care! Mordants can give off poisonous fumes, so work in a well ventilated room.

In the middle of the last century synthetic dyes began to be found quite accidently. Now a wide range of dyes suitable for every synthetic fibre as well as natural ones is available.

Different fibres take up dyes to different degrees, so interesting effects can be produced on blends or mixtures called **cross dyeing**. One dye may produce different shades on two types of fibres, giving a mottled effect. On the other hand two different dyes may have to be used to produce the same even colour all over a blended fabric or mixture.

Jacobean embroidery, using natural dyes.

Questions

1 **At what stages can colour be introduced into textiles?**
2 **Write briefly about how colour is brought in at each of the stages you named.**
3 **Where do natural dyes come from? As well as the ones mentioned above, name some colourful plants or plant products that might be used as dyes.**
4 **What is the function of a mordant in dyeing?**
5 **What is meant by cross dyeing?**

Dyeing

Dyeing can be done at home. There are many suitable commercial dyes available and new life can be given to a garment by changing its colour. Full instructions are included with the dye.

You can see clearly how fabrics absorb dyes to different degrees by preparing a dye and putting a collection of clothes made of different fibres into it. Follow the dye maker's instructions carefully. Note the variety of colour in the finished items.

Dyes must be evenly dispersed throughout the fabric so that streaking does not occur. However, if you want a streaky effect, you can tie pieces of fabric into knots or bind them with string to prevent the dye getting to that area. When you have dried and finished the fabric and you undo them, you will have a tie-and-dye pattern.

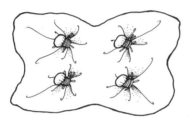 

When choosing a colour remember that you cannot dye a fabric lighter than it already is. You can only dye it darker. Make allowance for the colour that the fabric is before dyeing, unless you started with white fabric. The finished colour will be a combination of the original colour and the dye.

Colour fastness

It is always a good idea to test a strong coloured fabric for colour fastness before washing it **with** other items. It is absolutely essential to do this when you have dyed anything at home. To do this, wash the fabric, keeping it well away from any other items whilst damp. Place a small piece of the fabric between a folded piece of white cotton. Press well until the fabric is dried by the heat of the iron. Examine the white cotton carefully. There should be no marks of the dye on it.

Be careful with dyes. Wear protective clothing. Dyes stain!

▲ Using a natural dye

1 You will need a 90 cm square of white or neutral coloured cotton. You could try this experiment with several squares of different fabrics to compare the way each fibre takes up dye.

2 Prepare a dye solution of beetroot or elderberry:
Put 400 g cleaned beetroot or elderberries into a pan with two litres of water. Cut the beetroot up **in** the water, as they bleed and you do not want to lose the dye.

3 Boil until a good colour is obtained – about 30 to 60 minutes.

4 Strain the liquid into another large pan.

5 Wet the fabric to be dyed with warm water.

6 Immerse the fabric and stir it in the liquid slowly. Warm the dye to 70°C and soak well.

7 A mordant or fixative (see p.31) will set a dye in a fabric more firmly. **Alum** is a white mineral which fixes dyes. 15 g alum can be used and dissolved in some of the liquid. Then add it to the dye and stir it in well.
8 Leave the fabric in the dye overnight.
9 Rinse thoroughly until the colour has stopped coming out.
10 Half dry the fabric.
11 Test for colour fastness. Then iron dry.
12 Examine the colour of each fabric, if you have dyed several pieces. Compare how each has taken up the dye. You could use your squares of fabric to make a headscarf or a small tablecloth.

Printing

There are two main ways of printing a pattern on to fabric:

1 The colour is stamped on to the fabric as in lino or potato printing.

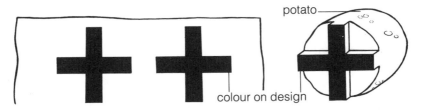

2 The design is treated so that the rest of the fabric takes up colour while the design does not. For example, to achieve a white design on a coloured background, the design is covered with a substance that will not take up the dye. When the fabric is dyed the treated part remains white while the rest takes up the colour. In **Batik** hot wax is used as a 'resist' to the dye.

Screen printing

Screen printing uses the same principle as potato printing. A light-sensitive nylon screen is exposed to the light, blocked by the transparency of the design to be printed. The part exposed to the light sets so that no dye can go through the screen except where the design has blocked the light out. When the screen is laid on the fabric and colour rolled over it, the pattern is dyed on. A different screen is used to add each colour to the pattern. Rotary screens are used commercially.

Patterns can be dyed on from both sides at the same time by a process called the **Duplex system**. Heated rollers ensure that the dye is held fast and penetrates the fabric evenly on both sides. In the home we use the same principle with a steam iron. The steam and warmth soften cotton and linen fibres and set the dye in them, so when the fabric dries, the dye is held fast.

Questions

1 **What limits your choice of colours in home dyeing?**
2 **Why is it important to test strong coloured or home-dyed items for colour fastness, and how is it done?**
3 **Coloured designs often look exactly the same on both the right and wrong sides of fabric now. What system has made this possible? What part does heat play in the dyeing process?**

Fabric properties

Throughout the process of fabric construction a manufacturer must ask:

- What properties does the fabric possess?
- Will the fabric wear well, and do what people expect of it?
- Does it need to have any treatment to give it extra qualities, or to help it retain the ones it already has?

Having thought about this the manufacturer may want to apply some 'finishes' to the fabric. The questions then arise:
- What might people do to the fabric in using and care that might spoil it, or ruin its good qualities?
- What advice should the consumer be given about caring for the fabric to help it keep its natural or added qualities and make it last well?

▲ Imagine you are a fabric manufacturer faced with these problems. Carry out a series of tests to check the characteristics of fibres, and see what qualities ought to be added.

Gather a selection of pieces of fabric. You need an untreated piece made from each of the main fibres. (Untreated means that it has had no particular finish already applied.) Include the following: wool, silk, linen, cotton, viscose, acetate, nylon, polyester, and acrylic.

Draw out a large chart giving plenty of room to write your conclusions and comments as you do the tests on pp.34–36.

	Texture	Lustre	Flammability	Absorbency	Stain resistance	Shrinking	Resilience
Wool	soft	hairy or matt	smoulders, does not flare up	absorbs water quite quickly	absorbs stains	shrinks and stiffens	does not crease. Springs back into shape easily
Silk							

Texture

Examine the look and feel of your fabrics. Are they soft or stiff?
Think about what the fabric might be used for. For example, cotton is suitable for shirts worn next to the skin because it is absorbent (takes in water). But should shirts be limp or stiff, or should some parts be stiffer than others? If so, which parts need stiffening?
The manufacturer needs a soft, absorbent fabric, yet one which looks crisp and smart in the places where it shows.

- Look at your fabrics. Which might require some stiffness to improve them in wear?

Lustre

Now look at the appeal of each fabric. Light shining on a smooth surface gives **lustre** and makes the fabric look rich and good. Furnishing fabrics will be either hanging or laid flat in use, and therefore lustre will be important. For example, linen may be laid out flat as a table-cloth and a lustrous fabric looks very attractive to complement a dinner service or glassware.

Look at each of your fabrics carefully. Hold each one over your finger at eye level. Small fibre ends are visible on some fabrics. These break up the light, giving a dull or matt surface, so there is no lustre.

● Write 'hairy', 'matt', or 'shiny' against each of the fabrics on your chart. Make a note of any you think might be used for curtains, table-cloths, or other furnishings, if they could be made more lustrous.

Flammability

▲ To test a fabric for flammability, you will need a taper and a pair of tongs. Put a piece of each of the named fabrics on a large metal baking tray. In turn hold each fabric by the tongs over the baking tray and ignite carefully with the taper.
Note how it burns:
● readily and quickly?
● smoulders, burning reluctantly?
● melts?

Flammable fabrics are dangerous.
● Do any require treatment to make them less flammable?

Brushed fabrics or nets are particularly flammable

Burns readily and quickly.   **Smoulders. Does not ignite.**   **Melts.**

Absorbency/water repellency

Put a drop of water on the surface of each of the named fabrics.
Note the reaction of the fabric in each case.

● Does the water stay on the surface, or is it absorbed?
● If it is absorbed, how quickly does this happen?

Repellent   **Time this one.**   **Very absorbent**

Sometimes we want fabrics to be absorbent.

● Why? Does this help in laundering them? How?

Sometimes we want a fabric that is water repellent, for use in wet weather.

● Which fabrics might be best for that purpose? Will they need any treatment to improve water repellency?

Stain resistance

Put a drop of oil on the surface of each of the named fabrics.
Note the reaction of the fabric in each case.
● Does the oil stay on the surface or is it absorbed?

Wash the fabric in warm soapy water.
● Is this sufficient to remove the oil from any of the fabrics?

Shrinkage

Does the fabric shrink?
Cut a 6 cm square of each fabric.
Soak overnight.
Wash and rinse.
Spin dry. Iron.

Examine each piece carefully.
- Has its texture changed?
Re-measure it.
- Has its size changed?
You had no particular instructions to follow about how to care for each fabric.
- Is the same method of laundering suitable for each, or would some labelling be helpful to the consumer?

Write your comments on the chart.

Resilience

Crumple each fabric in your hand tightly.
Does it remain crumpled or does it spring back into shape quickly without creasing?
A resilient fabric is one which resists creases.
Make a note of which fabrics crease badly, for this will happen when they are worn, unless the manufacturer applies a finish to make them crease-resistant.

Crease holding

A manufacturer will require some fabrics to hold creases.
What items might be pleated?
From which fabrics might they be made?
Would those fabrics retain pleats?
Press a pleat into each piece of fabric using a dry iron and a damp cloth.
Press well.

- How well does the fabric pleat?
Wash the fabric.
- Has the pleat been retained?

Questions

1   **Study your chart. Which fabrics are the most flammable?
    Would it be safe to use those for nightwear for children or old people, or
    should they be treated to make them flame-proof?
    How would you stop people from buying flammable fabrics for
    nightwear?**
2   **You can only take the minimum luggage for a month travelling, but must
    look smart in your job. Which fabrics would stand up to a long spell in a
    suitcase? Which fabrics would you avoid?**

Finishes (1)

Having woven or knitted a fabric, the manufacturer wants to make sure that it has the qualities that are needed in use.
Some qualities come from the fibre, such as warmth and strength.
Some come from the weave or knit, such as increased strength and elasticity.
Some come from the **finish** that is applied to the fabric.

Finishes are applied for several reasons:

1 To improve the look and feel of a fabric:
   - by stiffening
   - by increasing the lustre
   (the shine as it catches the light)
   - by giving nap – raising the surface.

2 To increase the fabric's life:
   - by making it flame-retardant
   - by moth-proofing wool and wool mixtures.

3 To improve the fabric in wear:
   - to make it water repellent
   - to make it oil and stain repellent
   - to give shrink resistance
   - to give crease resistance
   - to give power to hold creases for setting in pleats.

Finishes to improve the look and feel of a fabric

Good quality hard-wearing fabrics are made by weaving threads close together. A loose weave is not as serviceable as a close weave; and poor quality material would result from a low-grade fibre, loosely woven. To conceal this inferior quality a **filler** or **dressing** is sometimes used. This is a substance like washing starch which fills up the space between the threads and makes the fabric look better quality. In fact the filler will wash out, leaving a weak limp fabric. So beware of very cheap fabric which may have been 'sized' or 'filled'.Test it by rubbing the material between your knuckles and the 'size', a white powder, will drop out. Filling or dressing a fabric is similar to starching it.

▲ *Experiment*
1 Find a cotton traycloth or handkerchief.
2 Mix one tablespoon of powdered starch with two tablespoons of cold water. This is to distribute the starch grains evenly, as in making custard.
3 Boil about 500 ml water.
4 Pour the boiling water over the blended starch, stirring, and continue to pour until it turns clear. This is full strength starch.
5 Add 500 ml cold water.
6 Immerse the washed traycloth or handkerchief, and knead in the starch.
7 Spin or beat in a dry towel to soak up the excess moisture. Allow to half dry.
8 Using a hot iron (⬛ , 210°C), iron the cloth very slowly until all the steam has gone.
What do you notice about the cloth?

After starching (sizing, filling, dressing), fabric becomes much stiffer. It appears thicker. The heat of the iron cooks the starch. The starch grains swell and so the fabric seems much thicker. At one time this principle of starching a fabric was used for all cotton and linen fabrics where a good finish was essential. Table linen which must look thick, smooth, and clean, was always well starched. Nurses' and maids' caps used to be starched with full strength starch to make them stand well, and shirt collars, front bands and cuffs with slightly weaker starch to stiffen them, and give them 'body'.

Trubenizing

Today fabrics or parts of garments are given a permanent stiffening to avoid the need to starch them. This process is called **trubenizing**. It can be done in three ways. The parts to be stiffened – collars, cuffs, belts – can be interlined with a thermoplastic fibre or with cellulose acetate; or the fabric may be coated with synthetic resin.

Thermoplastic fibres melt when heated. They bond on to the garment material when pressure is applied, producing a stiffened fabric. Cellulose acetate can be softened by acetone, and that can also be heat pressed on to the fabric as a permanent stiffening agent. A coating of resin has a similar effect on fabric when heat pressed.

Calendering

Cotton does not have a natural lustre (p.34). This is because there are hairy fibre ends on the surface. When the cotton is freshly ironed these ends are flattened. The light catches the smoothed surface and it shines more than usual. To produce this sort of effect commercially, cotton (or linen) can be **calendered**. This means it is pressed round a series of rollers called a calender, which flattens not only the little ends on the surface, but the fibres themselves, making the fabric really very smooth. However, this is not a fully permanent quality. In washing, fibres gradually soak up water and regain their original more swollen state. So a dress, skirt, or blouse will always look better when new, and will lose some of its appeal as it ages.

Beetling

Linen has a natural glossy appearance. This can be improved for really good quality table linen by a process called **'beetling'**. This is 'beating' or hammering the fabric really hard with wooden hammers. It improves the lustre.

Brushing

To give a fabric a more hairy surface it can be brushed with very fine wire bristles. This draws up a nap. Air can be entangled in the nap, and so the fabric is warmer to wear because it retains the body heat better. Brushed nylon, used for nightwear, is a good example. Cotton can be brushed to make winceyette or flannelette – both warm and absorbent fabrics. However, raising a nap increases the speed with which cotton burns. During the early part of this century these two fabrics were used a lot for nightwear, until it was realized in the 1950s that this practice was really very dangerous. Many children died getting ready for bed in front of an open fire. Since 1964, winceyette has carried a label 'unsuitable for children's nightwear'.

Finishes to increase a fabric's life

Flame-retardant finish

If you look at the table on p.80 you will see that some fibres burn very easily and others do not. You will notice that cotton, linen, acetate and viscose burn well. These fabrics can be made flame-retardant but this may spoil their softness. Unfortunately some flame-retarding chemicals will react with soap and form a flammable substance on the surface of a fabric, so it is very important to follow the washing instructions carefully, and use a soapless detergent instead of soap if told to do so.

The flame-retardant finish is applied commercially by Pyrovatex CP or Proban treatment, and the care label tells you:

PROBAN
DURABLE FLAME–RETARDANT FINISH
HOT WASH WITH DETERGENT
DO NOT BOIL
NO SOAP OR SOAP POWDERS
NO HYPOCHLORITE BLEACH
DRY CLEANABLE

Do not bleach.

Fabric can be treated at home by using a solution of borax and boric acid. Unfortunately this washes out. But it is well worth applying it to curtains, loose covers, and other household furnishings, which are not washed frequently – particularly in cigarette smokers' homes!

Moth-proofing

Wool is attacked by the larvae of moths which feed on the fibres, making holes. Woollen fibres can be permanently treated with a chemical marketed under the trade names of Mitin, Dielmoth, or Eulan. Moths do not like these. Mitin and Eulan poison the larvae. Other fibres are quite safe from the ravages of moth larvae as it is only wool and wool mixtures that moths like for their egg laying. They are attracted by food on wool, so always store fabrics clean. Moth balls are useful in that they repel moths, but air clothes very well, for unfortunately they repel humans too!

Questions

1 **Name three ways in which a fabric gets the qualities the wearer need.**
2 **Name three ways in which the look or feel of a fabric can be altered.**
3 **What happens to a sized or dressed cloth when it is washed?**
4 **What does the word 'trubenized' mean on the care label of a shirt?**
5 **What is the purpose of calendering cotton?**
6 **How does cotton eventually lose its calendered effect?**
7 **Why might a brushed cotton be particularly dangerous to wear if untreated?**
8 **What is the name of the commercial treatment applied to fabric to make it flame-retardant?**
9 **Why is it important to read the care label of flame-retardant fabric very carefully, and carry out its instructions?**
10 **What steps might you take when storing clothes or blankets during the summer to prevent moths damaging them?**

Finishes (2)

Finishes to improve the fabric in wear

Water repellency

Rubber, PVC, and plastic are completely waterproof. This means that they keep out rain. However, it also means that they do not allow the body perspiration to escape, and so air holes must be provided in a waterproof garment or it will become uncomfortable to wear. These fabrics are also used outdoors for waterproof sheeting, buoyancy aids such as lilos, waterwings, and life jackets, and many other items concerned with the sea or weather. At one time fabric was treated by applying wax. Thus we get the name 'oilskins' for the type of rainwear shown here.

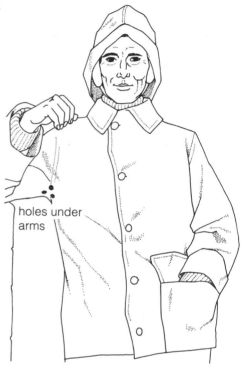

holes under arms

Of the more conventional fabrics used for the home and for clothing, nylon is one of the least absorbent, and a close weave will help to keep out water. A water-repellent finish can be applied and is particularly needed on cotton, viscose, and wool to prevent those fibres from absorbing water.

The process is done by treatment with silicone, and is called showerproofing. Showerproof garments are usually washable – care label – hand wash. All detergent **must** be carefully rinsed off or it will nullify the water-repellent quality. Always check the label of any showerproof garment, for some say 'dry clean only'. Others lose their water repellency during the dry-cleaning process, and have to be reproofed afterwards.

Stain resistance

We want to protect some fabrics against oil and water. Most fibres need to be treated so that they will not absorb. Zepel and Scotchgard are oil and water repellents. It is an expensive but permanent treatment. Fabrics which have been treated with these should need little cleaning beyond wiping and brushing.

Shrink resistance

The fabric most likely to shrink in washing is wool. This is because of the scales on each fibre, which will interlock unless the wool is very carefully washed, rinsed at an even temperature, and dried outdoors immediately.

It is possible to make wool shrink-resistant by removing the scales chemically (by chlorination), or coating the fibres with polymer or resin to give them a smooth non-scaly surface. The latter process can make wool machine-washable bearing the name 'Superwash'.

Wool fibres can also be treated with an enzyme called **papain**. (You have enzymes in your digestive system to act on proteins to make them soluble for absorption into the body.) Papain makes wool protein soluble. By careful treatment commercially, the little scales can be removed without weakening the rest of the fibre.

Cotton and viscose are stretched along the warp when woven. When cotton fibres are put in an alkaline solution, they swell and therefore shrink lengthways a little each washing, but most of all in the first wash. Wet fabric can be pre-shrunk by compressing it firmly into the size it is expected to shrink to after several normal washings. It is then dried in the compressed state and no more shrinkage will occur. A fabric shrunk in this way is said to be either **Rigmel shrunk** (the British method) or **Sanforized** (the American name). Fabrics treated in this way should be washed

In the home non-treated linen, viscose, and cotton can be shrunk before making up by soaking overnight and washing first. Most shrinking usually occurs in the first wash, but it must be remembered that some may still occur later on.

Crease resistance

Cotton, viscose, and linen crease badly. The fibres can be treated with resin to make them more resilient. This process (called **tebilizing**) also makes the fabric a little stiffer. The treatment is largely permanent, though with age, and repeated washing, the fabric will lose its crease-resistant quality. Synthetics and wool do not crease.

To crease permanently

Some fabrics retain creases well. Nylon, polyester, and acrylics are thermoplastic which means they can be heat set into shape, so they can be permanently pleated.

Linen and cotton pleat easily but the creases do not last. They fall out. Viscose does not crease as well as cotton, and it too loses pleats easily. There are commercial processes which give these fabrics the ability to retain pleats – Fixaform, Evaprest, and Tootaprest. The principle is that the fabric is pleated, and then coated with resin which is baked to hold the pleats in position.

Questions

1 **Which fabrics are completely waterproof?**
2 **How did 'oilskins' get that name?**
3 **Why is it important to read the label on a showerproof coat very carefully?**
4 **Why does wool shrink if it is not washed very carefully?**
5 **Describe briefly three ways in which wool can be prevented from shrinking.**
6 **Cotton and viscose sometimes shrink. Why?**
7 **Which fabrics crease badly and how can this be prevented?**

Further work on Chapter 2

1 Choose the correct description for each of the fabrics listed below.
   (a) A strong hard-wearing twill weave with coloured warp and white weft.
   (b) A lightweight fabric which is usually woven with white and coloured yarns in striped or check patterns.
   (c) A woven, shaggy looped fabric; white, dyed, or printed.
   (d) A hard-wearing woven fabric with ribbed pile running down the length.
   (e) A knitted fabric which drapes softly and is elastic.
   Terry towelling, corduroy, denim, jersey, gingham.

2 (a) Explain what is meant by a 'satin weave' fabric. (EAEB)
   (b) Name *two* fibres used for satin fabrics. (EMREB)

3 A desirable characteristic in clothing fabric is crease resistance.
   (a) (i) Name *one* fibre which has a high natural crease resistance.
       (ii) Name *one* fibre which creases easily.
   (b) Give a brief outline of a method of applying a crease-resistant finish during manufacture to fabrics of cellulose origin. (NWREB)

4 (a) What is understood by a 'fabric finish'.
   (b) What special property is given to a fabric by each of the following finishes?
       (a) Proban or Pyrovatex (c) Mercerized (e) Evaprest
       (b) Scotchgard (d) Sanforized (f) Trubenized
   (c) Name *one* item or garment to illustrate the use of each treated fabric.
   (d) How might these finishes affect general after-care?
   (e) Devise some simple tests that could be carried out on specimens of 'finished' fabric to show how the quality had been improved over similar untreated fabric.

5 Discuss the characteristics, properties, and usefulness of non-woven fabrics for clothing and general use. Relate your comments where appropriate, to food, family, and home as well as textiles. Explain how and why the nature of felt will affect the way it can be cut out and the method of construction used to make a toddler's toy.

6 Sketch a bonded fabric item of clothing with which you are familiar.
   Evaluate it with respect to its fitness for purpose.
   Briefly outline how bonded fibre fabric is made.
   Refer to any disadvantage caused by its construction.

7 Describe what is meant by a 'textured' knitting yarn.
   What are the differences between warp and weft knitting?

8 The following finishes may be applied to fabrics during manufacture:
   (a) sizing,
   (b) brushing,
   (c) calendering.
   What are the advantages or disadvantages of each?
   Explain how *one* of these finishes is applied to the fabric.

9 What is the meaning of the following terms used in weaving?
   Twill, hopsack, reed, heddle, weft.

Chapter 3

Understanding fabrics

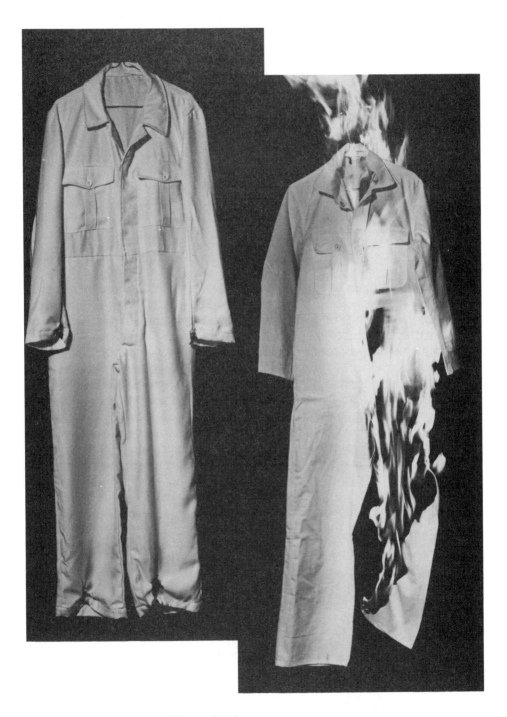

Testing the flammability of different fabrics.

Fabric qualities (1)

What qualities do we require from a fabric?

Fabrics for clothes need to be	Fabrics for household items need to be	Fabrics for industrial/agricultural purposes need to be
warm decorative functional comfortable absorbent	resistant to sunlight attractive decorative functional warm (curtains) noise-deadening (carpets) protective (oven gloves)	protective (against fire and radiation) water repellent safe – non-flammable warm strong

The above are not in order of importance. Place them in the order *you* consider most appropriate and add any further ideas of your own.

Certainly one of the most important qualities we require from clothing fabrics is warmth.

Warmth

We wear clothes to keep us warm. Our body converts food into energy and heat. The human body temperature is around 37°C. With activity more heat is generated by the body and we feel hot. Sitting still we may feel cold because we are not producing so much heat through physical activity. Lying in bed at night the body is performing no muscular activity and thus producing still less heat. So we need blankets to keep us warm by keeping in our body heat. Old people, who tend to be less active, are prone to **hypothermia** (a drop in the body temperature) and therefore need more warmth in their homes and bedding.

Air is trapped in some fabrics when they are woven or knitted. They are **bad conductors of heat**. They will not let heat pass out. So they keep the body heat in, and we stay warm. Fabrics that retain body heat include wool and cellular weaves like those on nylon and acrylic blankets. Air is trapped in by a cellular weave. The blanket therefore retains the body heat. There are also other methods of trapping air in fabric, such as raising a nap on flannelette or brushed nylon so that they are warmer than cotton or plain nylon respectively. But beware of the flammability of brushed cotton (see p.38).

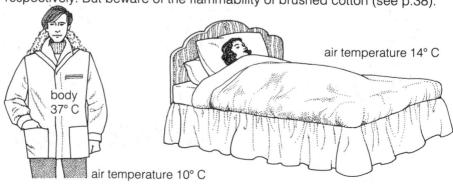

air temperature 14° C

body 37° C

air temperature 10° C

The natural **crimp** of wool and the crimp deliberately given to man-made fibres (see p.16) not only holds air but also makes them resilient (spring back into shape – see p.36). So in fact the air is not flattened out.

How well do different fabrics retain warmth?

▲ Try this group activity for seven people. Each person needs a small saucepan with a lid, and a thermometer.

Stage 1
Collect some pieces of fabric big enough to wrap round the small pans and some string to tie the fabric round the handle too.
You need samples of:
a woollen blanket fabric
b cellular fabric such as acrylic or nylon blanket
c cotton
d flannelette or brushed cotton
e nylon
f brushed nylon
Fill one pan with cold water. Measure the temperature. Heat it up to 37°C.
Put on the lid. Leave in a cool room.
How long does it take to cool to its original temperature?
Note the length of time.
This pan represents the body without clothes.

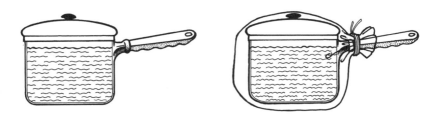

Stage 2
Fill all the other pans with cold water.
Warm all the pans of water to reach 37°C. Put on the lids.
Quickly wrap each pan in a single layer of one of the selected fabrics and tie it up.
Leave the pans for exactly the same length of time as the time you recorded in Stage 1. Then measure the temperature of the water in each pan.
Draw your conclusions. Place the fabrics in the order in which they will retain body heat best.

Questions

1 **When is the body likely to feel coldest?**
2 **Why is it particularly important for old people to have warm bedding?**
3 **Why is hypothermia so common amongst the elderly?**
4 **Why do blankets help to keep us warm?**
5 **Why is brushed nylon a popular fabric for nightwear?**

Fabric qualities (2)

Absorption and reflection of warmth

Heat can come from outside the body too. The sun warms us by radiation – the sun's rays passing directly on to our skin. It will also shine on to the fabrics we wear. Black and dull surfaces **absorb** heat and the body beneath feels the warmth of the sun's rays. White and shiny surfaces **reflect** heat. This is why white and light-coloured fabrics look and feel cool, and are associated with summer wear.

Fire-fighting suits with a top layer of aluminium foil are suitable for wearing near extreme heat because they reflect the heat away. So firemen can approach a fire a little more closely. We use this principle in the home too. Shiny **milium** ironing-board covers reflect heat. So less electricity needs to be used to keep the iron at the required temperature.

Cooling down

If we feel too hot we take off a layer of clothes to allow heat to escape. Clothes form a barrier between the body temperature and the temperature of the surrounding air, which is of course lower. When we take clothes off, we expose more surface area of our skin to the air. As the sweat evaporates into the air, we become cooler.

If too much surface area is exposed, we get too cold. Babies have a lot of skin surface area compared with their mass. So they feel cold easily. It is important to ensure that they are warm enough. Thin people have more surface area in relation to their weight than fat ones. This is why they usually feel the cold more quickly when swimming in the sea.

Wind will evaporate moisture from the skin more quickly. This is refreshing on a hot day, and when there is a window open. But it can be extremely uncomfortable in cold conditions. Notice how cold the exposed parts of the body get on a motor-bike with air rushing past!

The importance of absorbency

Wind-proof fabrics are used for most outdoor activities. They are closely woven. A close-weave material only allows minimum air through. A fabric which allows **no** air through is unsuitable for clothing because no perspiration can escape by evaporation. It is therefore uncomfortable and clammy to wear, and should only be worn for very short periods.

String vests are useful because they are knitted loosely with coarse yarn. This enables air to be held round the body to retain warmth. But if on the other hand you want to cool down, and you open your shirt neck, the string vest enables air to circulate round the body easily through the holes, and allows evaporation.

In a crowded room there comes a point when moisture will not evaporate into the air. This may be because so much sweat has already evaporated into the air that the atmosphere has become saturated (completely full) and will take no more. There may be no window open to create a draught of air (ventilation). Then beads of perspiration appear on people's foreheads. They feel uncomfortably hot and feel the urge to 'go outside and cool off'!

We lose about half a litre of moisture through perspiration each day. With exertion or heat we could lose half a litre in one hour! The skin perspires all over the body, not just on the exposed parts. Underclothes and socks should therefore be made of an absorbent fibre so that they absorb sweat and do not make the body feel moist and clammy.

There are other items which must be absorbent too. Towels take surface water from the body and from pots. Absorbency is increased if the surface area can be increased so that the fabric will take up more moisture. Terry towelling which has a looped surface will absorb many times more water than a smooth fabric.

Questions

1 **Explain why a white summer dress would look and feel cooler in hot weather.**
2 **Why should babies be kept warm?**
3 **Why should a thin, elderly lady be especially careful about keeping warm in bed?**
4 **Explain why string vests can be warm to wear and yet assist the body to cool down when overheated.**
5 **Why is ventilation important in a crowded room?**
6 **What qualities would you look for in:**
   (a) a motor-cycling jacket
   (b) underwear
   (c) a bath towel
   (d) a fireman's jacket?

Wool

Certification Trade Mark

Pure new wool

PURE NEW WOOL
The Woolmark guarantees the strength, shrink resistance, moth-proofing, and colour fastness of Pure New Wool.

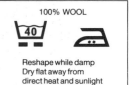

100% WOOL

Reshape while damp
Dry flat away from
direct heat and sunlight

What is Pure New Wool? How is it different from any other pure wool or woollen garment that we might buy?

This form of labelling is used because the demand for wool is so great that used woollen items are shredded and recycled to be made into yarn and cloth again. Even the wool from wool mixtures is reclaimed by dissolving away the cotton or other fibres. Old wool is called **shoddy**. It is mixed with wool from new fleeces for blankets and other woollen items.

Wool has been a major industry in Britain since early times. Through the ages our national financial state (economy) has been dependent on wool. In fact even now the Lord Chancellor sits in Parliament on the 'Woolsack', dating from the time when it was regarded as a mark of Britain's prosperity.

Wool comes from the fleece of the sheep. (Hair from the camel, llama, goat, and angora rabbit is also used to a lesser degree.) The best wool comes from the Merino sheep. These were originally a Spanish breed. They are now reared mainly in Australia and New Zealand. British people settled there in the last century to clear and utilize vast grazing lands and send wool back to the thriving woollen industry in Britain. South Africa and America also produce a great deal of wool.

Merino wool has fine, soft, white fibres. They are very tightly crimped. This makes the fibre very elastic and resilient – both extremely useful qualities in wear. Thicker, stronger fibres can be obtained from sheep of other types. Merino sheep have been crossed with other varieties. Fibres of varying thicknesses and crimps have been produced, and lengths can vary from 5–30 cm. Coarser fibres make thicker wools and fabrics.

A number of well-known varieties of knitwear take their name from the Islands. You will have heard of fine Shetland wool, Fairisle knitting, Harris tweed fabric, and Aran sweaters.

pattern knitted in using coloured wools

Fairisle   Harris tweed jacket   Bulky Aran sweater

Wool for carpets is coarser still. Although not soft enough for clothing, it is very warm and hard-wearing.

Production

When wool has been sheared it is baled. All of the wool from the 70 million sheep in New Zealand and most of that from Australia comes to British mills. There it is scoured to remove burrs, twigs, and dirt, and washed to remove the **lanolin**. This is the natural oil secreted from the sheep's skin. It keeps the fleece waterproof during life when the animal needs a raincoat! Lanolin is purified and used for cosmetics and ointments. The wool is then **carded** (brushed) between wire-covered rollers. It is a staple fibre (short), and is used to make two sorts of cloth: woollen and worsted.

The shorter fibres are used to make wool yarn. The fluffiness is due to the fibres running in different directions. This gives a pleasant hairy structure. Because air is trapped in its construction, wool always feels warm to the touch. Wool is spun to make yarn of various plys for knitting (see p.14), or for weaving or knitting into fabrics. Woven woollen cloths are flannel, nun's veiling (black), cashmere, blazer cloth, and tweed. Jersey cloth is knitted woollen fabric. It is of medium weight and is used for warm dresses.

The longer finer fibres are used to make worsted fabric. After carding they are combed to make them lie parallel. This gives an even texture and removes **noils** (short fibres). The long fibres are then spun into worsted yarn. This is woven to make good quality fine cloth such as suiting, gaberdine, and barathea.

Woollen fibres

Worsted – longer combed fibres

Properties

1 *Warmth*

Both the crimps in the fibre, and the fact that each wool fibre is covered by tiny scales, keep the fibres apart and trap air between them. This makes wool retain the body heat and so it is warm to wear. In addition air spaces are created by the structure of knitting. So hand-knitted garments are particularly warm to wear.

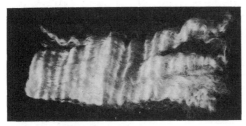

Crimps on fibres

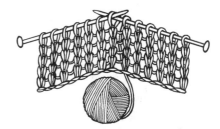

The structure of knitting traps air.

2 *Resilience*

Because of its natural crimp, wool is very resilient. Even when packed, creases readily shake out. Knitting also gives added elasticity.

3 Absorbency

Wool absorbs moisture readily. This is very useful when it is being worn next to the skin. As we saw earlier, babies have a lot of surface area compared to their size. It is particularly important to keep them warm, and woollen vests are therefore very suitable for them.

Even when wet, wool still feels quite warm to the touch. Moisture will only evaporate slowly from it. There is therefore no feeling of rapid cooling or chill as evaporation or drying occurs. These features are very useful in wear.

Because of its absorbency, washing wool can be quite a problem. The amount of water it takes up is much heavier than the wool itself, so wet wool should always be supported. Never hold it up or hang it, for wool will be forced to stretch. Because it takes up so much water it needs long thorough drying too.

Always spin dry well, to remove the weight of water. Then finish flat on a towel; or dry carefully out of doors. Wind removes moisture, raises the pile, and keeps woollens soft. Always support garments well by passing a tape through the sleeves, or by hanging the item carefully **over** the line to avoid stretching.

4 Washing

Superwash wool (see p.40) is stronger, will not felt, and can be machine-washed easily. The major problem with other wool is in washing it. The temperature must be evenly warm throughout at 40°C. A change of temperature, whether too hot or cold, makes the scales on the fibres interlock, pulling them together and causing the wool to shrink or felt. Rubbing, careless handling, and alkali also have the same effect on the scales. As soap is an alkali, a soapless detergent or soap flakes which are very mild are recommended for washing woollens.

The Care Labelling Code states:

40	MACHINE	HAND WASH
	Warm minimum wash	Warm Do not rub Warm rinse
	Spin. Do not hand wring	

or

Hand wash
(Do not machine wash)

A spin drier removes a considerable amount of water from wool. It is best to dry wool outdoors immediately. Wool left damp or dried in heat will felt. For this reason flat dwellers and working people on wet winter weekends have been grateful for the manufacture of acrylics!

5 *Effect of heat*

Wool will press well with a warm iron at ⌂ 160°C.

Being of loose construction it would scorch easily, so a damp cloth should be used to prevent scorching and shine. Steam assists in holding in creases, or shinking away slight fullness to shape fitted sections during garment construction – the 'easing-in' process. A special finish is required to make wool hold pleats permanently. This is called the Lintrak process.

6 *Strength*

Wool is not as strong as nylon, polyester, or the acrylics, and it loses its strength when wet. It is damaged by alkali substances and chlorine bleaches and needs care in washing. However, it resists acids.

White wool will turn yellow in prolonged sunlight.

Moths attack wool, and so moth-proof finishes need to be applied.

7 *Flammability*

Wool smoulders and is reluctant to burn. It does *not* flare up. There is the characteristic smell of burning feathers or hair (protein). Zirpro gives added flame resistance (to industrial clothes).

8 *Dyeing*

Being an absorbent fibre, wool takes up dyes well.

9 *Cost*

Wool is much more expensive to produce than cotton and synthetics. Wool costs the consumer about three times the price of cotton. One reason is that it is cheaper to grow a crop like cotton on land than to keep animals. Another is that the production of all natural fibres is subject to outside factors like weather conditions, which affect supply and demand, whereas the production of synthetic fibres from chemicals is not subject to weather conditions and can be geared to the demand much more easily.

Questions

1 **What advantages has a fibre with a natural crimp?**
2 **Explain the difference betwen woollen and worsted fabric in fibre, construction, and feel.**
3 **Explain the following terms in wool manufacture: shoddy, pure new wool, pure wool.**
4 **Where are the main wool-producing areas of the world?**
5 **Give three ways in which air is trapped in woollen fabric and becomes a good insulator.**
6 **Wool is very absorbent. State the ways in which this is a very useful quality. State any ways in which this fact creates problems.**
7 **What are the problems associated with washing wool? How can they be overcome?**
8 **Explain what substances and factors can harm wool in use and washing.**
9 **Worsted fabric is finer quality than woollen and therefore more expensive. How does the cost of these two fibres relate to other materials?**

Acrylics

For many years attempts were made to produce a man-made fibre which would be similar to wool in warmth and feel, but stronger and easier to wash. Acrylic fibres were the result. They go under the trade names of Acrilan, Courtelle, and Orlon. These fabrics are used for:

a knitwear, sweaters, dresses;

b simulated furs and fur fabrics;

c carpets;

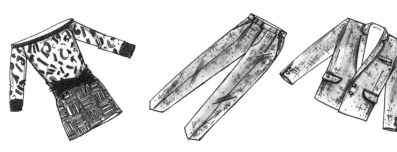

d woven and knitted fabrics such as Courtelle jersey;

e suitings.

They can also be blended with wool, polyester, viscose or acetate.

Acrilan is used to make carpets which are warm, hardwearing, easy to clean, and less expensive than wool.

Modacrylic is another one of the acrylic group. To produce this fibre 35%–85% of acrylic polymer (see p.62) is used, and so the name is short for 'modified acrylic'. Teklan and dynel are modacrylics.

The advantages of producing a man-made fibre like wool are enormous. It can be made to have better wearing and washing qualities than wool, and can be produced at a reasonable cost. Its retail price is similar to that of a moderately priced woollen fabric. Acrilan may not feel as soft as wool, but Courtelle and Orlon do.

Properties

1 *Warmth*

The fibres are generally used in staple (short length) form and this improves the warm quality. When knitted and woven loosely more air may be trapped between the fibres, thus providing a good insulating layer around the body. The fibre can be 'bulked' to produce varying weights of yarn for anything from thick knitted sweaters to woven fabrics.

2 *Absorbency*

Because of the fibre's low moisture uptake it washes easily and dries quickly. When loosely woven or knitted or when a cellular weave is used as in synthetic aertex, the fabric construction enables moisture to leave the body so that the garment remains comfortable to wear even though the fibres themselves are non-absorbent.

3 *Resilience*

Acrylics are soft to handle and lighter in weight than wool.They shed creases easily, so are useful for packing. They are fairly elastic and take up the body shape well.

4 *Washing*

	MACHINE	HAND WASH
40	Warm minimum wash	Warm
▬	Cold rinse. Short spin. Do not wring	

Easy washing and quick drying make Acrilan and Courtelle jumpers much more useful to working people who would find the careful washing and drying of woollens a time-consuming chore dependent on fine weather at weekends. However, acrylics stretch if left warm and moist. Therefore always rinse them in **cold** water before spin drying. Tumble drying should be done only with great care, using cold air. If ironing is necessary it should be done with a cool iron ⌕ on the **dry** fabric for the same reason.

5 *Effect of heat*

a At 210°C ⌕ the fabric will stick to the iron, and at a higher temperature it will decompose.

b The fibre can be heat-set into pleats, and so is suitable for dresses.

6 *Strength*

a Acrylic is stronger than wool but not as strong as nylon or polyester.

b Because the fibre resists acids, alkalis, bleaches, and solvents, it is suitable for a wide variety of purposes and normal washing is easier than wool, particularly as it dries quickly and needs little or no ironing.

c It resists sunlight and so is very practical for curtains and soft furnishings.

d It is not attacked by mildew or moths.

e Acrylics have a slight tendency to '**pill**' where the fabric is rubbed. Small balls of loose fibre collect and cling to the surface.

7 *Flammability*

Acrylics will burn, then melt. Modacrylics are self extinguishing. The acrylics can be recognized by shrinking and melting from the flame, forming a hard, roughly-shaped black bead. An aromatic smell is present.

Questions

1 **Name three fabrics which are in the acrylic group, and say what each is used for.**

2 **Give two reasons why acrylic clothes are useful for taking on holiday.**

3 **How would you wash and iron a Courtelle or Acrilan jumper?**

4 **Explain why a jumper made of Acrilan or Courtelle is much better for winter dinghy sailing than a woollen sweater.**

Silk

Silk has traditionally been worn and used by the wealthy and is still chosen for special occasions. It has always been highly regarded in royal, ceremonial, ecclesiastical, and legal circles. When lawyers reach the height of their profession they 'take silk'. This means that they are entitled to wear silk robes when they become a Queen's Counsel. When academic degrees are conferred, silken hoods are worn.

Silk ties, squares, and handkerchieves are given as very special presents. They are probably given more for their beauty than use, for real silk is very expensive. Why do people choose silk? Is it just tradition, or has silk some quality that other fabrics do not possess? Let's look closely at the fabric and find out.

Silk is made by the caterpillar of the silk moth (*bombyx mori*). This moth lays eggs which hatch in about three days into caterpillars or silk worms. They feed on mulberry leaves. Within about a month they are approximately 8 cm long. Each caterpillar then spins a cocoon by producing a long filament of thread which it winds around itself hundreds of times. This forms the case in which it sleeps for about a fortnight, after which it hopes to emerge as a silk moth.

Fully-grown silk worm surrounded by newly-hatched worms.

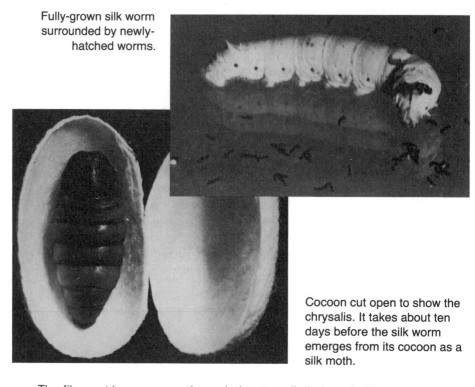

Cocoon cut open to show the chrysalis. It takes about ten days before the silk worm emerges from its cocoon as a silk moth.

The filament is very smooth, and about a mile in length. The cocoon is held together by the gum which surrounds the filament. In warm water this gum is loosened and the filament can be carefully unwound. This has been done in China for 4000 years and in Japan since AD 500. The breeding of silk worms for silk is done on silk farms. It is called **sericulture**. Japan and China produce most of the world's silk.

The cocoons are placed in a pan of hot water to soften the gum which holds the silk threads together. The ends float free and are caught on the revolving brush.

Raw silk is dull and creamy coloured because it has the gum still on it, but when the gum is removed the silk filament reflects light and has a beautiful lustre. In fact it is the most lustrous of all fibres.

Another variety of moth is called the tussah. It lives on wild oak leaves. It is not cultivated on silk farms. The silk it produces is called tussore or wild silk. Tussore is a slightly coarser filament, not quite so smooth, and it has a creamy colour. It does not take dyes as well as cultivated silk, and so is often left in its natural colour. Shantung and pongee are two wild silk fabrics.

Silk is the only natural fibre produced as a continuous filament. The fine filaments are twisted together in the spinning process and really strong fabrics result even though the threads are so fine. It was widely used as a fabric for parachutes until nylon was developed.

Spun silk is produced in a much kinder way from staple fibre. If the moth hatches out it emerges by breaking the cocoon. This leaves short silk fibres, called **noils**, which are used as staple fibre. It is carded and combed and then spun. Spun silk is not as strong and lustrous as continuous filament. Nevertheless it is a beautiful fabric, and is less expensive.

Tex and denier

The fineness of any fibre is measured in the unit of **tex**. This is the weight in grams of 1000 metres of fibre or yarn. The unit of **denier** was formerly used. This is the weight in grams of 9000 metres. So the denier of a fibre is 9 times its tex. In both units the smaller the number, the finer the fibre. (15 denier nylon is finer than 30 denier).

Properties

1 *Lustre*
Until the development of man-made fibres, silk was the only continuous filament. It has always been prized for its lustre.

2 *Resilience*
It is very resilient, and it drapes beautifully.

3 *Warmth*
It has a soft luxurious feel and is warm to handle. It is a poor conductor of heat and so retains the body warmth; yet being fine it is cool to wear in summer.

4 *Absorbency*
It is absorbent, but dries quickly. When wrapped in a towel the fabric is usually dry enough for ironing.
The beauty of cultivated silk is enhanced by the fact that it takes up dyes well. Being so fine, colours and prints go right through.

5 *Strength*

It is light in weight and fine, but in spite of that it is strong and wears well. However it is damaged by acids, bleach, and alkali. Sunlight and perspiration rot the fabric. For this reason protection should be put beneath the arms of silk garments.

6 *Washing*

Silk should be handled carefully and alkali used only with great care. Use cool water (hot water hardens silk) and mild soap flakes, Stergene or Dreft. Wash by kneading and squeezing in the water. Do not rub or twist the fabric as this separates the threads and spoils its appearance. Never wring silk as pressure would crease it badly.

Rinse it well, and add one tablespoon of vinegar per gallon of water to the final rinse to brighten the colour.

Lightly spin, and roll and press gently in a towel to dry.

Silk is not an 'easy care' fabric. It needs ironing.

Cultivated silk should be ironed damp with a moderate iron. It scorches easily. Do not iron over seams as this makes shiny marks on the right side.

Use a pressing cloth to prevent the silk becoming hard.

Wild silk however is better ironed dry. This is because it still contains some gum which will become hard or papery if ironed damp.

If silk needs to be stiffened, gum arabic can be used in the final rinsing water. It can be purchased from the chemist's.

Sometimes screen-printed silk is not colour-fast. It should be washed separately at 30°C. It also helps to soak it in salt water before washing.

As silk watermarks it cannot be dampened down if a part gets too dry. If a satisfactory finish is not achieved, and rough dry marks appear, the whole item should be re-wetted, rolled in a towel, and ironed again.

Do not press creases in as this will break the fibres.

Always air silk well as it is subject to mildew.

7 *Flammability*

Silk only burns slowly.

8 *Sewing*

Sewing presents some problems as silk is a slippery fabric. Machining is likely to pucker. This is because the feed dog is pushing the bottom layer of fabric through while the presser foot is holding the top layer down (see p.136). The two layers of fabric therefore slip apart, and the seam puckers. To avoid this happening, put tissue paper on the seam while machining, and tear it away afterwards.

Use pure silk thread for sewing and a size 11 needle.

9 *Cost*

Silk is the most expensive fibre there is. Sericulture is an expensive operation, for unwinding the silk is a highly skilled task.

The heaviest silk is **brocade** which is woven with a raised pattern. Silk velvet and brocade are used for very expensive drapes or curtains and can be seen today in many stately homes and castles. Lighter weight silks such as **Jap silk** (which is cultivated) and wild silk or **tussore**, **shantung**, and **pongee**, are used for dresses, blouses, and men's shirts. Ceremonial and ecclesiastical robes are made from either weight. **Chiffon** is a very fine silk.

Silk dresses for a royal wedding

Questions

1 **Which are the main silk-producing countries, and how is silk made?**
2 **What are the special qualities which silk has, that manufacturers try to imitate in other fibres? Why is silk expensive?**
3 **Explain how silk should be washed, and why.**
4 **Why is silk difficult to sew? How can this difficulty be overcome?**
5 **What do you understand by the terms: tussore, Jap silk, spun silk? Which would you expect to be the most expensive and have the most lustre? Which would be the least expensive?**

Nylon

▲ Nylon is a man-made fibre.
You can make nylon in the laboratory quite simply by using two solutions. The solutions can be made up by the laboratory technician.
You need: a 5% solution of adipyl chloride in carbon tetrachloride – call that solution A; and a 5% solution of diamine hexane in water – call that solution B.
(5% means 5 parts in 100 parts.)

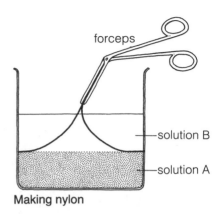

Making nylon

1 In a beaker put about 1 cm of solution A.
2 Carefully pour on to it about 1 cm of solution B. **Beware of the fumes**. Do not breathe them in, particularly if you are asthmatic. These two solutions do not mix. A skin forms where they meet as they react together.
3 With a pair of tweezers or forceps pick up this skin in the middle and draw it into a filament. Carefully wind it round a glass rod. This is nylon.

Nylon forms as a long smooth filament, but it can be cut into a staple fibre. All the chemicals are by-products of the petroleum industry so they are readily available to be made into nylon.

When Carothers and his team first discovered the polymer in 1935 they were hoping for a textile with properties something like wool. However they quickly realized that nylon was very light and smooth, more like silk, and extremely strong. In fact its production was very timely, because it could be used as well as, and instead of, silk for parachutes during the Second World War.

Nylon is a fine, smooth fibre. It can be closely woven and is extremely strong. It is used to make spinnakers for boats. A spinnaker is a sail used to billow out when the wind is behind. It draws the boat forward. It is not raised all the time, but only when the wind comes from directly behind the boat. When the boat changes course it must be dropped and stowed quickly.

Nylon is windproof and water repellent. This is an excellent quality for outer clothing because it will not absorb water. It also means that when fabrics are washed they dry quickly for they have not absorbed any moisture, and it simply drips off the surface. It was quickly realized that nylon had great possibilities as a clothing material and so it was cut as a staple fibre to give it bulk, and crimped to make it elastic. Bulk and crimp both give warmth by trapping air, and when a fabric is brushed to raise a nap that too traps air and gives warmth. The inclusion of air in the structure of a fabric assists in its absorbency even though the fibre itself is not absorbent. A wide variety of outdoor items, household goods, and clothes are made of nylon, for example: ropes, tents, groundsheets, jackets, swimsuits, umbrellas, nightwear, and sheets.

▲ Gather together some pieces of nylon fabric, and a selection of nylon clothes. You will find a variety of structures, textures, and weights: knitted, woven cellular, fine, coarse; some stretch nylon like Helanca; some bulked to give a warm fluffy finish, like nylon knitting yarn. Examine them all using the following suggestions, and write down your thoughts and conclusions as you do so.

1 Look at **warmth.**
  a Which of your items are perfectly smooth and shiny? They will have no warmth. But you may find that nylon is used for coats with an inner quilted or foam layer to give warmth.
  b Which ones have been bulked? How? What are they used for?
  c Have any got a cellular weave? What are they used for?
  d Have you a piece of brushed nylon (where the nap has been raised)? What is that fabric used for?
  e Have any been treated in any other way to increase their ability to hold air between the fibres, and make the fabric a bad conductor of heat? Will they be warmer than smooth shiny nylon?
2 Look for **resilience.**
  Crumple all your fabrics up tightly in your hand.
  What do you notice about their resilience?
3 What about **absorbency**?
  Weigh your fabrics. Wash and spin dry. Then weigh again. Has the nylon absorbed any water?
4 Is nylon **strong**?
  a Using your scraps of fabric, pull them hard. Are they strong?
  b Then wet them. Pull them hard again. Does wetting make any difference to the strength of nylon?
5 How does nylon stand up to **heat**? Use your scraps of fabric again here.
  a Iron at 120°C ⌐ . What is the result?
  b Fold the nylon. Cover with paper. Press well at ⌐ setting.
    The nylon melts enough to retain the crease because it is thermoplastic.
    It sets in its new shape as it cools.
    Wash the nylon. Has it retained the crease?
    Thermoplastic fabrics can be permanently creased.
  c Thermoplastic yarns can be permanently textured.
    Wind nylon thread around a knitting needle. Cover with a sheet of paper.
    Iron at ⌐ (hot), rotating the needle to warm all the thread.
    Take the thread off the needle. ᗧᗧᗧᗧᗧ You have given it a texture.
    Wash it. Does it remain textured?

Electrostatic charge

▲ Rub a nylon comb on the sleeve of an acrylic jumper. Then put a tiny scrap of paper on the sleeve or comb. What do you notice?
Find some dust. Rub your comb and fabric together again, then place them close to the dust. What do you notice?

On dry days non-absorbent fabrics like nylon become electrostatically charged when rubbing against the body or other layers of fabric. You may have come across an electrostatic charge on several occasions without realizing what it was. On a hot evening when you comb your hair, has it been attracted to the nylon comb or brush, and stood out towards it?

Have you ever noticed that when you take off a nylon slip in the summer it crackles, and is drawn towards your skin? If you do this in the dark you can actually see the sparks! Similarly if you wear a nylon dress, without a petticoat, the dress is sometimes drawn into your legs as you move.

These things happen because an electrostatic charge is produced by friction against the body, or against other layers of dry non-absorbent fabric. You can easily prevent the synthetic dress from being drawn to your body by wearing a cotton petticoat. (Why wouldn't a nylon one do?)

The reason why an electrostatic charge is produced is that we are using dry non-absorbent fabrics. Water is a conductor of electricity. So moisture in a fabric would conduct electricity away. But a dry fabric, which does not absorb moisture, will not conduct electricity away. So the charge stands still and is called static electricity. The fabric is said to be electrostatically charged.

Unfortunately dust particles are drawn to nylon, or any other synthetic, when it is electrostatically charged, and they stick. So the hem or sleeve of a dress or petticoat picks up dust or dirt more readily by actually attracting it, and the dirt is then difficult to remove. This is why white nylon or polyester underskirts or skirts so often look rather grey or soiled at the hem area even though they have been washed. So some makers favour dark colours like black for underwear. An 'Anti-Stat' finish can be applied to nylon, polyester, and the acrylics.

Fabric conditioners added to the final rinse after washing act as a 'wetting' agent on synthetics. With this on the surface, conduction of electricity is improved, and fabrics do not soil so quickly or cling.

Properties

1 *Warmth*
Nylon is a good conductor of heat. It has no natural warmth, but can be made warm by bulking or crimping the fibre to include air, or by brushing the surface of the fabric.

2 *Absorbency*
Nylon is not absorbent. It therefore dries very quickly.
It is not suitable for clothes worn next to the skin unless the structure of the fabric includes a lot of air to allow moisture to escape.

Its water repellency is of great value for outer wear and textile items for outdoor activities like tents and groundsheets.

3 *Resilience*
Nylon is very resilient. It does not crease. It springs back into shape immediately. It requires little ironing, and so is an easy-care fabric. It is quite elastic.

4 *Strength*
Nylon is very strong, even though light in weight. Wetting does not affect its strength. It resists alkalis, but can be harmed by bleach and mineral acids. Being of chemical origin it is not a food for mildew, mould, or moths, and is therefore unharmed by them.

5 *Washing*
As nylon is not absorbent, it does not soil easily.
Marks wash off in normal washing.

50	MACHINE	HAND WASH
	Hand hot medium wash	Hand hot
	Cold rinse. Short spin or drip dry	

6 *Effect of heat*
Nylon melts at 250°C.
It is a resilient fibre and does not require much pressing. When using an iron however it should be on ⌂ 120°C.
Slight softening is caused at a temperature between these two figures. This is how permanent creasing is done. The fabric is thermoplastic (melts in heat).

7 *Flammability*
Nylon does not burn; it melts. Nylon net includes a lot of air and will burn. It should be given flame-retardancy treatment on manufacture. Do not put net curtains in a kitchen, where they could catch fire.

8 *Dyes*
Although it is non-absorbent, nylon takes dyes well. The colour is added during manufacture, at the wet polymer stage, that is before the nylon is extruded and set into fibre. (See p.30.)

9 *Blending*
It is useful to blend nylon with other fibres to give the other fibre strength from nylon, and to obtain a quality that another fibre has. For example wool has warmth and absorbency; nylon has strength. Socks made of a mixture of wool and nylon wear and wash better than woollen socks. They are warmer, more absorbent, and more comfortable to wear than nylon socks.

Questions

1 **Why is nylon suitable for equipment used for outdoor pursuits? Name four such pieces of outdoor equipment, and in each case say why the properties of nylon make it particularly suitable for use in that way.**
2 **Nylon has no natural warmth. Name three ways in which the manufacturer can make it warm to wear.**
3 **Why is nylon called an easy-care fabric?**
4 **What substances can harm nylon in wear and washing?**
5 **Is nylon easily damaged by moths, mould, and mildew? Explain your answer.**

Polyester

In the early 1950s, **terylene** was produced. It seemed to have all the qualities of nylon, but was even better in many ways. Again it was produced from substances from the petroleum industry. It was named terylene after one of the chemicals involved in its production, but now it is referred to as **polyester**. This word comes from the group of chemical substances to which terylene belongs called esters. Because it is a polymer (a large molecule formed from a number of simple molecules) the word POLYESTER was coined.

The polyester group includes **terylene** and **trevira**. **Crimplene** is *crimp*ed tery*lene* (bulked polyester). **Polyester jersey** is a knitted dress fabric. **Dacron**, made in America, and **Tergal**, made in France, are trade names. You have probably seen these names on clothes labels.

Properties

1 *Strength*
Polyester is very strong and resists rubbing well. It is so strong that it is used for safety belts in cars. It is not harmed by alkalis, bleaches, or even acids. Mildew and moths do not like chemically-produced fabrics, so it is safe from those. It withstands sunlight very well and makes very good curtains.

2 *Warmth*
Polyester is not warm to wear, though it can be blended with wool to give the type of fabric the early researchers were looking for – one which is warm and washes well. Polyester can be used as a filling for duvets, quilts, and pillows. Because air is trapped within the filling it is very light and very warm.

3 *Absorbency*
Not only is polyester non-absorbent, it is hydrophobic – water hating. This means that it dries even more quickly than nylon. It does not absorb stains and is very easy to launder. This is one reason why it is mixed with cotton. Polyester is not used for underwear because it is so non-absorbent. A fabric that does not absorb moisture cannot be left damp. All modern sails (except spinnakers which need to be particularly light) are made from polyester, and this cuts out the chore of drying your sails after use, or after capsizing!

You probably found in your tests on p.32 that polyester did not take up dye very well. Again this is because it is not absorbent. Some dyes have been specially developed for synthetic fabrics. Commercially, polyester may be produced ready-dyed.

Because it is so dry, polyester becomes electrostatically charged and picks up dirt, so it should be rinsed in a fabric softener after washing.

4 *Resilience*
Polyester is particularly resilient. It requires very little ironing or pressing. It resists stretching and so polyester garments keep their shape well. Polyester is not as elastic as nylon so it has never been used for stockings and tights.

It holds pleats permanently. This is another reason why it is mixed with cotton and also wool. 45% polyester is mixed with 55% wool or worsted fibre to give a fabric which holds pleats, creases very well, wears well, and washes well. So men's trousers and suits made from this mixture are smart, resilient, warm, and easy to care for.

5 *Washing*

Polyester is very easy to care for. It should be washed at 🪣50 or 🪣40 if blended with wool. Drying is extremely quick and ironing minimized.

🪣50	MACHINE	HAND WASH
	Hand hot medium wash	Hand hot
▬	Cold rinse. Short spin or drip dry	

🪣40	MACHINE	HAND WASH
	Warm medium wash	Warm
▬	Cold rinse. Short spin. Do not wring	

6 *Effect of heat*

Polyester melts at a higher temperature than nylon and will withstand slightly more heat. Iron if necessary on setting one ⟙
It takes a hotter iron to permanently crease polyester items than nylon ones. Texturing can also be performed on polyester yarns, again at a slightly higher temperature.

7 *Flammability*

Polyester does not burn readily. It shrinks away from the flame. Because it melts at a higher temperature than nylon it is slower to melt. The flame becomes luminous and the smoke darker.
The flammability of polyester cotton is interesting. Because the cotton component prevents the polyester from shrinking away from the flame, the polyester burns readily. Polyester cotton is therefore quite flammable.

▲ *Try this experiment*

You will need samples of:
- polyester
- polyester and wool blend
- wool
- polyester and cotton blend
- cotton

You will also need a taper, two clamps, a wire, and a baking tray.

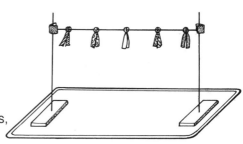

1 Cut strips of fabric about 2 cm wide and 10 cm long.
2 Tie each one on to a piece of wire long enough to leave space between them.
3 Put the wire between two clamps over a thick metal baking tray.
4 Carefully compare the ease with which these fabrics ignite, how they burn, melt, or smoulder, and the time it takes to destroy each one completely, and the residue. What are your conclusions?

Questions

1 **What is the meaning of the term hydrophobic? There are three ways in which this is a helpful property in fabric care. What are they? What is the disadvantage of a hydrophobic fabric in wear?**
2 **Why should polyester be given a final rinse in a fabric softener after washing?**
3 **List six advantages of using polyester fabrics for clothing.**
4 **How should a polyester skirt be laundered?**
5 **Name two fibres with which polyester may be blended.**

Cotton

Cotton can be produced much more cheaply and easily than wool. It is easier to devote land to the growth of cotton seed than to rearing animals. A crop of cotton also has by-products. Cotton seed produces vegetable oil for human consumption, and animal feed can be manufactured from the residue.

Cotton needs a tropical climate and wet soil. The West Indies produce Sea Island cotton, a soft, long-fibred, fine cotton of very good quality. Egyptian cotton is good quality too. A great deal of cotton is produced in the southern states of North America (in folk songs called the 'cotton-pickin' South); and in Russia, China, India, and Uganda.

The plants are about 1.75 metres high. The cotton boll forms after the flower has withered away, leaving the seed pod developing. This contains fibres, rather like cotton wool, surrounding the seeds. The seeds grow and swell. After about three months the pod bursts, revealing the boll which is ready for picking.

Black slave labour used to be used in the southern part of North America. The cotton pickers went amongst the plants many times as the boll ripened until they were all harvested. Now that is all done by machine. During the eighteenth century cotton came from America to Manchester. Cotton mills sprang up in the surrounding district and the Lancashire cotton towns grew up nearby to accommodate a new thriving industry rivalling the Yorkshire woollen industry, already in existence. Before the Industrial Revolution (the coming of machinery), women would spin yarn at home. Hence the meaning of the word spinster – a woman who spins.

After the Industrial Revolution in Britain, machinery speeded up spinning and weaving, changing them from cottage crafts (done at home) to large-scale factory concerns.

Hargreaves' 'Spinning Jenny', 1764

Natural fibres are subject to outside factors causing changes in supply and demand. The boll weevil is an insect which attacks the cotton boll. Bad weather conditions and a poor harvest can cause a shortage. The price of oil can raise production costs.

The thriving cotton industry in Lancashire was hit hard in this century by the development of the industry in China and Taiwan. Cheap labour in Asian countries was used to finish cotton goods, and these flooded the world market at very competitive prices. In addition the production of synthetic textiles during this century has had a considerable effect on the cotton industry.

Production

After picking, cotton is 'ginned'. This process removes seeds, stalks, leaves and any other material. Then it is compressed into bales and sent to local cotton mills, or exported. At the mill the process of carding brushes the long fibres into a thin film. This is separated into slivers which are drawn out, becoming finer and finer until they are ready for spinning.

The spinning process twists the fibres to give strength. Cotton is twisted with a Z twist for sewing thread. This is so that it does not untwist itself when being used in a machine.

When threading a needle for hand sewing, leave the cotton attached to the reel, and thread the free end. By doing this the twist of the cotton matches the flow of your work movement in sewing. So the thread will not twist up and knot itself.

Thread for sewing must be extremely smooth. So it is **mercerized** (see p.16) to make the fibres swell and untwist, shrinking them along their length. This makes them smoother and gives lustre. Embroidery thread is also mercerized making it very smooth. As it absorbs dyes well and has a lustre, it is as good as silk for fine decorative work.

Cotton fabric is likely to shrink because it is stretched in weaving. So the cloth can be pre-shrunk by the Rigmel method in Britain or sanforized in America (see p.41).

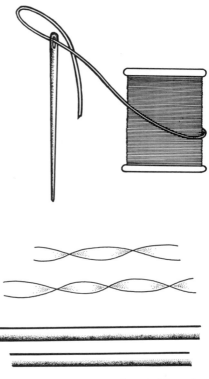

Mercerizing: fibres swell, untwist, and shrink in length

Properties

1 *Warmth*
Cotton is a good conductor of heat and is therefore cool to wear. Brushing increases its ability to hold air, and therefore makes it slightly warmer. But brushed cotton is flammable and must be given a flame-retardant finish.

2 *Absorbency*
Cotton is an absorbent fibre, and so it is very suitable to wear next to the skin. It is not as absorbent as linen, but is cheaper and is used a lot for tea-towels. By increasing the surface area with a looped warp thread on both sides (see p.25), more water can be absorbed. For this reason terry towelling takes up water extremely well. It is used for towels, beach wear, and babies' nappies.

Aertex is a cellular weave. This traps air and enables perspiration to escape from the skin. So, as well as being absorbent, the structure gives it wearing and comfort qualities for sportswear. See synthetic aertex p.53.

Cotton needs thorough drying. In all vegetable matter cell walls are composed of cellulose. Mildew is a mould which acts on dead vegetation – feeding on the cellulose. Leaving cotton damp invites this mould to attack, and so it is important to dry cotton. Mildew rots cotton, and is virtually impossible to remove.

3 *Strength*
Cotton is quite a strong fibre. Its strength increases when it is wet. It will withstand rubbing, boiling, change of temperature, alkali, and even bleach. In fact it will take really harsh treatment in washing. Any items likely to need boiling to kill germs and prevent infection such as sheets, handkerchieves, and bandages are ideally made from cotton. Hard-wearing items like boiler suits, denim jeans, and drill aprons are made from twill-weave cotton fabrics.

95	MACHINE	HAND WASH
	Very hot to boil maximum wash	Hand-hot or boil
Spin or wring		

Cotton without special finishes

60	MACHINE	HAND WASH
	Hot maximum wash	Hand-hot
Spin or wring		

Things which get very soiled and stained such as overalls were always traditionally made from cotton before nylon became so popular. Although cotton, being absorbent, does take up stains, they can be removed relatively easily because cotton is unharmed by most chemicals. However nylon is not absorbent and so does not take up stains in the first place. Most stains can therefore be removed by ordinary washing. Nylon is quicker and easier to care for, and so is very popular for overalls. But cotton is cooler to wear, and this is also a consideration for an overall.

Cotton is harmed by acids. These rot the fabric. Prolonged sunlight weakens the fabric and so cotton curtains should be lined.

4 *Effect of heat*
Cotton withstands a temperature of 210°C. A hot iron is needed ⬛ and it irons well without scorching. Ironing whilst damp, until the fabric is dry, gives a smooth crease-free result.

5 *Resilience*
Cotton has no resilience. When creased it remains so, until the crease is ironed or washed out. This is a useful feature when sewing. However, to retain pleats commercial treatment with resin is necessary. Trousers are creased in high temperature ovens to bake on a resin coating. Cotton is often blended

with 67% polyester. Cellulose fabrics like cotton do not hold pleats well, but a high percentage of polyester means that pleats or creases set in with heat are held permanently by the thermoplastic fibre.

6 *Flammability*
Cotton is flammable and flares up, particularly when the nap has been raised by brushing. It needs Proban treatment, especially for items for the young or elderly. As it is a cellulose fibre, it burns with the characteristic bonfire smell of burning wood or paper. It leaves a white outline of ash.

7 *Lustre*
Sea Island cotton has a lustre, but other types lack this. Manufacturers therefore treat it by mercerizing and by calendering (see p.38) to provide more lustre.

8 *Dyeing*
Cotton takes up dyes very well. Attractive colourful prints can be produced.

9 *Washing*
Although the cotton fibre can withstand harsh treatment, the finishes that the manufacturer may have to apply to it will not. Cotton may have had one or more of a number of finishes applied to it, and therefore require more care in washing.

It may have been:	given more lustre	calendered or mercerized	50
	made water-repellent	treated with silicone	see fabric label
	flame-retardant	Proban, Pyrovatex	see fabric label
	made stiffer	trubenized	see label or 40
	made crease resistant	tebilized	50
	set into pleats or creases	Evaprest, Tootaprest, Fixaform	50
	pre-shrunk	Rigmel, sanforized	50

So it will need more careful treatment, and must be washed at a lower temperature. Always look at the label on cotton goods and follow the care label instructions.

Questions

1 **What is the meaning of the phrase 'a good conductor of heat'?**
2 **Why is it important to wear something absorbent next to the skin?**
3 **Explain why aertex is suitable for sportswear.**
4 **What are the advantages and disadvantages of cotton and nylon overalls?**
   Say which you would choose and why for working in: (a) a restaurant kitchen; (b) serving at a petrol pump.
5 **Give *two* ways in which men's trousers can be permanently creased.**
6 **Why are cotton fabrics likely to need finishes? Give *four* finishes that can be applied to cotton garments, stating in each case two garments which might be treated in that way.**

Linen

In Chapter 1 we looked at how the Maoris used flax to weave into fabric. In fact flax was certainly the first plant fibre that was ever woven, and linen was probably the first fabric made. Egyptian mummies have been found in tombs wrapped in linen cloth. Six thousand years later the cloth was still intact! There is no doubt that linen is a very strong fabric. It can be either fine or coarse. The ships that sailed against the Spanish Armada had linen sails. At the same time fine linen was being made into delicate lace.

Flax grows in a cool damp climate. The main linen-producing areas are on a temperate line (with no extremes of heat or cold) in the Northern hemisphere – Normandy, Belgium, Holland, through Central Europe to Russia. China and Egypt also produce linen. The plant grows to about one metre high, and has a blue or white flower. In September the plants are uprooted by a puller, a machine which lays the flax out in parallel 'swaithes' on the fields. These are left for five to seven weeks whilst the dew, sun, and the occasional shower act on the straw. This process is called **retting**. It encourages the growth of micro-organisms, whose enzymes attack the pectin, a gum which adheres the flax fibre to the rest of the stem. The quality or fineness of the fibre inside the stem depends on the variety sown, the weather, the type of soil, and the degree of retting.

The flax is then gathered, dried, and scutched – a process of rolling and mechanical scraping. This reveals the fibres. They are then combed and are ready to be spun (twisted) into yarn. Flax fibres are long, about 30–50 cm. Harvesting, retting, scutching, and spinning all take a lot of time and effort. This is why linen, which is woven from flax, is expensive.

A smooth lustrous texture is given to linen cloth by calendering it using heavy rollers. (Beetling – beating with heavy wooden hammers – is less used.) Flattening uneven fibre ends means that light can shine continuously across the smooth surface giving the fabric its lustre (Damask, p.25).

Very fine bleached linen fabrics are lawn and cambric, both used for good quality handkerchieves and blouses. Linen sheeting is crisp and cool. Medium and heavier weight linen is used for embroidery, because it is easy to count the threads, so important for good neat decorative work.

Coarser linen fabrics are **crash** and **brown holland**. Occasional uneven threads are a characteristic of the coarser fabrics. This is known as a **slub thread**, and manufacturers have imitated it on synthetic fibres.

Properties

1 *Warmth*

Linen is a good conductor of heat. Clothes are cool to wear. Linen sheets have a refreshing cool feel.

2 *Absorbency*

Linen absorbs water well, so it is used for tea-towels. Absorbency is important for comfort in bed – another advantage of linen sheets.

3 *Resilience*

Linen is not resilient. It creases badly. This problem in wear is overcome by applying a crease-resistant finish, called **tebilizing**, after manufacture. It must then be washed at ⌷50⌷ to avoid damaging the resin finish.

Recent developments in blending flax means that it can now be blended with other fibres such as polyester to give the qualities that linen lacks, such as resilience. Linen has no elasticity.

⌷95⌷	MACHINE	HAND WASH
	Very hot to boil maximum wash	Hand-hot or boil
	Spin or wring	

Linen without special finish

⌷50⌷	MACHINE	HAND WASH
	Hand-hot medium wash	Hand-hot
	Cold rinse. Short spin or drip dry	

Linen with special finish

4 *Washing*

Linen is a very strong fibre. It is even stronger when wet, because of the length of its fibres. It will withstand boiling, rubbing, alkalis, and a very hot iron. But as we have just seen, when a finish is applied it must be washed and ironed at a lower temperature and with more care.

5 *Effect of heat*

Linen withstands high temperature ⌷iron⌷ , unless it has been treated to stiffen it. Table linen is usually starched to give a good finish. This means that a hot iron is necessary to cook the starch in the fabric. Linen should be ironed damp, dried with the iron, and then aired well to prevent attack by mildew.

6 *Strength*

Linen is a strong, hard-wearing fabric, but it is damaged by acid. Being a cellulose fibre it is attacked by mildew if left damp. It resists sunlight well.

7 *Flammability*

Linen burns with a yellow/orange flame giving a smell of burning grass and a grey skeletal ash.

8 *Dyeing*

Linen does not absorb dyes as well as cotton.

9 *Sewing quality*

Dress-weight linen has thick threads and so frays badly. It must therefore be carefully neatened. Three-step zigzag or overlocking are suitable methods.

10 *Cost*

Linen is an expensive fabric.

Questions

1 **Why is linen produced in Holland and Belgium?**
2 **Why is fine linen expensive, yet coarser linen available more cheaply ?**
3 **Name two linen fabrics from which handkerchieves are made. Which of the properties of linen make it particularly suitable for handkerchieves?**
4 **Why is it desirable to apply a finish to dress linen? What finish should be applied?**
5 **Explain why linen must be aired well.**

Regenerated cellulose fibres

Many attempts have been made to produce a fabric similar to silk more cheaply. A Frenchman, Chardonett, made the first artificial silk in the 1890s. This was a very shiny fabric, but unfortunately it was too flammable. Several other attempts have resulted in cellulose being regenerated (re-formed) in four ways to make **viscose**, **acetate**, **tricel** (another form of acetate), and **polynosic rayon**. It has also been discovered that by cutting filament into staple fibre, the fibre could be made to resemble wool or cotton.

Viscose

Viscose is pure cellulose. The raw material is wood or cotton linters. Linters are the short cotton fibres stripped off the ginned seed. After passing through chemical processes the cellulose is left in a more soluble form.

It is then forced through a **spinneret**. This is rather like a shower forcing out fine icing. The round holes make the shape of the filament.

If the extruded (forced out) substance is passed through a liquid to set it, the process is called **wet spinning**. If it passes into warm air and dries by evaporation, it is called **dry spinning**. In both cases a continuous filament is produced. It looks rather like silk in appearance.

Viscose can be cut into staple fibre to resemble wool or cotton, and then it is spun.

Properties

1 *Warmth*
Viscose is not warm to wear. It conducts heat well from the body.

2 *Absorbency*
It is absorbent and therefore suitable for wearing in hot weather. Viscose fabrics take time to dry. Dyes are absorbed well, and are fast.

3 *Resilience*
Viscose is not resilient. It needs a crease-resistant finish of resin, and then care must be taken not to wash this off or lose it by the heat of the iron. Viscose is not very elastic.

4 *Strength*
Viscose is not strong and is even weaker when wet. Being cellulose it is attacked by mildew. It is damaged by acids and strong alkalis.

5 *Washing*
Viscose is best washed carefully in mild soap or soapless detergent and warm water. As viscose is weakened when wet, dry cleaning is recommended for some types. Look at the care label and follow the instructions carefully.

6 *Effect of heat*

Viscose does not stand up to heat well. It should be ironed with a cool iron while damp. Beware of losing any crease-resistant finish which might have been applied by the manufacturer.

7 *Cost*

Viscose can be produced cheaply. It is used for items which are not going to be subjected to hard wear, or are not required to last.

As a continuous filament it has a good lustre resembling silk. As a staple fibre it is often blended with wool to reduce the cost of woollen items. Viscose and cotton blends are also available.

Softly draped viscose dress fabric: staple fibre

Viscose/cotton blend for curtains

100% viscose lining in sports jacket

Lining of lustrous viscose satin in fashion coat

Blend: polyester 67%/viscose 33% for school trousers

Non-woven viscose

The filament is spread out at random as a film and then imprinted with a thread-like appearance. In fact there are no threads in it. It takes colour quite well, and is made into curtain fabrics at half the cost of cotton. (It is also blended with cotton to make a pile fabric for curtains.) Having no resilience, this is not recommended for loose covers.

Modal and polynosic

Modern developments in viscose production have increased the strength of regenerated cellulose. The aim has been to make a fibre as strong or stronger than cotton. In addition the makers wanted it to have a good lustre, strength (particularly when wet), and the added advantage over cotton that it would not shrink.

Modal and polynosic have been the result, appearing on the market as **Vincel** and **Zantrel**. You may have noticed both these names, or the term polynosic, when looking at labels on underwear. Being a regenerated fibre it can be produced in whatever thickness is desired. As a continuous filament it can have whatever amount of lustre is desired. It can be cut into staple fibre, used alone, or blended with cotton or polyester. It is sometimes used with cotton as an underwear fabric for vests and pants for men, women and children. This blend reduces cost and prevents shrinkage.

Acetate

Cellulose is chemically changed by the addition of concentrated acetic acid to produce cellulose acetate. What is the common name for dilute acetic acid? You sprinkle it on your chips! Note the smell of vinegar in the burning test on acetate.

Acetone is used to make cellulose soluble during the process of making acetate fibre. In fact it will dissolve the fibre completely. Note the test used on p.83. Remember this when considering using anything involving acetone near acetate. Acetone is found in some glues, nail varnish, varnish remover, and some dry-cleaning and stain-removal materials.

Properties

1 *Warmth*
Acetate is a poor conductor of heat and so keeps the body fairly warm. Its warmth can be increased by trapping air in the construction of the fibre, and so it is used as a warm lining for coats. Cheaper winter dress fabrics and suiting cloth are made from acetate.

2 *Resilience*
Acetate is quite resilient, and somewhat elastic.

3 *Absorbency*
It is not very absorbent and therefore is not suitable for underwear or nightwear. In hot weather it feels sticky in wear. As it is not absorbent it dries quickly. After initial difficulties it can now be dyed quite well.

4 *Washing*
Acetate will not shrink or stretch in washing, but rubbing, twisting, or wringing will cause permanent creases, so it needs handling carefully.
It withstands wash powders.
Being a smooth fibre it does not take in dirt.

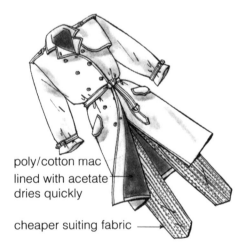

poly/cotton mac
lined with acetate
dries quickly

cheaper suiting fabric ⟶

	MACHINE	HAND WASH
40	Warm minimum wash	Warm
	Cold rinse. Short spin. Do not wring	

5 *Effect of heat*
Acetate is a thermoplastic fibre (one that melts with warmth). This means that it requires careful ironing on setting 1 only ⌐ to avoid melting the fibre. (Note that acetate is used to trubenize other fabrics – see p.38.)

Acetate should be ironed damp on the wrong side with care. It cannot be sprinkled with water to remove rough dry marks, because like silk, it water-marks. If dry patches appear the fabric must be re-wetted and re-ironed. Glazing is caused by ironing over seams. So acetate is not an easy-care fabric.

Cost
It is more expensive than viscose.

Tricel

Tricel dress, permanently pleated   Tricel blouse and matching lining in suit

A similar fibre called tri-acetate has been evolved which has improved qualities. It is commonly known as **tricel**. The main difference with this regenerated fibre is that it has a higher melting point and can be 'heat set'. This means that it can be permanently pleated, and can resist creasing. It will also accept a dye more firmly. In addition it is even less absorbent than acetate, and so dries quickly. It therefore has the easy-care properties found in synthetics such as nylon, polyester, and the acrylics, yet it is cheaper to produce than the synthetic fibres. It withstands washing better and does not shrink or stretch. It resists acids and alkalis, and does not even dissolve in acetone. As with many fabrics, tumble dry carefully, for over-drying in warmth causes creases to be heat-set in.

Tricel can be knitted as a fine jersey with a silky finish, or it can have a brushed surface. Both are attractive for dresses and blouses. It is the best of regenerated fabrics for dress wear.

Questions

1 **What is meant by the term 'regenerated fibres'?**
2 **Why are these fibres cheaper than others?**
3 **What are the chief disadvantages of**
    (a) viscose;
    (b) acetate?
4 **Explain why manufacturers use them**
    (a) for linings;
    (b) blended with other fibres.
5 **Look for viscose and acetate labels on clothes and other items. Why do you find a number of blends with viscose and acetate on market stalls?**
6 **Tricel and polynosic have superior qualities over other types of acetate and viscose rayons respectively. Discuss the advantages of these two regenerated fibres.**

Other materials

Elastomeric fibres

Elastic materials which are very strong, yet fine, are necessary for swimming costumes, foundation garments, bras, surgical stockings, and other items which give support.

A polymer (compound of many molecules) called **polyurethane** has excellent elasticity. Even when very fine it gives firm support and control. It is used to make elastomeric or spandex fibres. These have trade names such as **Lycra** and **Spanzello**.

outer layer

Elastomeric fibres are usually coated by another fibre being twisted around them. They are thus **core-spun**.

core of
elastomeric fibre

This both gives the elastomeric fibre a better appearance and feel and reduces cost by introducing another fibre.

Lycra and Spanzelle can be washed normally by machine or hand. It is not normally necessary to iron them. In any case they would not stand more than the lowest iron setting 🔺 .

Elastomerics may be dry-cleaned as they are unharmed by chemicals; but chlorine bleach would damage the fibre. As swimming pools contain chlorine it is always important to rinse a swimsuit after use. With these guidelines elastomeric fibres will give long service.

Leather

Leather is the hide of the ox which has gone through a process called *tanning*. This makes it waterproof and prevents it cracking. Leather is expensive but strong. It is used to make shoes, handbags, belts, and cases.

Shoes are exposed to dirt and need daily care, particularly to keep their waterproof quality. Clean them with a brush to remove mud. Apply polish regularly and brush the polish in well. Leather becomes dry and cracked if not fed with polish, or if dried in heat. Leather coats are extremely expensive. There are a number of good imitations for leather and suede.

Suede is a softer layer of inner leather which has been brushed to raise a nap surface. It is used to make shoes, slippers, waistcoats, and jackets. Again shoes need more regular care. Brush off dirt with a clean brush, and occasionally raise the nap with a suede brush.

Simulated suede fabric is sold in 90 cm width. It dyes well, does not fray, has no nap, is easier to sew, and is cheaper.

Simulated fur

As numbers of wild species have decreased, there is a leaning towards the use of simulated furs for humane and conservationist reasons. These are much more hardwearing, easier to care for, and far less expensive.

PVC

PVC is used for clothing and in the house. PVC is short for **poly vinyl chloride**. It is waterproof and so is used for raincoats, jackets, trousers, sou'westers, and life jackets. PVC cotton-backed aprons are useful, colourful, and popular. The fabric is non-absorbent and so will wipe clean. The material is reasonably tough, though it cracks if left folded.

Be accurate when sewing on PVC because pin or needle marks cannot be removed. Check the fit of hat or jacket sections *before* sewing. Use tissue paper to help the fabric go under the presser foot.

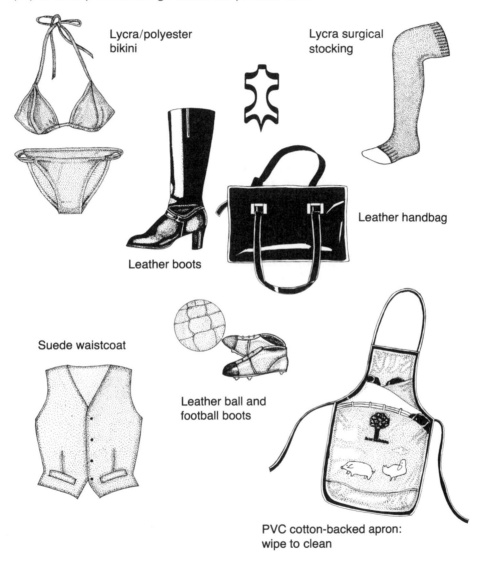

Lycra/polyester bikini

Lycra surgical stocking

Leather boots

Leather handbag

Suede waistcoat

Leather ball and football boots

PVC cotton-backed apron: wipe to clean

Questions

1 **Give *two* reasons why Lycra is commonly used for underwear. Name another type of garment which is sometimes made from Lycra.**   (ALSEB)
2 **What is a core-spun fibre?**
3 **Give *three* reasons for keeping shoes in good repair.**
   Describe how you would dry a pair of rain-soaked shoes.   (NWREB)
4 **What have suede and leather in common?**
5 **Explain the popularity of cotton-backed PVC aprons, and bibs for children.**

More fabrics

▲ Read through the section on each fibre in turn. List the various fabrics mentioned in each section under the heading of that particular fibre, and write a few sentences about each. You will amass quite a list of fabrics.

Find examples of them in wear. Look at them in the shops or market stalls, and compare their prices.

Here are some more fabrics in common use, not necessarily mentioned elsewhere, and a few facts about them.

Wool

Velour is a felt fabric with a raised nap (see p. 38). It is used for hats. It is also a one-way pile fabric (see p. 25) used for curtains.

Whipcord has a corded appearance. It is made of worsted but can also be made from cotton as cotton whipcord.

Gaberdine is a twill-weave, closely woven fabric. It gave its name to the gaberdine mac. It can be wool gaberdine, cotton, or a mixture of the two. When used for rainwear it is shower-proofed.

Cotton

Organdie is a very fine, plain-weave, stiffened cotton. It is used as a lightweight woven stiffening.

Holland is a brown fabric made from either cotton or beetled linen. It is a woven interlining used in tailored jackets and suits.

Drill is a closely-woven twill-weave cotton used for overalls, aprons, dustcoats, and the like. It can be khaki or white.

Denim is a twill-weave cotton. It has a blue warp and a white weft. Very hard wearing, it is used for jeans, skirts, and casual jackets.

Jean is a serviceable cotton twill used for overalls and jeans.

Calico is a closely woven plain-weave cotton, bleached or unbleached. It is used for household items such as ironing-board covers and mattress covers.

Corduroy has a cut weft pile. The cords run along the warp, parallel to the selvedge. It is made from cotton and can be printed.

Needlecord is a finer rib cotton fabric, made in the same way as corduroy.

Fabrics made from different fibres

A number of fabrics originally made in a particular way from a natural fibre have now given their names to a type of fabric made of either natural fibres or synthetics, or mixtures or blends. There are several reasons for this. They are:

1 The development of new synthetic fibres.
2 More understanding about making textiles.
3 New techniques of blending, weaving and knitting.
Here are some examples:

Jersey is a finely (warp) knitted fabric. Jersey cloth is a fine dress-weight wool. Synthetic fibres are warp knitted to imitate and improve on the original jersey cloth. Now we have fabrics called polyester jersey, courtelle jersey, and so on. Cotton jersey is used for tee-shirts. NB. It is essential to use polyester or pure silk thread for sewing knitted fabrics.

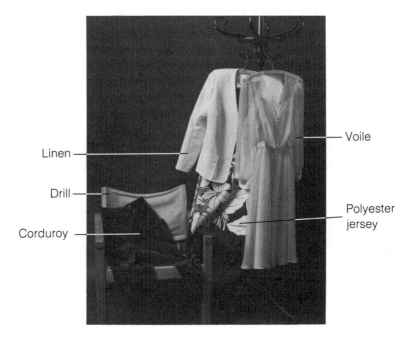

Linen

Drill

Corduroy

Voile

Polyester jersey

Bouclé means curled. The yarn has been curled and produces an uneven, rather loopy surface. Originally made with wool, synthetics can now be textured and very good fabrics are produced.

Lawn is a fine plain weave of linen or cotton. It is used for underwear and handkerchieves. Spun polyester is also woven as lawn.

Organza is a similar fabric to organdie, but made from silk. Organza is now also made from synthetics.

Seersucker consists of alternate areas of flat and puckered fabric. Cotton seersucker and nylon seersucker are popular. They are used for tablecloths and dress wear.

Satin and sateen The characteristic is the **satin/sateen** weave shown on p.24. Continuous filament is often used because the lustre is attractive, but even cotton and worsted will produce a very smooth surface.

Velvet is a pile fabric originally made of silk. Nylon velvet is similarly constructed. **Velveteen** is a pile fabric made from cotton. **Street velvet** is shower-proofed and used for coats.

Voile The name comes from the French word for 'veil'. It is a very fine, lightweight fabric. It was originally made from cotton or silk, but is now made from man-made fibres too.

Questions

1 **Name *three* lightweight fabrics and state the purpose for which they can be used.**
   For what would you use polyester lawn?
2 **Name *three* fabrics that can be used as interlinings, and say from what fibre they are made.**
3 **What are the differences between whipcord, corduroy, and needlecord?**
4 **Velour can be made in two ways. Describe them.**

Identifying fibres (1)

We can recognize familiar fabrics. We can name others if they have a label. But sometimes we cannot even guess what an unnamed fabric might be. How can we be sure what a fabric is composed of? There are a number of things that will give us a clue.

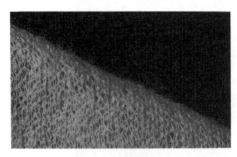 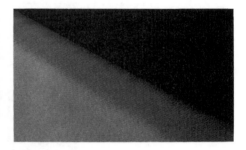

Hairiness on the surface of a fabric (see p.11) shows that a fabric is made from staple fibre; though that staple fibre may be wool, cotton, or linen, or a man-made continuous filament cut into staple fibre. If it is synthetic, the reverse side of the fabric will feel very smooth and even slippery to the touch. Natural fibres (with the exception of silk) are less regular and therefore can be gripped better. (The price of the fabric or garment could indicate whether silk – the most expensive fabric – had been used.)

Squeezing the fabric in your hand to see whether it creases provides another clue to its identity. Cotton, linen, and viscose crease badly; wool, nylon, and polyester do not. However, blends of fibres make it difficult to distinguish on these grounds, and even cotton, linen, and viscose can be treated to reduce creasing (improve resilience).

So the appearance, feel, price, and resilience may all give a clue to the fibre's origin, but not a definite answer. In order to identify the fibre, we can:
1 Use the burning test.
2 Look at the fabric under the microscope.
3 Use chemical tests.

The burning test

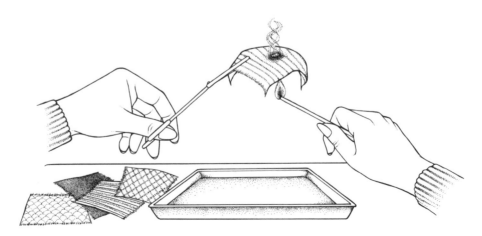

The burning test can be done in the kitchen, but must be carried out with care. If testing the fibre of a garment, take a small piece of the fabric from the inside of a facing where it cannot be seen, and always lay fabric to be tested on a large metal baking tray. A long taper is useful for lighting, and a pair of tongs or tweezers for holding the fabric to be tested. Try the test with a known fabric first so that you know what to expect, and can compare the unknown fabric with what happens to the standard pure fibre. The reaction to flame may surprise you in some cases.

At the same time we can notice the speed and ease with which materials burn – their flammability – for some fabrics are flammable and therefore dangerous for full garments likely to be near a fire, such as a child's nightdress.

Vegetable fibres

Cotton and linen are natural vegetable fibres, and viscose is man-made from wood chips. All these burn rather like the garden bonfire with a yellowish flame smelling of burning paper. Paper is also made from wood. They each leave a greyish white ash in a roughly crinkled shape of the fabric weave.

Animal fibres

Wool and silk are both animal substances like human hair and poultry feathers. They burn with a definite smell of singeing hair or burning feathers which you will recognize immediately; but an acrid (bitter) and pungent (strong) smell indicates the presence of another fibre blended with the basic one. Wool and silk burn slowly inside the flame.

Acetate

Acetate does not burn as quickly as viscose, but it does burn and melt. A vinegary smell is noticeable for it is made of acetic acid (vinegar) and cellulose (plant framework).

Synthetics

Nylon is not flammable, but will melt at 250°C. Therefore the heat of the flame melts it and it shrinks away, dripping.

Polyester

Polyester is difficult to light. It shrinks away from the flame but melts with its heat. The flame becomes a luminous red or yellow. Although polyester behaves in a similar way to nylon, the smell is different and the smoke darker. It melts at a higher temperature than nylon and is thus fractionally slower in shrinking away.

Acrylics

The acrylic fibres will burn rather more quickly than nylon or polyester, but less quickly than cotton or linen. The residue cannot be mistaken for cotton, linen, or viscose as the fibre slowly melts to form a hard black bead. Modacrylics (Teklan, Dynel) burn much less readily than acrylics; in fact they are self extinguishing.

The summary chart overleaf will help you to identify fibres. The most telling features are in italics.

A couple of other smells may occur. 'Bad fish' denotes the presence of a resin finish on cellulose; and 'burned milk' comes from a man-made fibre Azlon (fibrolane) made from casein – the milk protein. These are quite easy to pick out.

Burning test: summary chart

	Burning	Flame	Colour of smoke	Smell	Ash or residue
Cotton	*Burns readily* and quickly.	Yellow	White	*Burning paper*	Greyish white ash; *remains in the crinkled shape of the fabric.*
Viscose	Burns readily and quickly.	Yellow	White	Burning paper	Greyish white ash remains in the crinkled shape of the fabric.
Linen	Burns readily.	Yellowy orange	White	Bonfire smell of *burning grass*	Grey ash, skeleton of fabric.
Wool and hair fibres such as mohair	Smoulders; burns *slowly.*	Fibre burns inside the flame. Does not flare up.	White	*Burning feathers* or *human hair*	Black bead which *crushes* easily when cold.
Silk	Small brittle beads.	Fibre burns inside the flame. Does not flare up.	White	*Burning feathers* or *human hair*	Burns to an ash skeleton.
Acetate	Slower than viscose			*Vinegar* smell (acetic acid)	Melts to a hard shiny black bead.
Nylon	Not flammable; it shrinks away from heat of flame, melting and dripping.	Yellow	White	Strong *celery* smell	*Light coloured* fawn or white hard *round bead.*
Polyester	Difficult to ignite. Melts and shrinks from the flame. Hard beaded edges.	Luminous red or yellow	Darker *black smoke* with specks	Strong	Hard *round bead*, *darker* than nylon.
Acrylics: Courtelle Orlon Acrilan	Burns then melts.	Luminous reddish		Aromatic odour	Hard black bead of *irregular* shape.
Modacrylic	*Self extinguishing.*				Rubbery black irregular bead.

Under the microscope

Looking at a fibre under the microscope may help, for natural fibres are clearly recognizable when you look along the length of the fibre. All except silk are irregular in shape.

Wool has a scaly surface. It is these scales which become interlocked when wool is put into hot water and, because they cannot be disentangled, cause the fabric to shrink and felt.

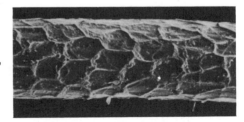

Linen has long irregular fibres rather like bamboo with cross-markings.

Cotton has twists in a ribbon-like fibre. This irregular shape is unsuitable for sewing thread which must be uniform in shape, so cotton is mercerized to swell the fibres, make them untwist and become smoother (see p.16).

Silk is smooth and fine and has no markings.

Man-made fibres are smooth. They can be distinguished by looking at a cross section (cut across the fibre). The synthetic fibre shown highly magnified below is Orlon.

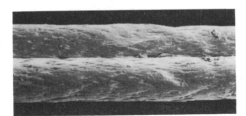
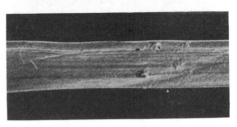

It is extremely difficult to recognize any difference between longitudinal views of continuous filament fibres. Thus, looking at a longitudinal shape of a fibre teased from a thread, and mounted on a microscope slide, will only establish whether it is wool, linen, or cotton with any degree of certainty.

Questions

1 **What factors might indicate the fibre in an unnamed fabric in a shop?**
2 **Put fibres in order of flammability, starting with the easiest to burn and ending with the least flammable.**
3 **What would indicate that a fabric you were burning might be polyester?**
4 **When fabric burns, a tell-tale smell is given off. Name some fabrics which can be recognized in this way, stating the smell you would notice.**
5 **How does the scaly surface on wool fibre affect its behaviour when washed?**

Identifying fibres (2)

Chemical tests

In the burning test and under the microscope the natural fibres are easier to identify, while the man-made fibres are more difficult to distinguish. The same can be said about the chemical tests. Chemical tests establish the presence of certain substances in the fibre. **Some of the chemicals used to test fibres are dangerous and need to be treated with great care. Always consult your teacher before using them**.

To do these tests you will need test tubes, a bunsen burner, tongs, and small pieces of white or light coloured fabrics to be tested. Dyes may run.

▲ Wool, hair, silk, and fibrolane (made from casein) all contain **protein**. This can be identified in the same way as when doing food tests – by the Xanthoproteic test.

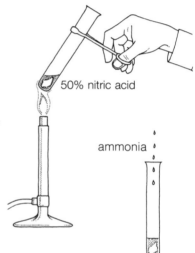

50% nitric acid

ammonia

1 Place a small piece of fabric in a test tube.
2 Cover with a 50% solution of nitric acid.
3 Heat very gently. If protein is present the colour turns yellow.
4 Cool the test tube under the tap.
5 Add a few drops of ammonium hydroxide (ammonia) and an orange colour appears, further proving the presence of protein.

Wool and hair contain sulphur. Silk does not.

▲ *To test for sulphur:*
1 Add 2–3 cm³ caustic soda solution to confirmed protein fibres.
2 Heat gently, then cool under the cold tap.
3 Add a few drops of lead acetate.
   • A brown-black precipitate shows the presence of sulphur.
   The fibre is wool or hair.
   • A white precipitate shows the absence of sulphur. The fibre is silk.

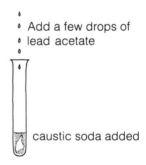

Add a few drops of lead acetate

caustic soda added

Cotton, linen, and viscose are all composed of cellulose.

▲ *To test for cellulose:*
1 Put a small piece of fabric into iodine solution; remove and shake off any surplus iodine.
2 Place the fabric in a test tube and cover with a 30% solution of sulphuric acid. A blue-black colouration shows the presence of cellulose.

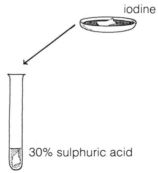

iodine

30% sulphuric acid

Testing for man-made fibres

Test the fabric by putting it in acetone.

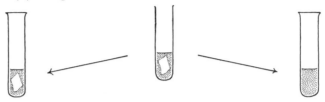

If it does not dissolve in acetone it may be nylon, acrylic, polyester, or PVC. PVC contains chlorine; nylon and acrylic contain nitrogen; polyester does not contain either.

If it dissolves it is either modacrylic or cellulose acetate. Acetate dissolves more quickly than modacrylic. A modacrylic contains chlorine.

To test for nitrogen:

1 Place up to 1 cm of soda lime in a test tube to cover the scrap of fabric.
2 Heat gently and place a moist red litmus paper over the top of the test tube.
3 If the fumes turn the litmus blue, nitrogen is present.

To test for chlorine:

1 Get a copper wire so hot in a bunsen flame that it stops burning green.
2 Touch the fibres with the hot wire so that some melt and stick to it.
3 Return the wire to the flame quickly.
4 If it burns with a green flame, again, chlorine is present.

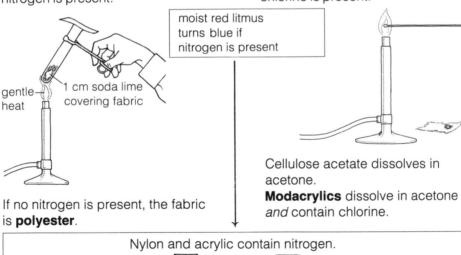

moist red litmus turns blue if nitrogen is present

gentle heat

1 cm soda lime covering fabric

If no nitrogen is present, the fabric is **polyester**.

Cellulose acetate dissolves in acetone.
Modacrylics dissolve in acetone *and* contain chlorine.

Nylon and acrylic contain nitrogen.

Nylon dissolves in a 50% solution of hydrochloric acid.

Add 50% hydrochloric acid solution.

Acrylic does not dissolve.

Questions

1 **How would you establish whether or not a fibre contains protein?**
2 **How would you distinguish between wool and silk?**
3 **How would you distinguish between nylon, acrylic, and polyester?**

Fabric investigations

Chapter 3 tells you about the properties of materials. You will also want to make comparisons and devise experiments of your own.
To do this keep a record in your file showing:

Aim	What you want to find out
Method	Equipment and techniques
Result	What was found out
Conclusion	What information you draw from the result and how the result affects your decision

This information will be useful in later work too.

All experiments must be (a) fair, (b) safe.

Reaction test

When testing a fabric's reaction to say, sunlight or washing, keep a standard piece of untested fabric to compare with the treated one.

Comparison test

This is to compare a fibre's or fabric's reaction with those of other fibre's or fabric's. To obtain fair and true results, all fabrics must be:
1   The same size   → use a template to cut specimens uniformly.
2   Treated in the same way   → list the equipment
                                   set out method clearly, and follow exactly.
3   Under the same conditions → use a stop watch/thermometer/scale card
                                   to achieve accuracy.

Grey scales for colour tests

Scale cards of varying shades of grey measure degrees of colour change. Compare the original coloured fabric and the resulting coloured fabric with the various shades of grey, to give a measure of the degree of fading.

Wear test

The Griffin and George wear-tester subjects fabrics to wear as it rotates.
Fix on uniform-sized fabric specimens.
Rotate either (a)   for a specific number of revolutions,
        or (b)   until the first fabric disintegrates.
Examine the specimens for comparative wear.

You can devise your own wear tests. For example, using sandpaper on fabric pulled taut over a jar, and secured tightly with string. When you test for wear or a fabric's strength make sure the experiment will be safe as you work. Consider the friction or pull you expose the fabric to, and don't be surprised when it breaks under strain or disintegrates. Could the sudden release of pressure cause an accident to you or the equipment?

Griffin and George
wear-tester

Be especially careful with flammability tests. Burn the fabric being tested well away from classmates, and support it securely.

Evaluating fabrics

The results of comparisons enable you to place specimens in order, for example weakest to strongest or quickest to burn to slowest to ignite.

If a measure is involved such as temperature, size, number of revolutions, or time you can use graph paper to show results as a bar chart. This not only shows *differences* clearly, but by *how much* the fabrics differ.

Stretch and elasticity

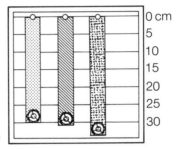

▲ Equipment: 30 cm × 3 cm pieces of fabric cut on the straight grain, metal nuts, needle and thread, graph paper on a board, drawing pins. Stitch a metal nut to one end of each fabric specimen. Pin the fabric at the other end to a horizontal line on the board, so that all the fabrics measure 25 cm from the line to the nut when laid out flat. Stand the board upright. Mark on the paper the distance that each fabric drops.

Leave overnight and mark the amount each fabric has stretched by next morning. Make a bar chart to show the extensibility of different fabrics.

Elasticity

▲ Remove the nuts by cutting the stitches. Does the fabric retract to its original length? Mark the new lengths of the fabric after retracting (a) immediately, (b) next day.

Which fabrics are most elastic? Compare the stretch and elasticity of a fabric cut on the cross with that of the same fabric cut on the straight grain. Make a bar chart to illustrate your results.

Resistance to sunlight

To test the effect of sunlight select similar coloured fabric pieces. Divide each piece in half. Place one half of each fabric in a drawer.

Fasten the other halves to the same sunny window, giving all specimens equal sunlight. Leave until they have been exposed to bright sunlight for some time, say two months.

1 Compare each fabric with its pair kept in the drawer.
2 Observe which fabrics and colours are affected most.
3 Carry out the wear test on each pair of fabric pieces to test their strengths.

You can devise tests to see the effect of agents on fabrics, or how fabrics react to their prospective environment. This is important in the selection of the right material for the job.

▲ Compare the effect of sunlight on two colours using a variety of fibres.
▲ Compare the effect of a natural dye (p.30) on white fabric pieces of various fibres. Mount the results and use them to explain why a variety of dyes are necessary in fabric manufacture.
▲ Devise a series of experiments to find out whether a given fabric can be labelled 'easy care'.

Care Labelling Code

The International Textile Care Labelling Code is found on packets of washing powders. It matches up with the labels which manufacturers are obliged to sew into clothes, stating how the consumer should care for the item. As the scheme is used in many countries, and as the labels are quite small, symbols indicate washing, bleaching, tumble drying, ironing and dry cleaning.

	Symbol	Meaning	Fabric
Formerly washcode **1** now	⌐95⌐	A tub without a bar – wash as cotton	White cotton and linen without special finishes
2 now	⌐60⌐	This is full wash time with maximum agitation; normal rinsing and full spin	Cotton linen and viscose without special finishes where colours are fast at 60°C
5 now	⌐40⌐		Cotton linen and viscose where colours are fast at 40°C but not at 60°C
4 now	⌐50⌐	A bar beneath the tub – wash as synthetics	Synthetics Cottons with finishes
6 now	⌐40⌐	This means a reduced wash with medium agitation; then a cold rinse and a short spin	Cotton blends
7 now	⌐40⌐	A broken bar – wash as wool	Wool and wool mixtures Silk
		This is a minimum agitation with a normal rinse and spin. Wool and silk are harmed by rubbing and twisting	

Loads in the first two groups can be mixed together and washed at the lowest temperature; but where there is a bar the washing action must be reduced too.

The broken bar process's gentle action is insufficient to clean fabrics normally washed as cotton. Knitted acrylics need the cold rinse in the synthetic wash, why?

Drying instructions

 Tumble-dry.

 Do not tumble-dry.

 Chlorine bleach may be used.

 Do not use chlorine bleach.

Ironing instructions are on p.140.

 Do not iron.

Dry cleaning instructions are given to guide the cleaners about which cleaning agent the fabric will accept.

 Any solvents.

 Perchloroethylene, Solv. R11. Solv. 113, white spirit.

 Solv. 113, white spirit.

A bar means that extra care is needed during the process e.g. specific drying temperature.

The Woolmark is the International Wool Secretariat's symbol for products made from pure new wool. Pure new wool garments may carry dry clean, hand-wash only, or machine washable (Superwash) labels.

Certification Trade Mark
Pure new wool

Wool blends carry this symbol:

Certification Trade Mark
Wool rich blend

Woolmark

Certification Trade Mark
Pure new wool

Fabric conditioners

Fabric conditioners such as **Comfort** and **Lenor** are added to the final rinsing water. They give natural fibres an added softness. They make synthetics free from static electricity, so that there is no crackle or cling (see p.60). They reduce creasing in cottons making them easier to iron. They add a pleasant fragrance to clothes.

Conditioners used in the tumble-drier
Bounce is a fabric conditioner added in the tumble-drier. It comes in sheet form in small packets. To use it, load the drier and set the control. Add one (or more) sheets of Bounce and start the drier. Remove the sheet after use.

Questions

1 **Name the process in laundering of clothing to which each of the symbols below refers:**

What does a cross through any of the above symbols mean? (ALSEB)

2 **(a)   Explain what is meant by each of the following symbols:**

(b)   Using four symbols write a care label for a coloured nylon smock.
(c)   The care label on a knitted garment often states 'dry flat'.
     Why is this advised?   (NWREB)

3 **What is the purpose of using a fabric conditioner on: (a) woollens;**
(b) man-made fabrics?   (SEREB)

Fabric detergents

▲ **Group activity on washing detergents for fabrics**

Collect as many different packs of washing powders, liquids and detergents as you can. Study the packs and see what they say about their contents.

1 How many actually say they contain soap? Put those in one pile.
2 How many do not mention 'soap' anywhere on the packet? Why?
3 How many advertise themselves as low-temperature detergents?
They may mention 'biological' or 'enzyme' action. Put those in another pile.
4 Are there some only intended for one type of washing? Sort those out into 'automatic' and 'hand washing'. For what type of machine are automatic powders used?
5 For what type of fabrics are hand-washing detergents used?
6 Do any say that they are suitable for removing greasy stains in particular?

List the detergents you have in each pile now.

Washing detergents for fabrics

1 *Soap powder*
A closer look at the packets of detergents shows that only Persil and Fairy Snow are soap powders. Lux is a very mild soap flake. You will remember that some fabrics do not respond well to soap (an alkali). Soap also forms a scum in the hard water found in some areas. Therefore much can be wasted.
    Soap must not be used on flame retardant finishes. In hard water soap not only removes flame resistance, but makes it even more flammable!

2 *Synthetic washing powders and liquids*
Manufacturers have found an alternative: synthetic washing powder. This is an advantage with wool. Blue and White Surf, Daz, and Tide lather well and leave no scum even in hard water. They can be used at all temperatures.

3 *Biological powders or liquids* such as Biological Daz, Bold 3, Ariel, Radiant. The biological action referred to is the enzyme action of removing stains by action on protein. You have enzymes in your digestive system breaking down proteins, and other foods too.

Enzyme action happens at body temperature. Biological powders work well around 40°C. They cannot be used for high temperature washing.

Biotex is a biological soaker and prewasher. It is particularly recommended for soaking nappies and blood-stained items.

4 *Automatic low-lather detergents* such as Persil Automatic, Bold Automatic. Front-loading machines need a low-lather detergent.

Over-lathering or too much powder prevents the machine from working well.

5 *Hand-washing detergents*
Stergene (a liquid) and Dreft (a powder) are soapless. They are used for delicate fabrics like silks and woollens. They condition the fabric too. Flame-retardant fabrics wash better in soapless detergents.

Front-loading automatic

6 *Grease-solvent powders*
Grease-solvent powders such as Drive are particularly effective in getting grease-held marks out during washing or soaking.

What Washing powders contain

Water softeners for areas with hard water. The most common is sodium carbonate (washing soda). Buy soap powder locally, as wash powders (like tea) are blended to suit the water in an area.

Flourescer This is a dye which absorbs ultra-violet light and reflects it as blue light. When an ageing yellowed fabric is washed it takes up the dye. The blue effect counteracts the yellowing appearance of the white fabric. Blue and yellow are complementary colours. So a yellowing white fabric appears whiter. Before washing machines became common a final rinse in 'washing blue' worked on the same principle.

Suspension agent

This is to suspend dirt so that it does not get back on to the fabric. It is added to soapless detergents in particular.

Bleach

Oxidising bleaches release oxygen to combine with the stain making it colourless. The stain is then soluble and can be washed out.

Oxygen in air and sunlight also has this effect. This is the principle of outdoor bleaching. Sodium perborate, in wash powder, is an oxidising bleach. It releases very little oxygen at low temperatures, but more and more the higher the temperature goes.

Bleach fades dyes. Sodium perborate has little effect on coloureds because they are washed at the lower temperatures 50°C $\boxed{4}$. But, it acts well on whites at 85°C – to boiling point in the high temperature wash.

Other ingredients

Perfume; colour; substances to prevent corrosion of washing machine parts.

Questions

1 **What type of powder would you choose to use for a boiler suit, or a pair of overalls used by a garage worker? Explain your answer.**

2 **What washing powder would you recommend for a family with a young toddler and month-old twins? What other substance might be useful for washing? Explain your answer.**

3 **You are amongst a group of volunteers mounting a display of historical costumes at the local museum. Some of the clothes given have been in attics for years and need washing. How would you do this?**

4 **Explain the reason for each instruction on the labels opposite. If a garment item or fabric carried a label like this, what fibre do you think it would be made from?**

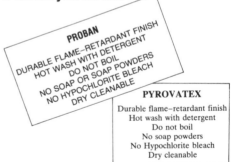

PROBAN
DURABLE FLAME–RETARDANT FINISH
HOT WASH WITH DETERGENT
DO NOT BOIL
NO SOAP OR SOAP POWDERS
NO HYPOCHLORITE BLEACH
DRY CLEANABLE

PYROVATEX
Durable flame–retardant finish
Hot wash with detergent
Do not boil
No soap powders
No Hypochlorite bleach
Dry cleanable

5 **It is your turn to do the household wash. You have an automatic front loading machine, and there are detergents in the cupboard. The following items are in the dirty linen basket.**

a pair of single cotton sheets; a pair of single coloured nylon sheets; a polyester cotton duvet cover; a tebilised colourfast viscose cloth; a tricel blouse; two fine courtelle jumpers; polyester/wool trousers; a fine hand knitted woollen top; two new unlabelled cheap red bath towels.

(a) **Study the ITCL code (p.86). Give the correct wash code for each item.**

(b) **Is there anything you would *not* wash by machine? Explain why. What treatment would you give, and what detergent would you use?**

(c) **Look at the advice on mixing loads on p.86 and say which items may be washed together and on what programme? List the washing in loads.**

(d) **What is the minimum number of loads needed to complete the washing?**

(e) **What detergent would you use? Explain why.**

(f) **Explain any reason for the advice 'wash separately' on a label.**

Further work on Chapter 3

1. (a) Give the names of four fabrics made from wool fibres and four fabrics made from cotton fibres.
   (b) Draw the magnified appearance of each of these fibres.
   (c) Briefly explain why wool is described as a good insulator and cotton is considered a good fibre to be used in sportswear.
   (d) Briefly compare the main differences between laundering cotton fibres and wool fibres. (OLE)

2. Give information on *four* of the following:
   (a) bulked and textured yarns   (b) regenerated cellulose fibres
   (c) staple and filament yarns   (d) non-woven fabrics
   (e) flame-resistant fabrics. (OLE)

3. (a) Explain the difference between a fabric which is a mixture and a fabric which is a blend.
   (b) Give *four* examples of mixtures or blends which are commonly used for household articles or clothing. In each case state *one* advantage of the mixture/blend of fibres. (SCE)

4. Explain your answer.

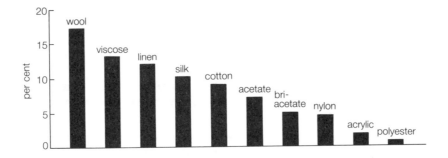

The bar chart shows the percentage of water present in the structure of textile fibres under standard conditions. Study it closely.
   (a) Name the least absorbent fibre.
   (b) Name four fabrics that would drip-dry quickly.
   (c) Which fibre absorbs the most water? What percentage has it here?
   (d) Name three fabrics which would take a long time to dry.
   (e) Give the percentage of water in a 50% viscose, 50% cotton blend.
   (f) Fabrics having little moisture produce static electricity with friction in dry conditions. Name four static-producing fabrics.
   (g) How does a fabric conditioner prevent the formation of static?

5. Analyse the human needs and material factors to be considered when choosing fabrics for: (a) underwear (b) sports clothes (c) children's play clothes (d) nurses' uniforms (e) car mechanics' overalls.

6. Your summer holiday is in Cyprus (temperature 32°C, 90°F). Explain the problems involved in choosing clothing fabrics for hot areas. Evaluate the suitability of two items from your own wardrobe which you might hope to wear.

8 Cellulose fabrics are often produced with a flame-retardant finish.
  (a) Name two natural and one man-made cellulose fibre.
  (b) Name a flame-retardant finish used on cellulose fibres and fabrics.
  (c) Explain with reasons any special care which is necessary in washing such treated fabric.

9 Identify the human needs and material factors involved in the choice of:
  (a) sleepwear (b) protective clothing (c) curtains.
  Refer particularly to health and safety in your answer.

10 During the colder months it is vital to keep warm.
  (a) Describe three ways of conserving heat (i) in the house (ii) at school.
  (b) Suggest four ways in which elderly people could protect themselves or be protected against hypothermia. Include reference to food, the family, home, and textiles.
  (c) Sketch a useful garment for an old person to wear at home during the day and suggest suitable fabric for it.

11 Why does a garment made entirely from nylon sometimes prove unsatisfactory to wear?
  You have been given a length of smooth, medium-weight woven blue nylon. Evaluate the fabric for making cushion covers, a kitchen overall, a child's summer blouse. What problems might you find in sewing it? How would you cope with them?

12 (a) How do you notice static electricity on synthetics in hot weather?
  (b) How does it affect the behaviour, hang, dirt resistance, and colour?
  (c) On which fabrics might static develop, and how is it caused?
  (d) What steps can be taken (i) by the manufacturer and (ii) in the home, to solve this problem?
  (e) In operating theatres and other places where flammable vapours are present it is risky to wear overalls which produce an electrostatic charge. Why?

13 Cotton jersey and polyester jersey are now in common use.
  Carry out a piece of investigative work to assess their popularity.
  What qualities do these fabrics possess which could account for this?

14 How would you investigate the truth of this statement: 'As humans grow their needs for warmth, and protection from physical discomfort, change.'
  Explain these needs and suggest suitable fabrics and items to meet them for each of the following cases: (a) a new born baby (b) a skater's track suit (c) an old person at night.

15 Copy and complete the following table on the results of tests you would use to identify fibres.   (SCE)

	Burning test result	Microscopic test result	Chemical test result
Wool			
Cotton			
Acetate			
Polyester			

Chapter 4

Looking after and choosing clothes

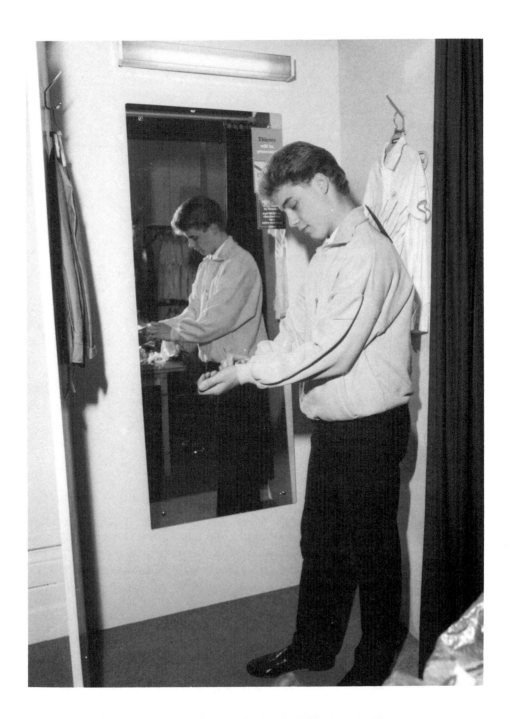

Looking after clothes

Home valeting

A clothes brush is useful. Keep it hanging near the wardrobe. You can give your clothes a pep-up by brushing them. Sponge and press woollen items like skirts, suits, and trousers.

1   Brush and shake well to remove dust and dandruff. Brush out pockets and turn-ups. Always do this before having trousers or skirts dry-cleaned too. Dirt in the pockets can stain if not removed.
2   Tack in pleats on the fold.
3   Wipe with a clean lintless cloth dampened in a bowl of water containing a tablespoon of vinegar.
4   Press on WS with a damp cloth. Dry with the iron. Dampness causes more creasing afterwards.
5   Air well.

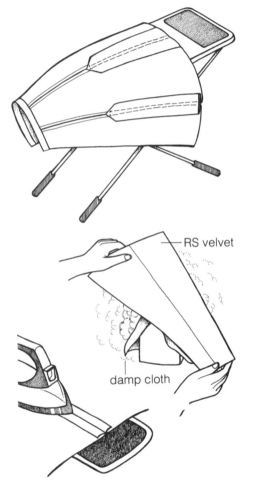

RS velvet

damp cloth

To press velvet

Stand the iron on its end. Lay a wet cloth over the hot iron to make steam. Pass the velvet over with the wrong side nearest the iron. The steam rising through the velvet raises the pile. Alternatively a velvet board, if you have one, allows room for the pile to be raised. The board is like an upturned hair brush with tiny bristles on which to lay the velvet right side down whilst pressing. Always lift the fabric when moving it. Do not pull it over the board.

Dry cleaning

Sometimes fabric cannot be washed. It may shrink. It may have a finish which would be removed by water; or the dye may not be fast. In these cases dry cleaning is used. Dust, dirt, and stains are usually held on to a fabric by grease. In dry cleaning grease is dissolved by a grease solvent, and the dirt and stains then fall out. Dry cleaning is done in rotary drums which look rather like automatic washing machines, in which the clothes are spun in solvents. Drying is done by tumble-drier to evaporate the solvents. Outdoor clothes may be limper after cleaning as dirt gives body to a fabric. The process of **retexturing** gives back the substance to clothes. A finish to stiffen the fabric slightly is applied. A showerproof finish also needs to be renewed after dry cleaning.

After cleaning, air clothes well before storing them.

Storage of clothes

In summer we do not need all our bulky sweaters and warm clothing. Store them in a separate cupboard or chest not in frequent use. Always store them clean. Moths attack woollens with food on.

Fold clothes neatly. Tissue paper helps to avoid sharp creases. Store in a polythene bag.

Always store shoes and boots clean and well polished. Shoe trees help to keep the shoes in shape.

Preparing for a special occasion

When going for an interview, or getting ready for a special occasion such as a wedding, think of the whole outfit. Make or buy the things you need to complete it well beforehand.

On the day before the special occasion, wash and style your hair. Press your clothes. Brush your coat or jacket. Clean your shoes. Check your tights. Take an extra pair in case they ladder.

Check buttons or fasteners. An important occasion can be marred by a button coming off, and hurried repairs.
Check your rainwear – it may rain. You will need an umbrella or waterproof to cover your best clothes. Wipe and pack a handbag to contain make-up and money.

Take a towel and overnight equipment, if necessary, in a small bag. Have a bath or shower either before bed or in the morning. Do you need to shave?

Put on clean underwear and socks.

Questions

1 **What treatment would you apply to a pleated woollen skirt before wearing it for a special occasion?**
2 **How would you press your young sister's velvet bridesmaid's dress?**
3 **Explain to your brother how he should prepare his best trousers to look very smart at the wedding. What preparation must he give his overcoat before dry cleaning?**
4 **(a)　What is meant by the term 'dry cleaning'?**
　　(b)　Why is it necessary for some fabrics to be dry cleaned instead of washed?
　　(c)　Sketch ιne care label symbol for a fabric which is dry cleanable.　(YHREB)
5 **List *eight* preparations which should be made the day before an important interview, to ensure good personal hygiene and a well-groomed appearance.**　(YHREB)

Stain removal

▲ Experiment

1 Take some scraps of different fabrics and on them put some common stains like shoe polish, grass, ball-point ink, and blood.
2 Cut your stained fabrics in half. Put one half of each fabric aside for three days.
3 With the other half see how many stains can be removed by water and washing powder only. Some members of the group can try a grease-solvent powder like Drive on all their stains. Others can try a biological powder like Daz or a liquid like Ariel on all their stains.
   In doing this part of the experiment you may notice that some of your fabrics are spoiled by hot water, or trying to rub out the stain.
4 Then try the appropriate method of stain removal suggested on p.97 on those stains that remain. There may be some that still remain after being in *hot* water even when you try the suggested method. Which are they? Can you account for this?
5 Three days later do the same experiment with the stained fabrics you put aside. The stains will be set into the fabrics by now.

What are your conclusions?

Dealing with stains

1 Stains should be removed *as soon as possible* before they have a chance to set on the fabric. If you act quickly the stain may come off by soaking in cold water. Never do this to wool or silk. Why?
2 Washing powder added to the water removes many stains such as fruit acids, tea, or coffee, but sometimes other agents are necessary.
3 To avoid the stain spreading make a 'tip' or point with it. Place it in a saucer with the reagent (stain remover) to soak. The stain and the remover must then be rinsed or washed off.
4 Grease solvents rubbed on lightly will evaporate and the stain can be brushed off.
5 It is important to know what the stain is: protein, grease, acid?
   The correct method and removal agent can then be used.
6 Remember what fabric the stain is on. Some agents damage fabric. (Acetone can be used to remove nail varnish or ball-point ink, but *not* on acetate. Why?) Synthetic fibres like nylon do not absorb stains. Even difficult marks like paint may be washed out with a detergent.

Using a grease solvent

open window

pad of rag

single fabric

grease solvent being applied, working inwards

Treatment for stains

Egg, blood, gravy, milk (protein stains)	Treat in cool water and enzyme wash powder/liquid. Enzymes work best at body temperature. The water should be no hotter than your hand. Hot water sets protein in the fabric. The stain cannot then be removed.
Grass, ball-point ink	Apply methylated spirit, then wash.
Writing ink	Soak in lemon juice or sour milk (lactic acid). This removes the fixative. The stain can then be washed out.
Iron mould (rust)	Use lemon juice and soak well. Then wash.
Mildew	Use bleach carefully. Rinse off immediately as bleach rots fabrics. Do not use bleach on coloured fabrics as it will remove the colour.
Grease stains (shoe polish, make-up, lipstick, oil)	If the fabric is washable use grease-solvent powder in the soak and wash (do not soak wool or silk). For other fabrics, use a grease solvent such as Dabitoff, turps or carbon tetrachloride. *Open the window. Do not use these near a naked flame.* Place the stained fabric on a pad of clean rag. Put the solvent on a second pad, and apply gently to the stain working from the outside inwards. This avoids the stain spreading. Air well to evaporate the solvent. Brush the stain off.
Chewing gum **Tar**	Pick off as much as possible. Freezing helps. Pick off. Then apply butter to soften tar. Remove either residue with a grease solvent as above.
Paint	Use turps, a paint solvent, as quickly as possible.

Questions

1 **What precautions must be taken before removing common stains from fabrics?**
Give clear instructions for the removal of the following stains: tea, ink from a ball-point pen, grass, lipstick, writing ink, rust marks, paint.

2 **For each of the following agents, name *one* stain which it will remove:**
(a) methylated spirits, (b) acetone, (c) an enzyme washing powder. (YHREB)

3 **If you prick your finger while sewing, how can you remove a spot of blood from the garment?** (SEREB)

4 **Careless use and storage of bleach and stain removers can have serious consequences in the home.**
(a) What accidents might involve young children?
(b) What might cause a fire?
(c) Devise a code of practice for the safe storage and use of these items in the home.

Achieving an effect

Colour and pattern within a room can give it an atmosphere and even appear to change its size or shape.

Rooms which face north often appear cold and cheerless because they get no sunlight. East, west, and south-facing rooms get sunlight either some or all of the day. This is because Britain is in the northern hemisphere.

The sun rises in the east and sets in the west, but passes on the southern side of Britain, so south-facing rooms get sunlight and some warmth during the day, but those facing north never get sun and are cold.

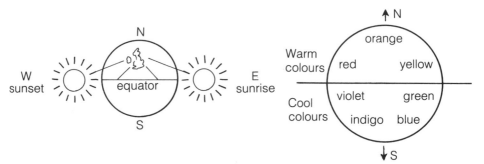

Look at the colour circle on the back cover of this book.

The warm cosy room
Reds, oranges, and yellows are called warm colours because they they give a warm cosy feeling; yellow is also a particularly cheerful colour. If one of these is used as the basic colour in a north-facing room, a cold cheerless place immediately takes on a warm cosy look.

The light airy room
On the opposite side of the circle are the cool colours: green, blue, indigo, and violet. Cool colours give an air of freshness to south-facing rooms, which will get a lot of sun.

The effect of different shades
A **shade** is a degree or depth of colour. Deeper shades draw walls in. Lighter shades give a feeling of more space.
This is how to make a narrow room look wider:

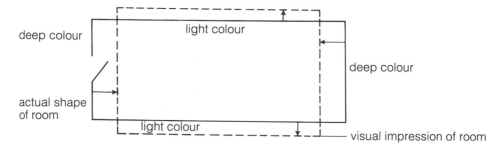

A deep colour on a ceiling makes it appear lower, while a light colour gives a higher, more airy effect.

Pattern

Having chosen the basic colours to give a good atmosphere and the right impression of size and shape, consider whether the use of a pattern somewhere in the room will improve it by adding interest, or detract from the finished effect.

1 A pattern breaks up a surface so it looks smaller. For example, a room papered with patterned wallpaper will give the impression of being smaller than one with plain walls.
2 If a room is normally a busy one with lots of items and equipment about, e.g. a kitchen, patterned wallpaper will add to the confused appearance. A calmer, tidier atmosphere is achieved with plain colours as a background.
3 Use only one pattern in a room. Two different patterns give a cluttered effect.
4 A pattern on the carpet has the advantage that it will not show marks as readily as a plain one.
5 Fabric is a good medium to introduce pattern. For example, it can be used for upholstery, bedspreads, and curtains.
6 Choose the size of pattern to suit the area. Small prints look attractive on cottage windows; large patterns are only suitable for large curtains.

The impression of a longer window can be given by curtains reaching to the floor, or by vertical stripes which take the eye up and down. Horizontal stripes give the impression of a wider window when curtains are closed by making the eye travel across the window.

Planning a room

By understanding what colours can do you can achieve the effect you want.

1 Consider the way the window faces, and the shape and size of the room.
2 Decide what effect is needed. Do you want the room to look cosy and warm? light and airy? smaller? larger?
3 Choose the appropriate colour and shades and decide whether a pattern will improve the effect or spoil it.

The finished result will have achieved the desired effect if the colour and pattern are chosen and used for the right reasons.

Questions

1 **Explain why rooms facing north are often cold and cheerless. How could the room be given a cheerful cosy atmosphere?**
2 **(a) Are south-facing rooms warm or cold?**
   (b) What colours would be suitable for decorating a south-facing lounge and why?
   (c) Design a pattern for use on the fabric in the room.
   (d) Where might you use the patterned fabric?
3 **Why might a large patterned fabric look very attractive in the department store, but rather ugly in your own small room?**
4 **An old mansion with rather lofty rooms has been turned into small flats and bed-sitting rooms. Describe how you would decorate and furnish one of the newly divided rooms, to avoid the feeling of height in a small room.**

Colour and style

Colour

Some colours suit a person better than others. This depends on the colouring of their features: hair, eyes, and skin.

Black hair contrasts well with strong colours, and so a person with very dark hair would look attractive in royal blue, scarlet, or emerald green – the strong colours. Blonde people often look their best in pastel shades, e.g. pink, primrose, light green, or pastel blue; men in muted shades of these colours

However, there are relatively few people who have such definite hair colour, and so many are puzzled by which colours suit them best. The clue to this lies in the colour of their eyes.

Blue-eyed people look at their best in blues. Those with green eyes find that green-based colours suit them best. People with hazel eyes feel best in the autumn shades: greens, yellows, browns.

People with pale skins look rather 'washed out' in dark colours like navy or black which appear to drain what little colour they have from the skin. On the other hand a suntan shows up much better against a pastel colour or white.

Neutral colours
Neutral colours such as grey, cream, and beige can look dull and uninteresting alone, but they do team well with a colour that suits the person worn near the face; for example a camel coat with a blue silk scarf or a green blouse or shirt with a grey skirt or trousers.

Teaming colours
Wearing colours together can produce different effects. Two colours of the same strength, e.g. scarlet and emerald green, would look vivid and gaudy, but two colours of different strengths from the same area of the colour circle can be teamed together and look attractive, e.g. deep green and light green, or brown and light yellow.

A *striking* effect is achieved by wearing either:

1 a single bright colour for the whole dressed shape, i.e. the top and trousers; the whole dress; the full length coat;
2 a fabric in which several bright colours are teamed together to make a gay all-over pattern (the colours are therefore in smaller quantities and so gaudiness is avoided);
3 a colour that suits a person well.

Style

Choosing the right style to complement the figure is extremely important if you want to achieve a good overall look.

The slimmer look
1 For a plump figure, take the emphasis away from the body width by making the eye travel vertically on pattern lines going from top to hem.
2 Colour going from top to hem makes the figure look longer, and so takes emphasis off the width.
3 A stitched pleat left open just above the hem edge can be a good way of incorporating a vertical line.

4   Use straight styles, or keep fullness lines flat by using darts and gores instead of gathers or unstitched pleats.
5   The longer the line from top to hem the taller the figure will look, so the longer hem line is better to achieve the slimmer, taller look.
6   Vertical stripes or a pattern going from top to hem on the fabric help too.
7   Avoid shiny fabrics; these make an area look larger.

To look taller

Points 1, 2, 5, and 6 above all serve to make the figure look taller and can be used by any short person, whether fat or thin; or by youngsters to give a more 'grown-up' look.

To look shorter

Conversely the figure looks shorter if the colour and line is broken at the waist, so separates look nice on very tall people. A shorter hem line gives a smaller total look.

To achieve more curves

The person who is 'skinny' can achieve an attractive 'total look' by using fullness wisely in several appropriate places.

1   Gathers give the best effect as they billow out and can emphasize the smallest curve.
2   Unstitched pleats have a similar effect to gathers, though they do not stand out quite so well.
3   Horizontal patterns carry the eye along them, and emphasize width.

New features

New features of fashion give interest to clothes and look very good on the attractive model girls chosen because their figure shows off that particular fashion well. It may be a shorter hemline, a wider shoulderline, or a frilly neckline, but the new line will not suit all figures equally.

This is one reason why people tire of a fashion quickly, as they realize that what looks good on someone else does not have the same effect on their own 'total look'. The wise person considers what the new feature will do to her figure *before* buying the dress or cutting out the pattern.

Questions

1   **Say what colour your hair, eyes, and skin are. Suggest a suitable colour scheme for a waistcoat, blouse, and check skirt.**
2   **(a) Describe your figure type. Name *two* style lines which will suit your figure type. Give a reason why each is suitable.**
    (b) Name *two* styles of clothes which *do not* suit your figure type and give a reason for each.
    (c) You are starting a job in an office. Sketch a suitable outfit to wear in the office. You should design the outfit to be part of a planned wardrobe. (EAEB)

Features

A feature is a mark by which something is recognized. It stands out and gives individuality. It can be a feature of fashion such as a frill, a collar, or even a total shape.

The fashionable frills of the early 1980s had been seen many times before – on men's clothes in the mid-eighteenth century and indeed on men's dress dinner shirts right up to the present day.

The soft lace collar worn by men in the mid-seventeenth century has been in and out of ladies' fashion many times since then. It returned once more in the early 1980s, together again with lace cuffs.

1750

1981

1981

1660
soft lace collar and cuffs

New Look 1948

Utility 1943   pencil-slim skirt 1952

The New Look of 1948 succeeded the 'utility' designs of the wartime period when fabric was in short supply. From 1940–1947 clothing was made from as little material as possible. The New Look gave added style, length, and width as more fabric became available.

In contrast 1952 brought the pencil slim skirt; popular again thirty years later.

Some features are of ethnic origin. They come from a particular race or people. Turkish trousers, the Afghan coat, poncho, kaftan, sarong, and sari have all appeared in the British fashion scene. Indian cotton, African prints, and Javanese batik (p.33) enliven modern fabrics. The **dirndl**, a full skirt gathered into a tight waitband, comes from Central Europe. The **magyar** style comes from Hungary. It features a plain sleeve cut in one piece with the bodice.
The **turban** hat has often been seen at Ascot in silk or fabric of a similar texture. It has also been featured in holiday clothes made in towelling to conceal damp hair after swimming.

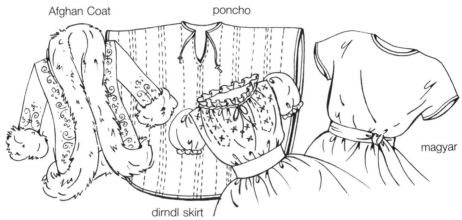

Afghan Coat poncho magyar dirndl skirt

The Japanese influence has been diverse. **Kimono**-style housecoats or pyjamas are particularly attractive. Eastern colours and designs in silk fabric lend authenticity to the style. The flimsy evening gowns of the late 1970s were a variation of the Kimono theme. Can you see the similarities? In complete contrast, judo clothes are also Japanese.

A **mandarin collar** gives a dress a Japanese or Chinese look. The garment can be further enhanced in the Chinese style with slits at the side. Rich colours of silk are associated with Eastern dress.

tie casing

flimsy soft fabric

Question

1 **Why are clothes different in other countries?**
What effect do factors like materials available; climate; local crafts; national sports and activities, have on the dress of a country or race?
Can you think of some examples of each factor?

Planning and buying

A major change in life, such as starting work, is an opportunity to plan a wardrobe. Instead of school clothes you will need daytime clothes for work. Although school uniform is not usually popular, you will probably find that even when you go to work you will wear certain clothes only in the daytime. Relaxing at home you may prefer to wear jeans. But you may have to conform to a certain standard at work and jeans may be frowned upon.

Working in an office it is important to look smart, and to try to look efficient. In a department store you may have to conform to a particular colour. On a food counter you will wear an overall and cap. As a nurse or police cadet you have a specific uniform.

Planning a wardrobe

1   Think carefully about the work you do. Select styles that are suitable. Long flowing hair, full sleeves, and hanging ties are particularly unsuitable for factory workers. Why?

2   Choose clothes in which you feel comfortable. Base your colour scheme on the colour that suits you most.

3   Clothes give a message. In a department store, on the cosmetics counter, you would be expected to look clean, smart, attractive, and have a pleasant air of efficient charm. Shoes are particularly important. In a standing job, footwear should be smart yet comfortable. It is very tiring for girls to wear high heels all day. You will look more attractive and be more pleasant to customers if you feel comfortable, so compromise with smart but lower heels.

4   Dress according to the temperature. It is often hot in centrally-heated offices and stores. Be sure that you are not too warm. Wear warm clothes to travel to and from work, but lighter clothing indoors.

5   Include a smart lightweight coat in your wardrobe. A full-length showerproof type with a matching or contrasting hat is practical in British weather. On a college campus involving outdoor walks between classes, a pac-a-mac with hood tucked into one's bag proves very useful.

6   Choose easy-care fabrics or make sure you can launder them, particularly at the beginning when you may have only a limited number of clothes.

7   Select an outfit that has two or three different parts. A pinafore dress is versatile, and quite easy to make. Wear it with a jacket, a jumper, a blouse, or alone according to the weather. Buy jumpers that tone or contrast, and later, when you have more money, buy or make a skirt of a different style and colour, to tone with the first set of tops. Gradually enlarge your wardrobe. A matching sports jacket, pullover, shirt, and tie can be warm travelling to work, and smart or casual later, depending on which is removed.

Study the outfits above and think of your own wardrobe combinations.

When buying clothes decide on the features that are important. Is the item: smart, fashionable, serviceable, durable, warm/cool, easy to launder and care for, part of a planned wardrobe, within your price range? Put these factors in order of importance. When choosing disco clothes your order will be different from when you are choosing working clothes.

▲ Answer the questions and compare buying ready-made clothes with making them. Boys may have a different viewpoint to girls as lots of men's clothes are shaped by tailoring processes. Some boys may not feel so confident with a sewing machine, but practising is fun!

	Ready-made clothes	Making clothes
Advantages	1 Can you see the item and try it on before purchase? 2 Can you have it altered to fit exactly? 3 Can you wear it immediately? 4 Do cheaper synthetics, and machine decoration on female wear make underwear a good buy? 5 Are men's tailored clothes more difficult to handle? Are they better made by an expert? 6 Are men happier than women to wear identical mass produced clothes?	1 Is it cheaper? 2 Can you make the item fit you? 3 You can choose both fabric and style, so have you got more individuality? Are you less likely to meet someone dressed identically? 4 Can you make seams and fastenings more secure by sewing them better? 5 Would you get pleasure and satisfaction from wearing something you have made well, and would you enjoy making it?
Disadvantages	1 Is the ready-made item *exactly* what you want? Do you have to pay a lot for it? 2 In ready-made clothes might you meet someone wearing the same item? Would you mind? 3 Do you find fastenings on ready-made clothes come off easily?	1 Not all designs are easy. Do you need practice in tailoring to achieve good results on coats or jackets? 2 Is underwear cheaper to make or to buy ready-made? 3 The materials are far cheaper than the ready-made item. What is the other part of the cost?

Choosing clothes

Decide on the features that are important. Then put them in order.

Children's day clothes

1 Easy for the child to learn to fasten.
2 Pretty for party wear/Serviceable for play or school/Tidy and smart for Sunday Family Service.
3 Durable and hard wearing.
4 Washable fabrics, preferably easy-care.
5 Warm/cool to wear.
6 Choose a style that allows for growth with fullness; good hems; adjustable fastenings like velcro.

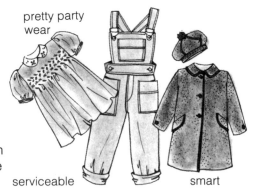

pretty party wear

serviceable

smart

Place these factors in order.
Then choose the fabric, style, and colour which best matches up with the factors you list.

A mother-to-be

yoke features quilting, piping, and toggles

1 Loose, comfortable, and expandable, yet smart.
2 A yoke is a useful feature as the waist and lower part of the body will expand.
3 Give emphasis to an interesting feature on the collar or yoke to divert attention away from the size of the waist and stomach.
4 Warm or cool to suit the season of the pregnancy.
5 Colour to suit the person to make them look at their best.

Alternative ways of buying textile goods

Consider the factors relevant to what you want to buy and then make up your mind how to buy it.

Mail order catalogue
This enables you to shop from home. It is useful for people who cannot get out. You can try the item on at home, and send it back if you don't want it.

Disadvantages:
1 You would have to find someone to alter it, or do it yourself if any adjustments need to be made.
2 You cannot compare it with other items.

Boutique
These specialize in highly fashionable clothes for the younger age group. There is usually plenty of scope, as stock is confined to young fashion.

Magazine offers
Magazines offer ready-to-sew clothes. These are useful for inexperienced sewers who find difficulty in cutting out. That job is already done.
Read the advertisement carefully. Notice the type of fabric. Is it likely to fray, or be difficult to handle? Compare the offer with the cost of buying similar fabric, or buying a similar ready-made item.
Look and consider before you buy.

Market stalls
Cheap fabrics and clothing are offered on market stalls. There are several reasons why they may be cheaper.

1 A stall has fewer overheads than a shop.
2 The stallholder may have access to good quality fabrics or clothes not passed as first quality. A small flaw means it becomes a 'second'. Real bargains can be secured by using fabrics carefully and avoiding the flaws in cutting out. Occasionally flaws in clothes are in an inconspicuous place. Always find the flaw or fault before purchasing. Bigger faults in fabrics or clothes may be no economy, even if they are cheaper.
3 The fabric or clothing may be made of cheap fibre which frays badly and is weak in wear.
4 Inferior quality fabric is dressed or 'sized' (see p.37) to improve the texture. Rub it to see if white powder falls out.

Customers' rights

The Sale of Goods Act covers all forms of trading. You should know what your rights are.

1 The Act states that all items must be of suitable quality to perform the job for which they are being sold.
2 The facts stated about them on the labels, or verbally by the seller, must be true. Shoes can only be called 'leather' if they really are leather. Synthetics cannot be labelled 'silk'. This is part of the Trade Descriptions Act 1968 too.
3 The goods must be in working order.

Always ask about goods before purchase. Keep receipts. If you think the law has been broken, go back to the shop with your receipt and goods as soon as possible after the fault is discovered. Discuss it with the shopkeeper, who must give you your money back, or change the item if you prefer to have another one. *But*, if an article was reduced because it had a fault, you cannot complain about *that* fault. You bought it cheaply for that reason. (However, if there is another fault, then you can complain.) This is why it is always a risk buying goods which have been reduced in price.

Questions

1 **(a)** **List the advantages and disadvantages of buying clothes from a boutique specializing in teenage fashion.**
   (b) **Sketch a double-breasted winter jacket which could be worn with both trousers and a skirt.**
   (c) **Suggest a suitable fabric for the jacket.**
   (d) **What are the benefits of making the jacket yourself?**
   (e) **Give instructions for sewing on a jacket button.** (NWREB)
2 **(a)** **State *three* advantages and *three* disadvantages of buying clothes by mail order.**
   (b) **Magazines often advertise cut-out and ready-to-sew garments. Suggest *two* advantages and *two* disadvantages of these offers.**
   (c) **A pair of boots guaranteed waterproof start to leak within one month of purchase. What steps could the consumer take in this situation?**
   (d) **What are the *three* main provisions of the Sale of Goods Act?** (SCE)

Further work on Chapter 4

1 Sketch *two* different outfits, one showing the effect of horizontal stripes and one showing the effect of vertical stripes. Suggest a figure type and state suitable fabrics and colour for *each* of the outfits.
In each case give reasons for your choice of style, fabric, and colour. (AEB, 1981)

2 How has the introduction of co-ordinating wallpapers, paints, and furnishing fabrics affected the homemaker's opportunity for original home decor?
Take one room in your home and suggest how you would use co-ordinating materials to create a particular mood or impression.
How would you make a piped cushion cover for use in this room? (London)

3 Name four ethnic items that have influenced modern British fashion. Say how two of them have been influenced by shape, colour, or fabric. Sketch garments or fabric items to show two different ethnic influences. Explain the origin of the influences.

4 The fifth and sixth form students at your school are staging a fashion show for charity. Sketch *two* contrasting outfits which you could make to illustrate your skills, giving details of styles, fabrics, and colours and the accessories you will wear with each outfit. (London)

5 You are going to the local further education college next term. Discuss the points to consider when choosing clothes for your new life.
Sketch an outfit which would form the basis of your wardrobe.
Name the fabrics and colours chosen.
List the order of work for making up one of the garments. (AEB, 1982)

6 Sketch a suitable garment or outfit for each of the following, naming the fabric(s) to be used in each case.
(a) A cosmetic consultant in a department store to wear at work,
(b) A seventeen-year-old at a special social occasion.
Give reasons for your choice of styles. Describe *two* of the fabrics you have chosen and compare their properties. (London)

7 (a) Sketch a two-piece outfit which a child of six could wear for:
either a birthday party in winter; *or* playing in the garden in summer.
Give reasons for your choice of outfit.
(b) Suggest and name suitable fabrics for the outfit and list the haberdashery required to complete it.
How may the outfit be lengthened when the child grows? (AEB, 1981)

8 (a) What points would you consider before deciding that a dress you propose to buy is good value for money?
(b) Sketch a dress for a mother-to-be showing interesting collar or yoke detail.

9 Explain briefly what is meant when fabrics or garments are described as 'seconds'.
State *two* points for each item below, which are important to check when buying 'seconds'.
(a) a market remnant of towelling,
(b) a ready-made Shetland wool sweater. (NWREB)

Chapter 5

Grain and patterns

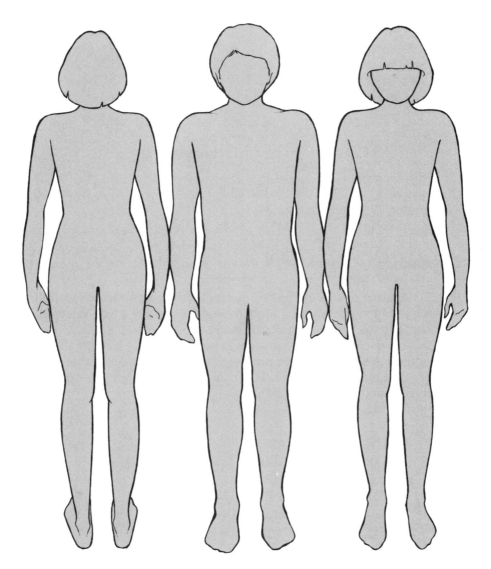

Use these body shapes to help you draw sketches of garments and outfits. They are a good size to show any features you wish to illustrate, and they will keep your drawings in proportion.

To make templates

1 Trace the outlines by placing thin plain paper on the page. Draw the outline.
2 From the paper, transfer the outline on to card using carbon paper.
3 Cut out your figures in card using scissors.
   Keep them safely – flat in your book.
   When sketching designs of clothes, draw round your templates faintly on the paper, and then clothe them.

Grains

Have you ever played the game where you cut out half a dancing doll shape in folded paper, and you have a line of dancing dolls?

This is the principle used in pattern making. A half pattern shape laid on the folded edge of fabric forms a whole piece which is exactly the same on both sides of the fold line. It is said to be **symmetrical**.

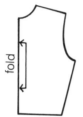  

Pattern pieces are usually symmetrical, so generally a half pattern piece is used, and cut double on fabric. When placed on a fold, like the dancing doll, it forms the whole piece without a join. A piece placed on double material without a fold will require a seam to join it (for which a seam allowance is added). A seam may be desirable if you need to make an opening in it.

Seams which are not on the straight grain (the warp) help flat fabric to take up and flatter the body shape.

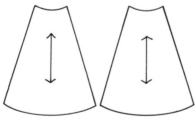 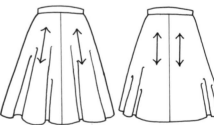

The two sides of this skirt seam are cut on the **bias** grain, so that when the skirt is worn, it will hang evenly and flow from the hips, as in the middle sketch. The right-hand sketch shows how it would hang if the seam were joined on the straight grain.

Bias grain is between warp and weft, but not on the true cross.

The **true cross** is found by folding the weft on to the warp.

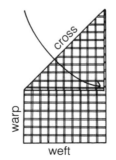 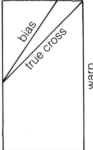

In Chapter 2 we found that the warp was the tightly spun, strong thread running the length of the fabric. Being strong it can carry the weight of the garment, and hang without stretching. This is why it is used to run from top to toe. The weft is composed of less tightly spun thread.

Experimental work

▲ 1 Cut a 20 cm square of fabric, marking carefully the warp and weft.
2 Holding it in both hands, pull it sharply along the warp; then give it a sharp pull along the weft.
Do you notice a sharp snap as you pull the warp? This is because there is no 'give' or stretch in the warp. On the weft you will hear a duller sound for there is slightly more 'give' in the fabric along the weft.
3 Now fold your fabric (as in diagram) to find the true cross, and cut along it. Cut a strip about 2 cm wide.

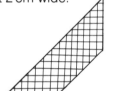

Pull this.
What do you notice?
Does it stretch easily?
You can see from the diagram why the fabric is said to be 'cut on the cross'.

Because this strip is so stretchy it can be used to fit round curved edges to neaten them. We often need to join strips, but because the fabric stretches when sewn on the true cross, a simple join like the one below would give a very misshapen result.

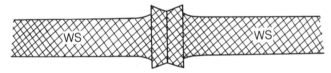

The line of stitching *must* follow the line of the threads. Cut another strip of fabric the same width on the true cross. Can you work out how to join it *sewing on the line of the thread* and putting right sides together? (For the answer, see p.223.)

Bias binding

Commercially, binding is cut on the bias and joined into lengths. This is not quite as stretchy as that cut on the true cross, but it is quite adequate for most curves. A 0.5 cm turning is pressed on both sides to make it easy to use. Nainsook, a fine cotton, makes the best bias binding. It is soft and pleasant to handle. Other cotton binding is coarser, and may have a dressing which gives rather a harsh feel in use.

Questions

1 **What is meant by the term 'symmetrical'?**
2 *Asymmetrical* **is the opposite of symmetrical. Explain what this term means when referring to a pattern. Sketch a blouse or dress which is asymmetrical.**
3 **Give two reasons why a seam might be used to join two symmetrical pattern pieces, instead of cutting them on the fold.**

Pattern lays

▲ On the next two pages are the pattern pieces for a pair of shorts and trousers; and for a dress, with more alternative skirt styles on the next page. Any of these styles could be set on to a waistband to make a separate skirt.

Trace the patterns on to greaseproof paper and label them. You could then make templates (cut-outs) from thin card, or cut them out in coloured sticky paper.

The scale of the pattern pieces is 1 mm to 1 cm. Cut out greaseproof paper on the same scale to represent fabric.

9 cm will represent	90 cm width.
11.5 cm	115 cm
14 cm	140 cm
15 cm	150 cm

A long strip of paper will represent a roll of fabric.

A **pattern lay** is a plan of the most efficient way to lay all the pieces for a garment on to the fabric. You can work out a pattern lay by placing the pieces on the paper as economically as you can. Remember the straight grain line, which goes from top to toe of the garment, must run parallel with the selvedge or warp. You can fold the fabric crosswise or lengthwise to make two thicknesses. Each piece is usually cut double,
either because it is a half piece (see p.115);
or because we need two (sleeves, cuffs);
or because it is a double part (collar).
When only one piece is needed it should be cut on single material (waistband).

It is useful to position the largest pieces first, and to fit the others round like a jigsaw. Sometimes it helps to put a piece face side down to fit it in. You will still get two symmetrical pieces from it. Put the pieces as close together as you can. The best arrangement is the one where there is as little space as possible left between the pieces.

When you have made the pattern lay you can measure the amount of fabric needed for each garment. Then use the scale to convert it to metres.

▲ **How much fabric do I need?**

1 Pick out the pattern pieces you would need to make the pair of trousers in the sketch.
Using the paper 'fabric', work out how these pieces are placed on the fabric to use the minimum amount to make the trousers from 90 cm material.
How much fabric would be needed?

2 Pick out the pattern pieces you would need to make the dress in the sketch. Work out a pattern lay which uses the minimum amount of 90 cm fabric. Find out how much fabric would be used.

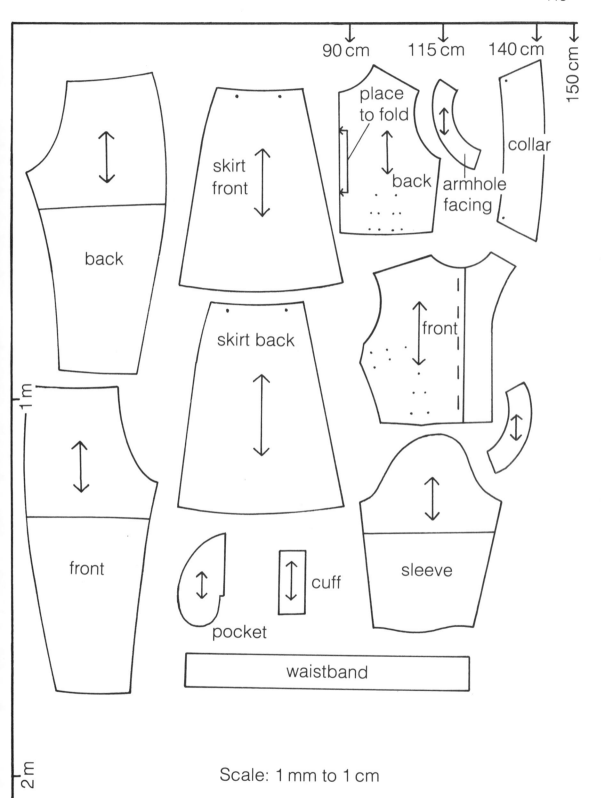

90 cm 115 cm 140 cm 150 cm

place to fold

back

armhole facing

collar

back

skirt front

skirt back

front

front

1 m

2 m

pocket

cuff

sleeve

waistband

Scale: 1 mm to 1 cm

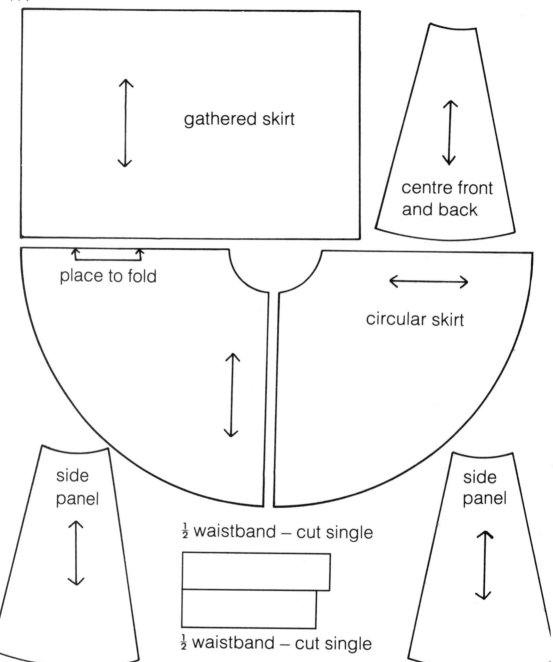

gathered skirt

centre front and back

place to fold

circular skirt

side panel

side panel

½ waistband – cut single

½ waistband – cut single

Nap

A **nap** forms when the surface of material is raised by brushing. Brushed nylon, winceyette, and flannelette have a nap. A **pile** on fabric such as velvet, corduroy, or needlecord is formed by loops in weaving, which are then cut. The pile is brushed so that it lies one way. As pile and nap look best going in one direction, pattern pieces must all be cut out the same way up, with the pile or nap stroking from top to toe. Pattern makers refer to pile and nap fabrics collectively as 'with nap'. Also use the 'with nap' lay for a one-way design. Usually 'with nap' requires more fabric.

3 Pick out the pattern pieces you would need to make the skirt in the sketch. Work out the pattern lay which uses the minimum amount of fabric. (A crosswise fold on the fabric might be useful here.) The skirt pieces can be placed whichever way up fits best, provided that the straight grain lines are parallel with the selvedge to make the skirt hang right. The waistband need only be cut on single fabric as it is a complete waistband pattern. What is the minimum amount of fabric required?

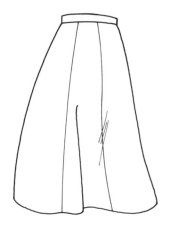

4 Now imagine your fabric has a nap (see p.114) or a figured design where the flowers go one way only. To make it look right all the pattern pieces must run the same way. How much fabric are you going to need?

In doing these exercises you will realize that you need to place the largest pieces first and the smaller ones fit in.

As each half piece is on double fabric, a front or a back of the bodice or skirt can take up roughly the width of 90 cm fabric. Other small pieces may be fitted beside the bodice back. The amount of fabric is therefore usually twice the full length including hems, *plus* the length of sleeve or any other large part such as a frill.

Now try the same patterns using a different width of fabric. With a wider fabric you may find it helps to fold the fabric partway across, leaving some single fabric. Then you can place two halves separately on single material, turning one face side down to get two symmetrical halves. You will find that you need less fabric, because pieces will fit side by side.

5 Can you work out how to put the two quarter circle patterns on double material to make a circular skirt using 90 cm fabric economically? You can place one quarter to a crosswise fold.

6 Select the pattern pieces for the sleeveless dress in the sketch. You will need the armhole facing patterns. Work out the pattern lay and the amount of fabric needed for:
   (a) The dress with a plain gathered skirt (a dirndl) using two widths of fabric.
   (b) For a full gathered skirt using three widths of fabric.

7 Using the patterns for a pair of shorts work out the amount of fabric required to make them from (a) 90 cm fabric, and (b) 150 cm fabric.

Checks and stripes

What is wrong with this skirt and pair of trousers?

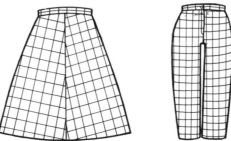

How can this problem be avoided?

▲ 1 Use some 5 mm squared paper to represent 90 cm checked fabric.
2 Fold it lengthwise on the middle line so that the check lines on the lower thickness are exactly beneath those on the top layer. Why?
3 Place the pattern pieces for the four-gored skirt on the 'fabric'.
How can you make sure that the checks will match at the seams?
4 Watch the position of the squared lines. They must be in the same position on the seam line on each piece that has to join together. It is quite useful to match them by the notches and ends of seams.
5 Cut round your patterns on the squared paper fabric and see if your checks match, by placing the centre front, side seams, and centre back together. Do the checks also match on the pieces from the under layer that you couldn't see?
Now you will realize why fabric must be folded carefully to put the lines of the under layer exactly beneath the top one. This is quite easy on paper because you start with a straight edge of paper along the weft. Unfortunately fabric is not always cut like this, so you must match the weft lines together at the ends of the length of material. Checks are usually formed by the weaving of different coloured threads, and so that may be easy. But difficulty may arise in two cases.

1 If the fabric has been pulled unevenly as it comes off the loom, when you fold it, the weft lines do not lie together. To correct this you must pull the fabric back into shape.
   Grip the short corner (that's the one that lies short, see diagram) and the one diagonally opposite (when the fabric is laid out flat). Pull firmly and carefully to get the fabric back into shape.

2 Sometimes a check may be printed on to fabric, and on cheaper materials it may not be printed on the straight grain. Always check a printed check before purchase. Avoid bad prints as matching is extremely difficult.

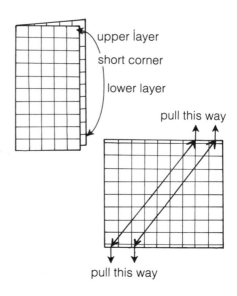

upper layer

short corner

lower layer

pull this way

pull this way

From this activity you will have learned that much of the attractive appearance of what we wear or make is achieved in the pattern cutting.

When cutting checks, stripes, or large prints:

1. Fold the fabric so that the warp lines, stripes, or motifs lie together, even if this means that because the fold is not quite central, there is a little fabric left over on one side. Keep the selvedges parallel.
2. Follow the weft line across and pull into shape if necessary.
3. Pin the weft check line at the selvedge edge.
4. Match the position of lines at notches and corners so that they will meet each other at seam lines.
5. Where a dart fits into a seam line to be matched, for example on the side seam of the bodice pattern, match the largest part of the seam.

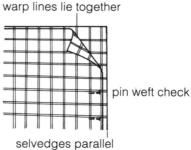

warp lines lie together

pin weft check

selvedges parallel

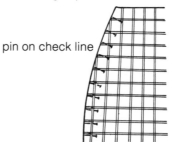

pin on check line

Sewing checks, stripes, and large motifs

Having cut out carefully so that the lines match, place them right sides together and pin *on* the check lines, on the fitting line, at right angles to the seam edge. This will ensure the lines do not slip out of position while sewing.

Furnishing fabrics often have large motifs. These need to be matched well as they are in constant view. Some floral curtains may be particularly difficult because all the flowers should be growing upwards. Some checks do not look exactly the same upside down. In both these cases beware of a crosswise fold. Cut the fabric across on the fold and turn the lower layer so that the pattern matches the upper layer exactly, before attempting to lay on and cut pattern pieces.

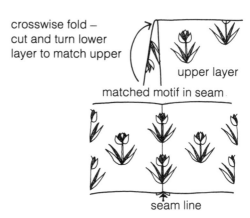

crosswise fold – cut and turn lower layer to match upper

upper layer

matched motif in seam

seam line

Questions

1. **How do you deal with a woven check which does not lie flat even if you match the checks of the two layers of fabric?**
2. **Where do you match pattern pieces to make sure the check will match on the garment?**
3. **What additional care is necessary when working with checks?**
4. **Name two cases where a crosswise fold of fabric may mean cutting and turning the lower layer. Explain why.**

Measurements and alterations

Body shape and size

When choosing a pattern look carefully at the style drawings in the pattern book, and select a style that suits your build. Bear in mind any features about yourself that you wish to highlight or conceal. Whilst growing, take all your measurements periodically, especially before buying a pattern. Measure yourself over underclothes only. Why? Girls add 5 cm ease on bust and hip; boys on chest and seat.

To take measurements

Measure **bust** or **chest** around the fullest part of the body above the waist.

Measure **hip** around the fullest part of the body below the waist. Find the waist by tying a tape around yourself tightly and wriggling about a bit. The tape naturally falls into the narrowest part of the body – the waist. Note the difference in the male body shape on p. 109. The male waist is lower.

Note where it is, and feel which spinal vertebra is on the waistline. Some length measurements should be checked whilst you have a marked waistline.

Measure **nape of neck** (the most prominent vertebra when you bend your head forward) **to waistline**. Measure **waistline to ankle** for trousers and long skirts. (Boys will need **inside-leg** too.) Measure **waistline to hem** (where you want it) down centre back with a friend's help (don't bend to look).

Waist measurement: remove the tape *before* measuring on that line. Why?

Boys may need **neckband:** using nape and collar bone; and **neck:** round neck. Why

To measure the shoulder length

This is important to detect any fitting problems before they arise. Measure the pattern NP to SP and compare with body size. Measure from the corner of the neck to the sharp bone at the top of the arm, on *both* sides. You may find one or two centimetres difference between the two shoulder lengths. Note this down. This is why we need to check the fitting of *each* sleeve as it is put into the armhole. We also check sleeve fittings because some people's shoulders slope more than others. Sloping shoulders make the bodice crease. This can be avoided by sewing the shoulder seam just below the shoulder point.

To measure the sleeve length

Bend your arm. Measure from the sharp bone at the top of the arm to the wrist bone *around the bent elbow*.

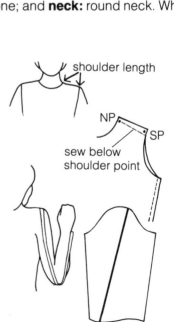

Choosing a pattern

Buy a pattern according to the width measurement.
For an item worn above the waist buy according to the bust or chest size.
For an item worn below the waist only, buy according to the hip or seat size.
Selecting the standard size nearest to your figure, by these measurements, avoids difficult alterations.
Having selected the pattern buy fabric that will drape or hang well in that style, and be serviceable for its use. The pattern envelope suggests fabrics, and states the amount necessary, for the view and size you have chosen.

▲ Compare standard size measurements from a pattern book with your own. See if any adjustments would be necessary. *Always* do this *before* cutting out to avoid alterations later. This example shows a girl's pattern envelope.

Standard body measurements						Own measurements
Size	**8**	**10**	**12**	**14**	**16**	
Bust	80 (31½")	83 (32½")	87 (34")	92 (36")	97 (38")	87 (34¼")
Waist	61 (24")	64 (25¼")	67 (26½")	71 (28")	76 (30")	63 (24¾")
Hips	85 (33½")	88 (34¾")	92 (36")	97 (38")	102 (40")	90 (35½")
Back – neck to waist	40 (15¾")	40.5 (16")	41.5 (16¼")	42 (16½")	42.5 (16¾")	41.5 (16¼")

To alter length

Is it the nape of the neck to waist, or waist to hem or ankle that needs some alteration? How do you know?
Alter the pattern on the pattern **lengthen or shorten** lines. These are at right angles to the straight grain line. They are placed where they will not interfere with any other line such as the dart, the armhole, or the neckline.

Trousers require alteration in two places; on the crotch seam and the lower leg. This keeps them in proportion.

To shorten

Fold on the line on each pattern piece and make a double tuck. Re-draw the pattern line.

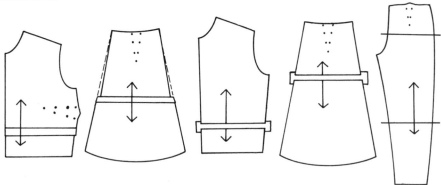

To lengthen

Cut the pattern along the line and pin a piece of paper in.
Note: always keep the straight grain line straight.
Join the seam line above to the seam line below the adjustment to make it flow evenly again.

To adjust the waist

If the waist is too large, this will only matter on a fitted skirt or trousers that hang from the waist. To adjust the waist, divide the difference in measurements by the number of darts. Make each dart that amount wider at the waistline.

Then adjust the length of the waistband pattern to match, by taking identical small tucks so that the pattern markings match.

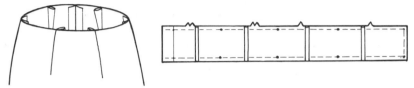

To alter the width

If you buy a pattern by the bust size and the hip measurement is too small, this will only matter on a straight fitted skirt.

Width alterations are done parallel to the straight grain line, and where it will not interfere with any pattern line.

Divide the alteration into four (there are two half backs and two half fronts). On each half back and half front add in a quarter of the amount needed.

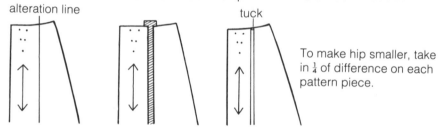

To make hip smaller, take in $\frac{1}{4}$ of difference on each pattern piece.

The above method will also make the waist wider or narrower.

How would you adjust that to make it fit?

Choosing the right lay on a bought pattern

There are a number of different lays on an instruction sheet.

You will use only one. To decide which one to use, look for your view, your size, and your width of fabric. Which view have you chosen? (e.g. View 2) Ignore the rest.

That narrows it down to considerably fewer diagrams.

You will find they are labelled by the *width of fabric*: 90 cm, 115 cm, 140 cm, 150 cm. What is the width of your fabric?

Look at the 'View 2' lays labelled with the width of your fabric. That narrows it down even more. Now look for the lay for your *size*. Now you are left with one lay. Make a circle round it.

Questions

1 **List your own body measurements. State the appropriate size of pattern you should buy. Compare your measurements with the standard ones, and say what alterations you would need to make on the patterns of a fitted skirt, trousers and waistcoat.**

2 **Why is the lengthen or shorten line placed so low down on the female bodice? Could it be higher? What would happen if it were?**

3 **Could the lengthen or shorten line be lower on the skirt?**

Pattern markings

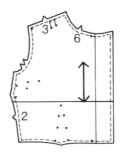

The straight grain line is used in laying the pattern on to the fabric. It should be placed straight along the grain parallel to the selvedge.

This mark means place the pattern edge to the fold along the straight grain.

The thick line running at right angles to the straight grain line is for lengthening or shortening the pattern.

Small triangles on the cutting line are **notches**, sometimes called **balance marks**. Cut around these. They have a number. They indicate which pieces fit together later. If you place the pattern pieces very close together, or the notched edge to the selvedge, you cannot cut round the notches. Either mark these with chalk, or tailor tack. (See below.)

Dots on the seam line indicate shoulder point, centre front, centre back, and so on. These markings should be transferred on to the fabric. The position of darts, tucks, and pleats are marked by dots joined by lines.

Tailor's chalk is a quick and efficient way of transferring markings on to fabric. Use this for items to be made up immediately. It brushes off. Where fabric is handled a lot, markings may be lost before they have been used. Carboned tracing paper and a **tracing wheel** mark fabric quickly too, leaving a line of dots. **Tailor tacks** are made with double thread.

1 Pick up the dot stitching through both thicknesses of fabric with a small stitch. Leave a 2 cm end and a finger-width loop, then leave another 2 cm end.
2 When all the tailor tacks are done, unpin the pattern piece.
3 Pull the pattern lightly away from the tailor tacks and remove it.
4 Draw the layers of fabric apart and snip between.
5 Always leave the pattern on the fabric until you are actually ready to use the piece so that you can read the information.

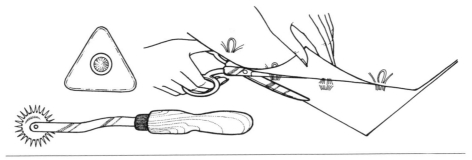

Questions

1 **What are notches or balance marks? What are they used for?**
2 **At what stage in the preparation of a garment do you use the straight grain line?**
3 **Why is it useful to leave the pattern pieces on the fabric after unpinning, until they are actually used? What guidance can you get from them?**

Further work on Chapter 5

1   Study the body templates on page 109. Illustrate the basic body measurements which should be taken to ensure a well-fitting outfit. Give instructions on how best to take them from the figure.

    (a)   State three ways in which a person's figure may differ from standard measurements.

    (b)   Having bought the pattern as near the measurements as possible, explain how you would check the pattern for size before laying it on fabric.

    (c)   Why do you need to consider lengthening (or shortening) trouser patterns in two places?

    (d)   Use labelled diagrams to show how you would make the following pattern alterations on a waisted dress with long fitted sleeves.
        (i)   increase the bust measurement by 4 cm (1½″)
        (ii)   decrease the waist measurement by 2 cm (¾″)
        (iii) decrease the sleeve length by 2.5 cm (1″).

3   (a)   Give two reasons why a pattern should be bought before the fabric.

    (b)   What is meant by the words 'with nap'?

    (c)   Why is a separate layout needed for cutting out fabric with nap?

    (d)   State two fabrics, other than napped ones for which you would use the 'with nap' lay.

▲4   Use a shirt pattern. List the size, fabric width and view of each lay given. In each case say why you would or would not use that lay to cut out your size on 90 cm napped fabric. Circle the lay you would use.

▲5   Investigate the different fabric markers found in the textiles room. Evaluate three methods of short-term marking suitable for transferring pattern marks to fabric. Say which is most efficient. Why?

▲6   Kay has a size 12 dress pattern (bust 87 cm, waist 67 cm, hips 92 cm, finished back length 110 cm). She measures bust 87 cm, waist 63 cm, hips 90 cm, and wants a finished length of 114 cm.
    Using tracings of the pattern pieces on page 113, and mounting them with explanatory notes, show how the pattern may be altered to make sure of a successful fit to the finished dress.

▲7   Devise a pattern lay for a tailored shirt in a one way checked fabric.

▲8   Using traced shapes or cut-outs from magazines, explain and illustrate how the body's shape changes during growth.
    How do other factors affect size and shape? Refer in your answer to food, family, health, and fitness.

▲9   You intend to make a pair of child's dungarees. You plan to use a pattern given to you by a friend. The pattern is too short and needs lengthening before use. To allow for growth, use an adjustable fastening to join the straps to the bib. Include a decoration in the item. Lengthen the pattern to give an increase of 16 cm in the *overall* length. State with reasons the most suitable fabric for the summer dungarees. Work out the amount of fabric needed to make them up using width (a) 90 cm (no nap) (b) 115 cm (no nap) (c) 115 cm (with nap). Give details of the notions/haberdashery needed to complete them.   (NEA prac.)

Chapter 6

Aids to good needlecraft

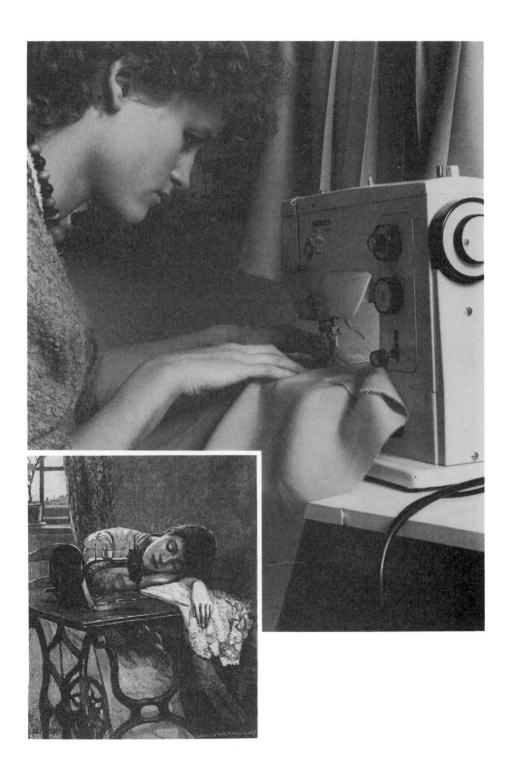

The sewing machine

Threading the machine

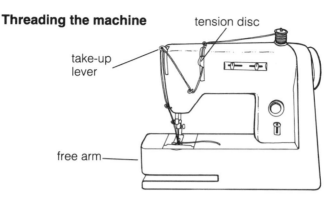

tension disc

take-up
lever

free arm

Each make and model of sewing machine has slightly different features, and so some parts may be in a slightly different position, but the basic threading of a machine is always in the same order.

The top thread comes from the **reel** via one or possibly two **thread guides** and then goes between the **tension discs**. From there it goes through the **take-up lever**, and then via thread guides to the **needle** itself.

The position of the last thread guide indicates which way the needle is threaded. It is always important to consult a diagram or instruction book when using a new machine, as incorrect threading results in a poor stitch.

Always test a machine on a scrap of the fabric to be used, folded double, and if the stitch does not appear perfect, recheck the sequence of both the top and lower threads.

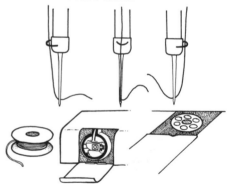

The lower thread is wound on to the **bobbin** or **shuttle** and the instruction book indicates which way the bobbin must be inserted into the bobbin case. Take care to get this right! Put the bobbin in position and close the door, leaving the end of the thread hanging out. To get the bottom thread to go through the hole beneath the needle, hold the top thread and turn the **balance wheel** towards yourself once. As the needle goes down it interlocks the bottom thread, and that too can be drawn up easily. Before starting to machine, place both threads away from you. This keeps them clear of the machining line.

Tension

Machining is a stitch formed by two threads interlocking in the fabric, one from the top and the other from the shuttle or bobbin beneath the fabric.

The tension of the top thread is governed by the tension disc, which is numbered 0–9 or 10. Between 4–5, that is, halfway, is regarded as normal tension (check your instruction book). At this setting the threads meet in the fabric, so the stitch looks the same from both sides (diagram **a**).

The thread runs between two discs. When the number is lowered these discs are loosened so that more thread flows through easily. The thread then goes right through the fabric instead of meeting the bottom thread in the fabric. This is not a firm stitch. It does not make a secure seam. The thread can be pulled along, and this is why the tension is loosened for a gathering stitch (diagram **b**).

	loosened top tension	top tension too tight
a normal tension	**b** pull to gather	**c**

On the other hand, if the tension is tightened to a higher number the discs are screwed more tightly together, and the top thread has more difficulty in getting through. There is less thread to form the stitch at the top so it lies as a straight line on the surface. Therefore loops from the bottom appear on top for the top tension is too tight (diagram **c**).

The bottom tension (a small screw on the shuttle case) is not usually altered except during servicing.

Stitch length

The stitch length can be adjusted by moving a lever on older machines, or by turning a knob on newer models. On old straight stitch machines the number represented the number of stitches to the inch. Since metrication, numbers relate to the mm length of the stitch itself: 1 mm to 5 mm.

1   2   3   4   5

The general rule is: the thicker the fabric, the longer the stitch should be. So use the longest stitch for thick or heavyweight fabrics; for making a gathering thread (and loosen the top tension as explained above); for machine basting.

Use a medium stitch for medium and lightweight cottons and wools. While fine fabrics require a suitable stitch, beware of using too fine a stitch for seams. It is very difficult to remove should unpicking be necessary. This is another reason for testing the stitch on a double thickness of spare fabric of the type to be used, before starting to sew.

Questions

1 **Why is it important to thread the machine in the correct order?**
2 **How do you get the bottom thread of a machine to come up through the hole beneath the needle?**
3 **Why is it important to test a machine on double fabric each time it is used? Give several reasons why a stitch might not appear perfect. In each case say what you would do to remedy it.**
4 **How would you prepare to make a gathering thread?**
5 **What is the general rule about the length of stitches for machining?**

Types of sewing machine (1)

The changing design of sewing machines

The older machines, built to last a lifetime, do straight stitch, and may be extremely satisfactory for that. Natural fibres have been worked with straight stitch machines throughout this century – and grandmother's sixty-year-old sewing machine, still in working order, may be found in many homes today. Most synthetics too can be satisfactorily worked in straight stitch, though a ball-point needle is necessary to roll off the fabric thread. A pointed needle would spear the fibre and pull threads.

But the manufacture of synthetic fibres, and their widespread commercial use in ready-made clothes, has revolutionized domestic sewing machine design during the last forty years. There are now other types of machine available and the decision about which to choose may be a difficult one.

Choosing a machine

How much sewing do I do? What am I going to sew?
If the answer to these questions is: simply the construction of clothes and household furniture using natural fibres, then a straight stitch machine can be adequate. But today:

1 Many modern fabrics are stretchy and require swing-needle treatment.
2 The use of the swing needle streamlines construction by speeding up neatening, buttonhole making, and other processes.
3 Quicker construction means greater interest in fabric use and thus more sewing being done.
4 A wide range of swing-needle stitches have been evolved to streamline processes, such as three-step zigzag for patching or sewing on elastic and blind hemming to remove the need for hand sewing.
5 Instant decorative finishes or embroidery can be produced.
6 The use of an automatic 4-thread overlock reduces the process of sewing, trimming, and neatening to one quick operation, and brings the speed and method of commercial dress construction into the home.

Older straight-stitch machines may be hand operated. The treadle machine, worked by a swinging foot pedal attached to the balance wheel to drive the machine, was the forerunner of the electric foot-controlled machine. It freed both hands whilst machining, and this of course is the advantage of an electric machine.

The shape of the machine has also changed from being a flat bed to a free arm, for easier working of shaped sections. The fabric, other than the part being machined, can be kept out of the way under the arm as the item fits round it.

1859

There is now a wide range of sewing machines on the market. When spending such a large amount of money, it is worthwhile looking closely at each model to see what it offers, to compare the price, and to watch a demonstration of its use.

Electric machines may be **semi-automatic**, **automatic**, or **electronic**.

Semi-automatic machines

A semi-automatic machine will perform straight stitch and zigzag using a swing needle, producing a limited number of different stitches. The stitch length and width can be adjusted to provide suitable stitches for a variety of processes. Stitch length numbers relate to the mm length, from 1 to 4 or 5. Stitch width is graduated 1 2 3 4 or 1 to 5 relating to mm width. By varying the length and width of stitch the correct one can be obtained for the job in hand.

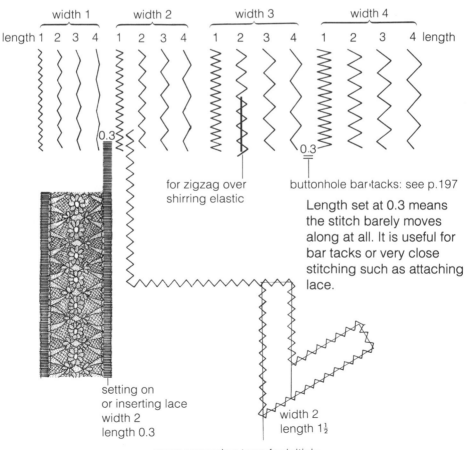

for zigzag over shirring elastic

buttonhole bar tacks: see p.197

Length set at 0.3 means the stitch barely moves along at all. It is useful for bar tacks or very close stitching such as attaching lace.

setting on
or inserting lace
width 2
length 0.3

width 2
length 1½

monogramming tape for initials

Three-step zigzag

Three-step zigzag has a number of uses. The winding line of machining can stretch when pulled on a seam line and so is particularly useful on stretch fabrics, see p. 154; or when attaching elastic, see p. 169.

Bias binding
Bias binding can be attached in one operation by placing the centre line of the binding to the edge of the fabric. The greater width of stitching reduces the chance of missing the binding altogether on the underside. That is the difficulty encountered when trying to attach both sides simultaneously with straight stitch.

Lapped seam
One layer of fabric overlaps the other to make the seam. A lapped seam sewn with three-step zigzag on terry towelling gives a ready neatened flat finish (see p. 155). Interlock or locknit materials (made with a smooth warp knit, see p. 27) do not fray. Three-step zigzag can therefore be used for all seams and hems, considerably reducing time normally taken on these processes.

Patching
The stitch length and width for patching can be varied according to the type of fabric used. The stitch should be suitable for neatening the raw edge of fabric as well as securing the patch firmly into position.

To neaten the edge of loose-weave fabric
Three-step zigzag is often useful for loose-weave fabrics where normal zigzag is not so suitable.

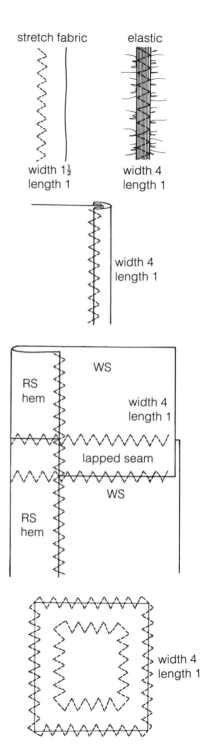

stretch fabric   elastic

width 1½   width 4
length 1   length 1

width 4
length 1

RS
hem   WS

width 4
length 1

lapped seam

WS

RS
hem

width 4
length 1

Blind hemming

Blind hemming is a series of three or four straight stitches, followed by one zigzag stitch. This produces invisible hemming.

Press the measured hem up and then fold it back on itself leaving the hem protruding 1 cm. The line of stitching is machined along the protruding edge, so that the zigzag just catches the folded fabric.

It must be carefully positioned, for sewing too far on to the fabric makes the stitching show on the right side, while sewing too far away will not catch the fabric.

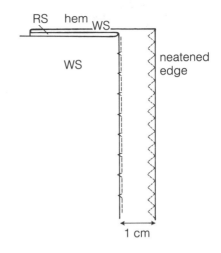

Automatic machines

An automatic sewing machine can be set to produce a variety of patterns of machine stitches and does these without further adjustment of stitch length or width.

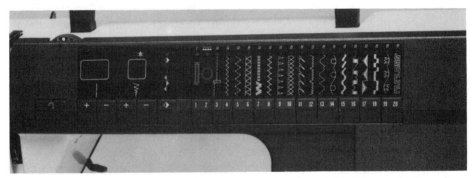

Questions

1 **A semi-automatic or fully automatic machine can speed up needlework by reducing the amount of hand sewing. Using diagrams show four processes which can be done by swing-needle machine and in each case name the hand stitch which it replaces.**

2 **What factors would encourage you to buy a swing-needle machine?**

3 **Study what your machine can do. Devise and sketch a design to be worked on to a collar and cuff made in plain fabric. Explain what adjustments you would make to your sewing machine and how you would stitch your design.** (SUJB)

Types of sewing machine (2)

Electronic sewing machines

The advantage of an electronic machine is that when set to do a particular job, it will adjust its own needle position, speed, and sequence of stitch, and also allow for the thickness of fabric.

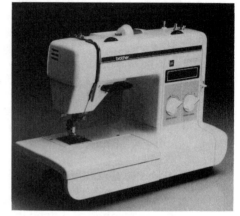

All modern machines are electrically operated, either by foot or knee control. Handicapped people, finding this a problem, will be pleased with the Brother Superstar Electronic which has no foot control, and is operated by a lever on the arm to start and stop it. A button touch gives a choice of three speeds. Slow speed is useful when first getting used to the various processes, or learning to machine; while medium and fast can be used for full efficiency.

Additional pieces of equipment can be linked in to electronic sewing machines. For example, the Electronic Brother Compell Ace has a button-hole foot into which a button can be fitted, and the machine will make the hole to its size. Individual features like these mean that from the wealth of models and makes on the market, one should be able to choose the model most suited to one's own requirements and pocket.

Computer-controlled sewing machines

Computerized sewing machines such as the Pfaff Creative, Bernina Record 930, Husqvarna Prisma 990 and 950, and Frister Logica offer speed and versatility; performing a variety of processes on modern fabrics.

By programming the keyboard for a process, the electronic circuits set the machine to the correct stitch in a suitable length and width, for stretch or non-stretch fabric, of the weight indicated.

Individual models vary. They feature topstitching, overlocking, edging, a twin-needle for raised seams, decorative stitches, numbers and letters. Round-ended, keyhole, reinforced and corded buttonholes can be programmed. On the Husqvarna 990, simply set the size by working the first one, and it will repeat a series identically.

When attaching buttons by machine a clearance plate can be used to form a shank. Machine darning is strong and quick to do. (See instruction book.) Darn over the whole worn area running on to strong fabric. Material placed on the wrong side, reinforces the darning on really worn areas.

All models have a wide work-surface area, part of which can be removed to give a free arm for easy handling of sleeves. Look for variations and useful features. Pfaff Creative and Husqvarna machines can sew very slowly. This is helpful to boost the confidence of first-time users. On the Prismas, bobbin rewinding can be done directly from the needle without re-threading.

Overlocks

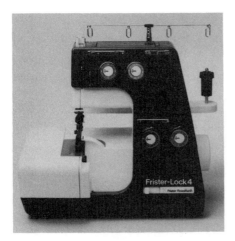

Frister-Lock 4

An overlock considerably streamlines the processes involved in needlecraft and brings industrial efficiency and speed into the home. It combines the separate processes of machining a seam, neatening, and trimming all into one. A four-thread overlock machine has two needles and the seam is made with a double chain stitch, while a strong and serviceable finish is given to the turnings by the overlock stitch. Simultaneously the edges are trimmed off by the cutter. Each of the processes can be performed separately if desired.

Obviously the cutter is sharp so take care with it. When choosing a machine make sure the cutter is safe whether in or out of use, so that no accident could occur. In use, position work with particular care to avoid getting any other part folded in the way of the cutter. Further, because the cutting is done on the machine, more regular defluffing of the machine is essential.

Overlocks may have only two or three threads. Two threads simply overlock edges making a very narrow seam. Where there are three threads the seam will be a little more secure. Because there are more threads it is important to run the machine on for 5–7 cm after the end of the seam, in order to get the work out easily.

Although two needles and four threads may sound complicated, the colour code on Frister-Lock 4 leads threads to the correct positions with diagrams facing the worker on the front of the machine as it is being threaded. Another good feature is the two speed foot control for the new or nervous worker.

Some machine manufacturers, such as Elna, advertise, quite wisely, the fact that there is nothing to lose like a removable bobbin case. Where would this feature be particularly useful?

Questions

1 **Name the features of a sewing machine that you would look for if you intended to make most of your own clothes, using modern fabrics.**
2 **How does an overlock reduce time spent on a garment to hours instead of several evenings?**

Care of the machine

Any equipment will last much longer and give better service if it is looked after and treated well.

1   Try to keep your machine in a dust-free place, and when not in use keep its cover on.

2   If possible keep it where it is going to be used, to avoid moving and bumping it. Older machines are heavy, and need handling carefully to avoid damage.

3   Clean the machine regularly. To do this, remove any lint and dust from around the bobbin case with the little brush. Electronic machines need no oil but other models should have a drop of oil applied in the oil holes shown in the instruction book. Remember every moving part must have regular oil. After this run the machine for a few minutes so that the oil can reach the bearings. Then run a scrap of fabric through, to avoid oil being deposited on your sewing.

4   Take care not to damage the machine by careless use.
(a)   Always make sure the needle is in its uppermost position before removing work. You may bend the needle by pulling work out hastily. Then it will break by hitting the pressure foot or base plate.
(b)   Only move the needle position or stitch width control *with the needle right up*. Why?
(c)   Let the machine draw the work through naturally. Undue hand interference spoils the stitch.
(d)   Use the correct needle and thread for the fabric. A ball-point needle is important for synthetic fibres. Make sure the needle is put in the right way round; the instruction book will indicate this.

5   Look after electrical equipment. There are a number of important points about the care of all electrical equipment and these of course apply to irons, sewing machines and all other electrical sewing aids.
(a)   Do not twist wires or flexes tightly as this may break them. Frayed, broken, or exposed wires are particularly dangerous. Do not use them. They should be repaired or replaced at once by a qualified electrician.
(b)   Always use good quality plugs. Cheaper ones break easily if dropped, and will need immediate replacement, so it is no economy to buy them.
(c)   See that plugs are wired correctly.
(d)   Avoid using or overloading an adaptor.
(e)   Always bend down and pick up the foot control carefully. Never lift it by the flex. Why?
(f)   A fuse is the weakest link in the electrical circuit. If something is wrong it will 'blow'. It is easy to replace a fuse, but *that is not the end of the matter*. First find out *why* it 'blew', and put *that* matter right. If may have been due to overloading or something similar. If it is not corrected the fuse will blow again – and again – and worse will happen!
(g)   Learn about electricity so that you know what you are doing. Do not attempt to rewire a plug or mend a fuse unless you are sure about how to do it. Get it checked by an expert before screwing up.
(h)   The BEAB mark of safety should be on every electrical appliance you buy. This is the mark of approval given by the British Electrotechnical Approval Board, and it will have a British Standards number on it.

(i)   Look after electrical equipment and it will continue to be safe and will last much longer.

(j)   Always switch off before disconnecting.

(k)   **Never** touch anything electrical with wet hands.

Attachments

A number of attachments can be bought or are provided with a sewing machine.

Zipper foot

When stitching has to be done very close to a zip or to corded piping, the normal presser foot would keep the stitching the width of the toe away. So it is replaced by a zipper foot which has only one toe and the stitching can be sewn right up to the edge of the cord or zip. The cording can be placed either side and the foot can be adjusted so that the needle goes through the hole on the desired side of it.

Quilter

A quilting foot has short upturned toes so that it can run easily over padded fabric. A bar with a guide to run along the previous line of machining can be set to the required space and keep quilting parallel.

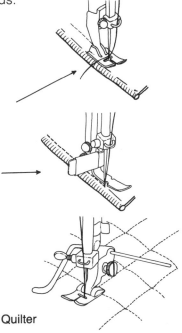

Quilter

Binder

Straight-stitch machines can have a binder which fits on instead of the presser foot. Bias binding can be fed through the scroll-shaped slot which actually takes the binding round the edge of the fabric to be bound. As the fabric passes under the needle, the two edges of binding are joined to it simultaneously.

Binder

Questions

1   **Explain how and why you would oil a sewing machine.**

2   **Damage is often caused by carelessness. Give some examples of how careless treatment can damage (a) a sewing machine, (b) any piece of electrical equipment.**

3   **What is the purpose of a fuse?**

4   **What type of machine needle should be used for synthetic fibres?**

5   **What is the advantage of using a zipper foot? Name two occasions when it would be essential.**

6   **What do the initials BEAB represent when found on a label attached to an electric sewing machine or iron?**   (SUJB)

7   **Give examples of _two_ processes carried out on a sewing machine which require the use of a foot other than the normal presser foot.**   (SUJB)

Machine needle and thread

A machine needle and the thread in it are subjected to enormous friction during sewing. Each piece of thread passes through the eye of the needle as many as 30 to 40 times during machining. This means that the thread must be strong, and the tiny eye of the needle carefully rounded so that the edge is not sharp enough to cut through the thread.

There is a groove running down one side of the needle. This is for the thread to slip into when the needle goes into the fabric. The grooved side of the needle should be facing the last thread guide. In other words it is on the side from which the needle is threaded. As the thread must fit into the needle groove it must not be too thick for the size of needle.

Both needle and thread should be the correct size for the fabric, and the stitch size selected to suit the material and the purpose – tacking, gathering, or making a firm seam (see p. 125). It should also be the right type of thread to match the fabric.

Fabric	British needle	Continental	Stitch length	Thread
Suede **Leather**	12–18	Spear or Leather point	3–4	40 Gütterman Dewhurst Star
PVC	16	100	3–4	
Heavyweight fabrics Wool: tweeds Cotton: sailcloth, twill, denim Furnishing fabrics	14–18	100	3–4	Sylko 40
Synthetics	14–18 Ball-point	100	3–4	Gütterman Dewhurst Star
Medium-weight fabrics Wool: (suiting) Cotton: corduroy, poplin Linen Jersey knits	14	90	2	50 Sylko
Synthetics	11–14 Ball-point	90	2	Gütterman Dewhurst Star
Lightweight fabrics Cotton: gingham, muslin, fine poplin Silk	11	80	2	50 Sylko Gütterman
Synthetics	11 Ball-point	80	2	Gütterman Drima Dewhurst Star Drima Trylko
Fine fabrics Cotton: organdie, lawn, voile	9–11	70	$1\frac{1}{2}$–2	50 Sylko
Fine synthetics	8 Ball-point	65	$1\frac{1}{2}$–2	Gütterman Dewhurst Star

Problems

Problem	Reason	Caused by	Advice/Explanation
Missing stitches	(a) Blunt needle	Needle hitting part of the machine, for example: presser foot loose and out of position; needle loose in clamp; needle not fully up in clamp.	Change the needle. Check and tighten position of needle and presser foot.
	(b) Threads of top and bottom tension not the same thickness.		Always use the same thread for upper and lower tension.
Needle unthreading repeatedly	Thread unable to slip down groove.	Needle put in wrong way round.	Set needle in correctly.
Needle unthreading occasionally	Thread drawing back.	Machine is being stopped when the needle is not in its *uppermost* position.	To understand this watch what happens to the threads when starting slowly. The take-up lever takes up thread as it travels upwards and pulls it from the needle. Remember thread goes *back* and forth through the eye many times before being stitched down. The needle thus becomes unthreaded.
Needle breaking	Side pressure on needle	Swing needle position moved sideways whilst needle is in down position.	Always check that needle is in its uppermost position: (a) before altering stitch width. (b) before pulling work out.
	Bent needle	Work being pulled out of machine before needle was in its uppermost position – thus bending needle.	
Thread breaking	Top tension too tight	Needle wrong way round.	Loosen top tension. Correct needle setting.
		A sharp eye in the needle cutting the thread.	
Seams puckering	Tension too tight	Needle wrong way round.	Loosen tension. Set needle correctly.
Fabric threads snagging	Bent needle	Needle hooks threads and pulls them.	Change needle.
	Blunt needle	Needle pushes threads instead of entering fabric between them.	Change needle.

Puckering

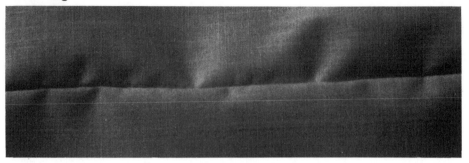

There are a number of reasons why seams pucker.

1   The fabric threads of very closely woven or knitted fabrics are so close together that there is no room for the machine threads too. So the fabric puckers.
To remedy this use a finer needle and a larger stitch so there are less stitch threads in the fabric.
Puckering occurs mainly on seams on the straight grain because in fabric cut on the cross or bias grain there is more room for the threads.
Remember how a crossway strip stretches! (See p. 111.)
On industrial machines and overlocks, a chain stitch is used. This stitch does not interloop *in* the fabric but *on* the surface, and so it is very useful for close weaves or knits.
2   On fine fabric a large needle will cause the fabric to appear puckered.
3   Smooth or slippery fabrics may pucker for a different reason. As a seam is put under the machine, the feed dog pushes the lower layer of fabric forwards. The presser foot however exerts a holding influence over the top layer. If the fabric is smooth or slippery, the two layers slip apart causing puckering. A good idea is to insert a piece of tissue paper. This will easily tear away when the seam is completed.
4   We can get rid of slight fullness on woollen fabrics easily by easing it in (see p. 165) and pressing the seam with a damp cloth. Synthetics do not 'ease in' like wool (and to some extent cottons) do. Slight fullness cannot be pressed away. Seams on synthetics may appear puckered if the two parts are not exactly the same. Therefore cut pattern pieces more exactly to size on synthetics. Do not rely on 'easing away' even slight fullness.

Questions

1   **You have to replace a needle in a machine. By looking at the machine how can you tell which way to insert the needle?**
2   **You are using an unfamiliar sewing machine. How can you tell which way to thread the needle?**
3   **Your friend keeps breaking needles on her sewing machine. What might this be due to? Give her some advice about how she can avoid this happening again.**
4   **Explain why the following faults might occur when machining and how they can be avoided: (a) machine needle unthreading repeatedly; (b) threads snagging; (c) seams puckering.**

Hand sewing

Needles

What jobs do we want needles to do?
Which is the most suitable needle for each purpose?
Needles size 6–9 are in general use. The higher the number the finer the needle. You will find some needles leave holes in fine fabrics. Some threads look clumsy and make big ugly stitches on fine or medium-weight fabric. Some needles and threads make small neat stitches, but are too fine for coarser fabrics.

A **sharps** needle has a round eye and a sharp point. It is used for most sewing.

A **between** needle is shorter than a sharps. Some people find short needles easier to work with, especially for hemming, or if they have small hands.

For embroidery we need a needle with a sharp point and a long eye through which to thread several strands of embroidery silk. This is called a **crewel** needle.

A **darning** needle is long and has a large eye.

A **bodkin** is thick and is used to pull elastic through a casing.

Curved needles are needed for repairing upholstery, chairs, car seats, tents, sails, and lampshades.

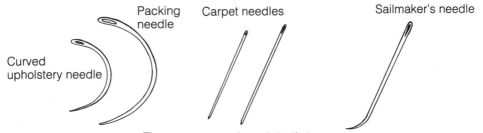

Packing needle   Carpet needles   Sailmaker's needle

Curved upholstery needle

These are approximately half size.

Pins

Fine steel pins are best as they do not rust. Being fine they do not make holes in fabric. Lillikin pins are very small and suitable for delicate fabrics.

Hand stitches

Tacking stitch Used for temporarily holding seams together. Start with a knot and end with a double stitch.

tacking

Running stitch Used for gathering. Begin securely with a knot or firm double stitch. When fastening off also use a double stitch.

running

Back stitch Used to replace machine stitch or to fasten off other stitches.

Blanket or loop stitch Used for neatening edges and making bar tacks. Work from left to right, keeping the needle upright when sewing.

Buttonhole stitch This strengthens and neatens a raw edge such as a buttonhole. It is also used for sewing on press studs or hooks and eyes securely.
To work the stitch: hold the work in your left hand and insert the needle towards you. Wrap the needle thread around the point. Draw needle through then away from you, so that a knot forms on the raw edge.

Oversewing Used where two folded edges are sewn together, for example at the end of a waistband, or when sewing on tapes.

Hemming Used to hold a folded edge down firmly and permanently. Small stitches should be invisible on the right side.

Slip hemming A speedier method of hemming, and one which is easy to remove, should the hem need to be altered to suit fashion or growth. It is firm yet invisible on the right side. The needle runs inside the folded edge for up to 1 cm between hemming stitches.

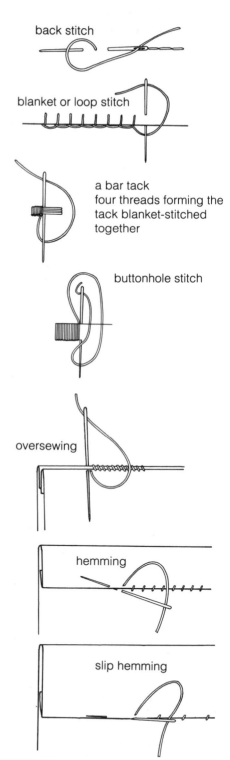

back stitch

blanket or loop stitch

a bar tack
four threads forming the tack blanket-stitched together

buttonhole stitch

oversewing

hemming

slip hemming

All these stitches are shown for a right-hand worker. *If you are left-handed* use a mirror on the drawing or trace the drawing on thin paper, then turn the paper over, and draw the lines on the reverse side.

Herringbone stitch Used to secure hems on thick fabrics where no second turning is taken.
To work the stitch: Make a single running stitch alternately on the upper and lower line as shown.

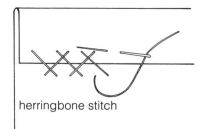

herringbone stitch

Slip stitching Used to hold two folded edges together, for example the lower folded edge of a front facing on a coat or blouse.

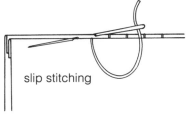

slip stitching

Feather stitch An embroidery stitch often used on baby wear and in smocking. The needle points towards the worker, yet slants alternately in opposite directions. Double feather stitch is formed by two consecutive stitches done in each direction.

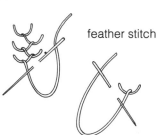

feather stitch

Questions

1 **What difficulty might be encountered when machining a fine sheer nylon and how would you overcome the problem?**
2 **Describe the following types of needle and say when they are used: sharps; crewel; bodkin.**
3 **What hand stitch would you use when making the following repairs to ready-made garments:**
   (a) to fasten off machining that was coming undone
   (b) to sew on loose hooks
   (c) to bar tack a back neck facing
   (d) to refix the hem of a tweed coat pulled away by a shoe heel.
   Draw a diagram to show how you would work the stitch in each case. (State if you are left handed.)
4 **What is the difference between hemming and slip hemming? Give *two* examples of where you would use each stitch.**
5 **Modern sewing machines have removed the need for a great deal of hand sewing. Draw *three* hand stitches, and in each case name and draw a similar stitch which can be done by machine more quickly.**
6 **Look on coats, jackets, blouses, and dresses to find examples of where slip stitching is used. List the places where you find it. Is there a lot of strain on the place where this stitch is used?**
▲7 **Work some herringbone, buttonhole, and feather stitches on hessian. Draw each stitch using the position of the needle to show how each is formed.**

The iron

Modern irons have three temperature settings indicated by one, two, or three dots.

⌁ (one dot)	120°C	cool	nylon polyester acrylics acetate tricel viscose
⌁ (two dots)	160°C	warm	wool silk polyester mixed with other fibres
⌁ (three dots)	210°C	hot	cotton linen

Thermostatic controls

The thermostat inside the iron keeps the temperature at the required setting by cutting off the current so that it goes no higher when that temperature is reached. As on an electric cooker, a pilot light indicates that the iron is switched on and warming up. When it reaches the required temperature the light goes off. Occasionally it may flash on again briefly. This is when the temperature is likely to drop below the setting, and the current is automatically restored to retain the correct temperature.

A sewing aid

The iron is of great value in needlecraft because good pressing can give a really professional finish and speed up your work. Press the garment on completion and when carrying out the following processes:

1 Seams which are pressed open lie flat and are less visible.
2 French, double-stitched, and overlaid seams all need pressing during construction to achieve a good finish. (See p. 152.)
3 Darts pressed flat and to a point become almost invisible.
4 Tucks and pleats can be positioned quickly and neatly.
5 Pleats can be pressed with the paper pattern still on them for accuracy and greater speed, removing the need to tailor-tack.
6 Iron-on interfacing is quicker to use than sew-in interfacing.
7 Cottons respond well to ironing. The seam edges and the free edge of facings can be turned up for edge-stitching with the iron, and will stay so well that it is unnecessary to tack.
8 Facings have a crisper joining edge when pressed open then folded exactly on the line of machining.

9 Bound buttonholes must be pressed to fold the binding down on the wrong side, and give a straight edge to the buttonhole.

10 An iron is needed to turn collars through, achieve sharp points, and get a good edge in the same way as on a facing.

11 The turnings of patches, mitred corners, patch pockets, and the like are pressed to give a straight edge.

12 Cuffs and waistbands need pressing to turn them through neatly.

13 Press the two turnings of a hem separately. Do not press the completed hem on the hemmed edge as this would make it visible on the right side.

14 An elastic casing can be pressed into position. For speed, pressing and *vertical* pinning can replace tacking (the machine needle will go over pins at right angles to the line of stitching).

Irons and their care

1 A **steam iron** is useful because it heats water into steam as it irons; but it is cheaper to use a dry iron and a damp cloth.

2 A **spray iron** sprays a jet of water on to fabric.

3 As water is hard in many areas, distilled water should be used in a steam or spray iron to avoid the calcium deposit (like that which builds up inside a kettle) blocking up the holes from which the steam should come.

4 Always empty the water out of the iron after use.

5 Keep the iron sole clean, using scouring powder if necessary, and wiping well after cleaning.

6 If standing the iron up on its base plate, take care not to knock it off the ironing board.

7 Cool the iron standing up, and take care not to melt the coating of the flex by winding it round the iron when hot.

8 Also refer to care of electrical appliances, p. 132.

Questions

1 **What is the function of a thermostat?**

2 **Explain why an iron is regarded as a sewing aid.**

3 **(a) Give three examples of processes which are carried out much more *quickly* with the help of an iron.**

   (b) Give three examples of processes which are carried out much more *neatly* with the help of an iron.

4 **Explain the stages at which the hem of a cotton dress should be pressed. Give reasons for your statements.**

5 **Give four rules for looking after a steam iron.**

6 **Give reasons for each part of the following code of practice.**

   (a) Use distilled water in the steam iron.

   (b) Empty the water out of the steam iron after use.

   (c) Do not wind the flex around the iron after use.

   (d) Check the flex and plug regularly. (NWREB)

7 **Using words or symbols state the iron settings for dry ironing each of the following fabrics.**

   (a) gingham (b) polyester/cotton mixture (c) brushed nylon (d) tricel (e) linen.

The ironing board

An ironing board must be firm and stable. Put it up well away from doors or where people walk, and close to the power point. A trailing flex is an accident hazard and can cause the iron to be knocked off the board.

Stand with the iron and iron stand at your right hand side if right-handed. If you are left-handed, stand the other side of the board, with the iron and iron stand on your left. This means that the flex does not pull over ironed work.

The padding on the board should be blanket or foam for softness, and covered with cotton, usually bleached calico, for smoothness. Cotton withstands heat well. **Milium** is a good alternative. Milium covers have a shiny metallic surface and make efficient use of heat by reflecting it. This saves electricity. Therefore the iron can be used at a lower setting. Foam padding is bonded to the underside, and ties secure the cover to the board. The surface merely requires wiping over. It is an easy-care surface and does not absorb stains.

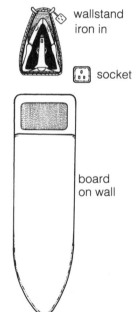

wallstand
iron in

socket

board
on wall

The board is shaped to allow skirts and shaped garments to be ironed over it. A sleeve board is useful for achieving a good finish on narrow items. Free-standing ironing boards must be put up and taken down with care to avoid trapped fingers. Boards which are connected to the wall and slide up into position are extremely convenient and safe. The iron can be stored on a stand above the board.
Ironing is the slow movement over a damp fabric after washing to smooth and dry it without creases.
Pressing is a static action on dry fabric to make it hold a position, flat or folded.

Pressing cloths

A pressing cloth is extremely important when standing an iron on fabric to press it. It is necessary:
(a)   to protect the fabric.
(b)   to prevent shine.
(c)   to use a damp cloth on woollen fabrics (i) to achieve a good finish and (ii) because steam can help to shrink away slight fullness when 'easing in' woollen material.
(d)   to raise the pile on velvet. See p. 94.
A lintless cotton is the best fabric for a pressing cloth. It must be a fibre which will withstand a high temperature. A piece of muslin about 90 cm square is cheap and effective. Turn narrow hems on the raw edges so that the cloth lasts well. Iron dry after use. Cotton is subject to mildew if left damp. Wash the cloth regularly.

Sleeve boards

A sleeve board serves a similar purpose to the free arm on the machine. It makes it easy to press one layer of small sections of garments without pressing the under layer at the same time. It is padded and covered in the same way as the ironing board.

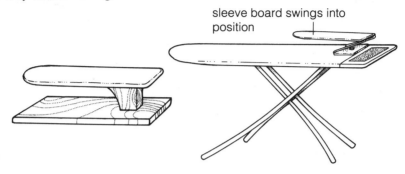

sleeve board swings into position

Pressing hams

This is a ham-shaped, solidly stuffed pad, covered with calico. The shape gives wide and narrow curves. Rounded sections of garments, such as sleeve heads of various sizes, can be pressed over these curves. A ham is essential in tailoring.

Pressing ham

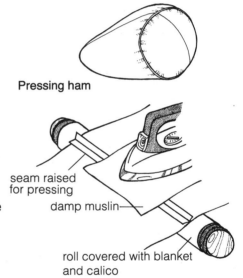

seam raised for pressing

damp muslin

roll covered with blanket and calico

Although not tailored, fashionable boutique clothes like unlined tweed jackets can be reproduced at home for comparatively reasonable cost. The finish can be obtained by very good pressing to achieve the right shape. Good sewing and shaping over a ham gives that professional touch.

Seam rolls

A seam rolls can be improvised from a rolling pin covered with blanket and calico. This is useful for pressing seams. It brings the part we want to press under the iron, without making an imprint of turnings on the right side.

Questions

1   **List five points, other than cost, which you should consider when choosing an ironing board.**   (YHREB)
2   **(a)   Give four reasons for using a pressing cloth in dressmaking.**
    (b)   Name a fabric suitable for use as a pressing cloth. Give two reasons for your choice.   (YHREB)
3   **List the equipment required for pressing wool. How would you prevent the imprint of seams showing on the right side?**   (NWREB)

Textiles equipment

Brief: Design a pair of shears for cutting out.
Specification: A pair of shears to cut all fabrics.
Analysis: What qualities are needed in cutting out shears? Factors would probably (though not necessarily) be in this order:

1 Sharp blades to cut fabric.
2 Strong durable construction.
3 10 cm blade for long smooth cutting.
4 Reasonably light weight.
5 Blade low to the table to lift fabric as little as possible when cutting out.
6 Comfortable handle for convenient use; thumb hole smaller than hole for most fingers.
7 Maximum leverage for hand size.

Bearing in mind these desirable qualities there are a number of possible solutions. Some solutions are discarded because: the metal may be too heavy; it would rust; the shears might lift the fabric too high, and so on.
We are left with the chosen solution which is the working drawing.
This is used for the **realization** – the finished article.
The working drawing would look like this:

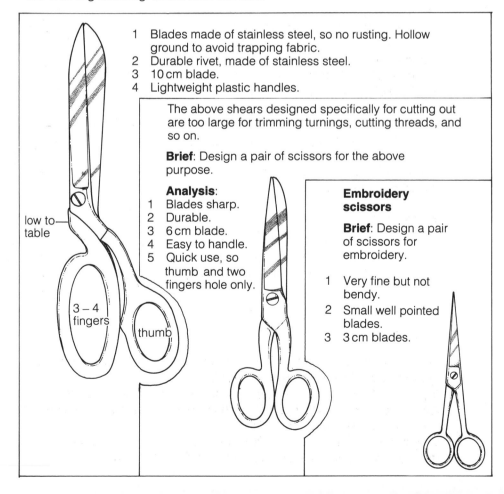

1 Blades made of stainless steel, so no rusting. Hollow ground to avoid trapping fabric.
2 Durable rivet, made of stainless steel.
3 10 cm blade.
4 Lightweight plastic handles.

The above shears designed specifically for cutting out are too large for trimming turnings, cutting threads, and so on.

Brief: Design a pair of scissors for the above purpose.

Analysis:
1 Blades sharp.
2 Durable.
3 6 cm blade.
4 Easy to handle.
5 Quick use, so thumb and two fingers hole only.

Embroidery scissors

Brief: Design a pair of scissors for embroidery.

1 Very fine but not bendy.
2 Small well pointed blades.
3 3 cm blades.

low to table

3 – 4 fingers

thumb

Useful aids for measuring

A **tape measure** should be made of substantial fabric so that it does not stretch or fray. It should be clearly marked on both sides. It can be used for measuring curved lines on patterns by standing it on its edge.

A **metre rule** is very useful for drawing straight lines when altering pattern lengths and for measuring fabrics.

Skirt marker
A skirt marker is a useful item for marking a level hem line.

1 Put on the skirt and with the aid of a mirror decide on a length which is suitable and fashionable. Do not bend forward to mark the skirt. Why?
2 Set the measure, and holding the puffer bag, turn round slowly so that each section of the skirt faces the marker in turn. Don't be tempted to look down but keep erect whilst doing this. By squeezing the bag chalk is puffed on to the skirt. This will brush off after use so turn the hem up immediately.

Measurement marks
It is helpful to make a 10 cm and 1 m mark on a table for quick measurement of fabric. This can be done with coloured adhesive tape on a formica or veneered table edge measuring from one corner.

The right-angled corner of a table is helpful in checking whether fabric needs to be pulled to straighten it before cutting out.

Seam marker
▲ Make a seam marker from card for small measurements in regular use. Larger card markers are useful when doing hems or pleats.

Embroidery ring
Embroidery is kept flat if an embroidery ring is used. The fabric is fitted between the inner and outer rings. This prevents the stitches being pulled too tightly and puckering the fabric.

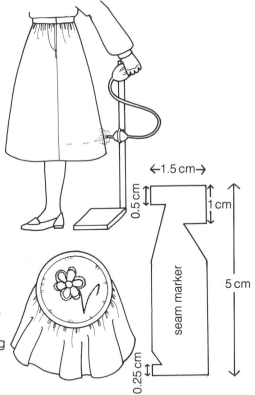

Questions

1 **What features would you look for when choosing cutting-out shears?**
2 **Why are scissors made of stainless steel?**
3 **Your brief is to design a sleeve board (see p.143). Work out the analysis specification, and what the realization should be like.**
4 **How would you measure the exact distance around a curved line on a pattern?**

Interfacing and bonding

Interfacing

Vilene can be bought at fabric or haberdashery counters in large stores and in most drapery shops. It is used to give body or to stiffen parts of a garment. It can be bought by the metre or in packs. As it is a non-woven fabric it can be cut in any direction. (See p.29.) Various weights are available. The finest may be used on silks and lightweight synthetics. The heaviest is firm enough for curtain pelmets or waistband and belt interlinings.

Vilene comes in both 'sew-in' and 'iron-on' forms. When using 'sew-in' vilene, apply it to the wrong side of the pattern piece and tack into position. When the seams are completed, trim the vilene down to 3 mm from the machining line. In this way the seams are not made more bulky than necessary, yet the seam machining line holds the vilene in position firmly.

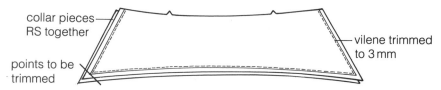

collar pieces RS together
vilene trimmed to 3 mm
points to be trimmed

To apply iron-on vilene

1 Cut the pattern pieces out.
2 Lay the rough side to the wrong side of the fabric.
3 Fuse with a hot iron and a damp cloth on to the smooth side of the vilene.
4 Press well all over the surface to be covered, and leave it for about ten minutes to set well before checking.
  The setting of heat for iron-on vilene is governed by the fabric being used. For example, the vilene must be pressed on wool for *longer* at a lower temperature than for cotton to achieve a satisfactory bond. Try all iron-on products on a spare piece of fabric first.

Transparent iron-on vilene should be used for transparent fabrics. Superdrape iron-on vilene is for knitted and stretch fabrics.

Bonding

Wundaweb is a sewing aid for turning up hems.
It has a fine soft nylon fleece that bonds the fabric together.

To apply Wundaweb

1 Measure the hem and turn up a single turning.
2 Place the Wundaweb in the fold of the fabric.
3 Cover with a damp muslin cloth.
4 Press well. The use of muslin protects the fabric from the hot iron, as well as producing steam to assist the bonding process.
5 Press until dry, and leave for ten minutes to cool and set before checking.

50	MACHINE	HAND WASH
	Hand-hot medium wash	Hand-hot
	Cold rinse. Short spin or drip dry	

This bonding will withstand washing and dry cleaning. To lengthen or shorten the hem later it is necessary to soften the adhesive again by pressing with a damp cloth. Then peel the adhesive away carefully while still warm.

Before using Wundaweb, test a little on a spare piece of fabric. It cannot be used on pile fabrics like velour, velvet, cord, or for fibreglass. Hems on trousers, sleeves, dresses, and curtains are quickly done. Wundaweb can also be placed inside pleats to make them stay in place.

Bondaweb

Bondaweb can be used to bond fabrics together. It is useful for putting on patches, badges, and motifs, and can be used for facings too. It is a soft adhesive attached to special paper. You can draw on the paper.

To apply a patch or motif

1. Cut out the Bondaweb required.
2. Iron it on the fabric.
3. Leave it to cool.
4. Cut out the patch. Peel off the paper from the Bondaweb and place the patch on to it on the main fabric.
5. Cover with a damp cloth.
6. Press with a hot iron until the cloth is dry.
7. Cool well before testing.

RS blazer

Apply Bondaweb to WS. Peel off paper.

tear

WS blazer

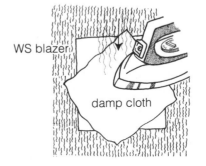

WS blazer

damp cloth

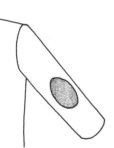

Bondaweb reinforcement on the right side.

Questions

1. **Why are interfacings used?**
2. **(a) What is fusible fleece, e.g. Wundaweb?**
   (b) Give two different examples of where fusible fleece can be used. (NEA).
3. **How would you repair a small tear in your blazer caused by catching it on a nail?**
4. **How would you apply a new school badge to your blazer pocket?**
5. **Name a bonded, lightweight woven and heavyweight woven interfacing and suggest a use for each.** (SUJB)
6. **Describe the difference in the construction of bonded and woven interfacing.** (YHREB)

Further work on Chapter 6

1 (a) What are the benefits of owning a sewing machine?
  (b) State *four* points you should consider before deciding which model of sewing machine to buy.
  (c) Name *two* faults which can occur in machining and state the remedy in each case.
  (d) Devise a code of practice to keep the machine working well.
2 The correct thread, machine needle, and stitch size all contribute to good results when machining. Use the chart on page 134 to provide the following information.
  (a) What thread should be used to machine:
      (i) cotton lawn (ii) medium weight polyester jersey (iii) tweed?
  (b) State the correct needle size and stitch length for:
      (i) PVC (ii) linen (iii) organdie (iv) heavy duty nylon.
3 What accidents causing damage to (a) yourself (b) your fabric, and (c) your machine, could occur whilst working with fabric? Devise a simple code of practice which could be used to avoid damage in the textile area. Explain the reason for each point.
4 (a) Choose a modern sewing machine. State its make and model.
  (b) Investigate and report on ways in which your machine can help in using the wide variety of textiles and yarns now available.
  (c) Plan, make, and evaluate an item to illustrate the scope and versatility of your sewing machine.
5 Name a particular model of sewing machine with which you are familiar. List four features on it which you find helpful. Say when and why you would use them.
  Sketch suitable articles and label the drawings to show any special processes made possible by each of the features.
6 What role does each of the following machine parts play:
  (a) a presser foot (b) feed dog (c) take up lever?
7 You need simple cool nightwear for a Summer holiday in Spain and have a length of plain flame retardant cotton lawn. Discuss a suitable design for the climate.
  Show how the sewing machine can be used to turn plain fabric into a colourful, attractively decorated piece of nightwear.
8 Give the make and model of one known sewing machine and describe how you would care for the machine.
  Discuss the advantages and disadvantages in use and care of a fully automatic and a basic swing needle sewing machine.
  Suggest the causes of the following faults:
  (a) missed stitches (b) broken needle (c) thread breaking (d) material not moving under the presser foot (e) puckered seams. (London)
9 (a) List *three* points to consider when buying a sewing machine. Give a reason for each point.
  (b) Prepare a set of instructions for the successful use of a sewing machine.

(c) Suggest what might have caused the following machine fault and how you might correct it.

 ← Fabric

(d) List three problems you may encounter when machine stitching polyester jersey and suggest how you could overcome them.   (SCE)

10 (a) You have won the sewing machine of your choice in a competition. State what your choice will be and give *six* reasons for this.

(b) Give details of the machine needle, thread, and stitch suitable for:
(i) cotton needlecord trousers; (ii) a fine tricel jersey dress;
(iii) top-stitching a twill weave Trevira jacket.

(c) Give advice on topstitching a pointed collar on the jacket.

11 Familiarize yourself with the following pieces of equipment:
(a) an embroidery ring   (b) a zip foot
(c) a seam roll   (d) a dress form
(e) a ball point machine needle (f) Velcro
(g) a hem marker   (h) a metre rule
(i) a free-arm sewing machine   (j) a velvet board.
Sketch and label each item. Try it out. Say for what processes or fabrics each is particularly suited. Evaluate its use in modern textile work.

12 How can damage to yourself, your fabric and your equipment be prevented (a) in the positioning of the machine and iron (b) during the processes of machining and ironing.

13 There is money available for back stage equipment at the Youth Drama Club.
(a) Prepare a list of useful items for making and altering costumes. Place the items in order of priority. Justify the cost of each. What points would you look for in choosing them to get good value.

(b) With safety in mind draw how you might arrange the working area and store the equipment and costumes in a small L-shaped room with two electric sockets.

(c) Write a concise advice notice on borrowing clothes hygienically.

14 The choice of needle is an important factor in good hand sewing. Carry out an investigation using various types and sizes of needle on heavy, medium, and fine fabric to prove or disprove this statement.

15 List three points apart from cost, to consider when choosing:
(a) a dressmaker's tape measure (b) dressmaker's pins (c) cutting-out shears.   (NEA)

16 Compare electric cutting-out shears and hand ones with respect to cost, efficiency and safety in use.

17 Choose a different commercial preparation to solve each each of these problems:
(a) the worn elbow of a school blazer
(b) a three-cornered tear on a cotton poplin skirt
(c) a loose hem on a pair of trousers. Justify your solutions.

Investigating tools

A worker is only as good as her tools.

Before starting any piece of work, make a list of the tools and equipment you will need. Choose each item carefully so that it does its job well.

Here are some design briefs. Specify the needs of the brief, develop your ideas, and sketch a solution.

In each case, make a list of the equipment and haberdashery that you would need to realize the brief. Say what qualities you would look for in each item you name. State what you would choose and why.

Later you can realize the brief fully and evaluate your design.

18 **Ethnic features have influenced decoration as well as the modern British fashion scene.**
    Design a disco top, a piece of household furnishing, or a useful domestic article using ethnic features as sources of inspiration.

19 **A human's need for warmth changes with age.**
    Design and make a useful item to meet this need.
    State the age group you have in mind, and give details of how and when the item would be used.
    Explain how your fabric's construction helps in the provision of warmth.

20 **Sketch and make a protective garment for yourself or a relation to wear for a Saturday job as a hairdresser.**

21 **A teenage magazine is sponsoring a fashion competition which you have decided to enter. Competitors are asked to design and make an item of clothing for themselves showing an interesting and decorative use of fabric. The total cost of the finished result and the instructions for a care label must be considered.   (WJEC)**

22 **Sketch an outfit of two or three separates suitable to be worn at college by a sixteen year old. Show front and back views. On the main lower garment show the disposal or suppression of fullness and a decorative feature such as a yoke, pocket, top stitching, etc.**
    Say what human needs and material factors govern the choice of style, fabrics, and colour. Name suitable fabrics to meet these requirements.

23 **Sketch and describe a fabric item which could be used or worn in the kitchen. Explain the wear it will have to withstand and the problems involved. Suggest with reasons, possible solutions to minimise the effect of these problems on clothes and other textile items in the kitchen. Your solution should relate where appropriate, to food, family, and home as well as textiles.**

24 **Design an item of attractive winter wear for a very tall, slim teenager. Suggest suitable fabrics to enhance his or her appearance. Evaluate your design.**

Chapter 7
Taking shape

Seams

Understanding textile work means learning to choose the most efficient method – that is, the one that gives the best result, in the shortest time, with the minimum effort. Seams and fullness are considered together in this unit because sometimes it is easier to deal with fullness before seams are joined; and sometimes the seams must be joined before the fullness is treated. We can decide which is the most efficient method of doing a job by considering all the important relevant factors.

Seams

A seam is a join between two pieces of fabric. Consider:

1 *Finish*
Usually we want a flat, invisible finish, but this is not all.

2 *Treatment of turnings*
Enough turnings (usually 1.5 cm) must be taken to prevent the seam from pulling apart, yet the raw edges must not show; they must not be bulky; and they must not be allowed to fray in wear.

3 *Fabric*
(a) Is it fine?   (d) Does it fray badly?
(b) Does it press well?   (e) Is it stretchy?
(c) Is it bulky when folded?

4 *Fullness*
Are the two pieces of fabric of equal size or is one bigger than the other? If so, how is the fullness being treated before the seam is made, and how can the full edge be worked into the seam and neatened?

5 *Pull*
Will the seam be pulled by having a weight hanging from it, as a waist seam has? Is one line of stitching sufficient?

6 *Wear*
Is the seam being used on a garment subjected to heavy wear?

7 *Speed*
A swing-needle machine can join and neaten simultaneously.

In most cases when making a seam, the first two points apply. But the remaining five factors each call for slightly different methods to be adopted to achieve the most satisfactory result in every case. Let's examine the various answers to our questions.

Fabric

Is it fine?
If so a **French seam** can be the most suitable and serviceable one to use.

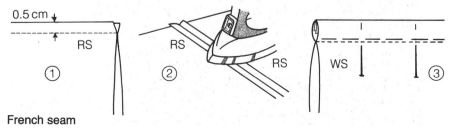

French seam

1 Place both raw edges wrong sides together. Sew 0.5 cm in.
2 Press open.
3 Fold right sides together on the machining line. Pin, tack, and machine.
4 Press seam towards back (side seam) or left (centre seam).

Does it press well?

Cotton print does. An open seam is useful here.

Open seam

Press open

1 Put right sides together. Pin and tack 1.5 cm in.
2 Press open.
3 Press 0.5 cm turning on each side. Machine stitch right on the edge (this is called **edge stitching**).

Is it bulky when folded?

Wool and thicker fabrics may be. An open seam may be neatened by swing needle. The stitch length and width are adjusted according to the coarseness of the fibre.

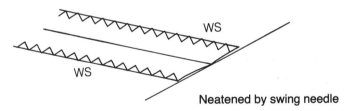

Neatened by swing needle

Does it fray badly?

A loose weave can be treated with three-step zigzag, or bound with bias binding.

3-step zigzag

Bound

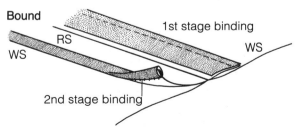

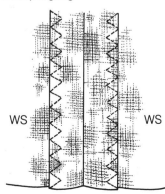

To attach bias binding
1 Open out one folded edge of the binding. Lay it on the seam edge. Pin, tack, and machine on the binding crease.
2 Fold the binding over the edge.
3 Hem into machining.

Is it stretchy?

If so use a zigzag or three-step zigzag stitch so that the seam can stretch too.

Stretching seam

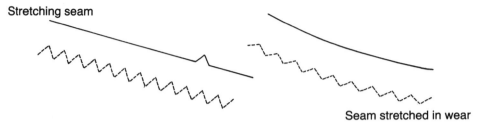

Seam stretched in wear

Fullness

Where one piece is bigger than the other, for example a bodice and skirt, the fullness on the larger section will have been treated before the seam is made. To work the full edge into the seam and neaten it, an **overlaid seam** is used. This means that the smaller section is folded and *laid over* the fuller one.

Overlaid seam

1 Using the iron, fold the 1.5 cm turning of the smaller section towards the wrong side. Lay the folded edge over the gathered section as far as the seam line. Pin, tack, and machine on the right side.

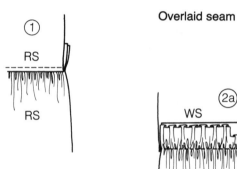

2 To neaten fine fabrics, trim the gathered turning down to 0.5 cm.

3 Make a small crease on the other turning. Fold it over so that the folded edge meets the line of machining. Secure by hemming.
An alternative method of neatening, for fabrics which are not so fine, is to use the swing needle, or overlocker. (See 2b.)

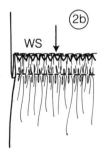

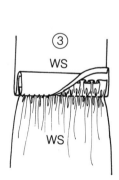

Pull

If there is weight hanging from the seam, one line of stitching may not be sufficient. The skirt may be very full or heavy. Again an overlaid seam is needed.

Wear

Is the seam being used on a garment subjected to heavy wear, for example a skirt, boiler suit, jeans, or children's wear? If so a *double-stitched seam* should be used, sometimes called a 'machine and fell'.

1 Place *wrong sides* together. Pin, tack, and machine along the fitting line.
2 Press open. Trim the back (on a side seam) or left-hand turning (on a centre seam) to 0.5 cm.
3 Fold the remaining turning in half and press the folded edge over the cut edge. Pin, tack, and machine.

Double-stitched seam

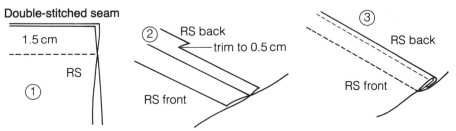

A double-stitched seam is turned towards the back, or towards the left if it is a centre seam. Where two seams meet, the minor seam is folded the opposite way so that the bulky joins are not one on top of the other. A double-stitched seam used on fine materials gives a particularly flat finish. This is very useful for pyjamas.

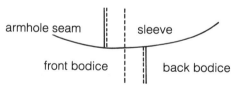

Speed

A swing needle can join and neaten simultaneously.

A **lapped seam** is a simple join where one edge is lapped over the other and sewn by two lines of three-step zigzag to hold down both edges. It is used on terry towelling for beach robes, shorts, etc. where the loops of the fabric make stitching invisible.

Lapped seam

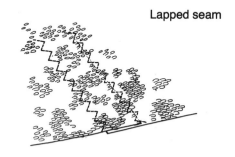

Questions

1 **Giving your reasons, say what seams you would use to make a nightdress in cotton polyester lawn. How would you attach the yoke to the body of the nightdress?**
2 **Give four ways of neatening an open seam, stating on what garment and fabric you would use each method.**
3 **Explain how bulkiness is avoided when double-stitched or French seams meet at the armhole. Use diagrams to illustrate your answer.**

Shape

Fabric is flat, but the things it is used to cover – our bodies and the furniture in our homes – are not. So fabric has to be given shape and encouraged to drape or hang well.

Pattern shape

Fullness can be given by the way the fabric is cut.

The size of the waist of a circular skirt is a great deal smaller than the hem circumference because of the way the skirt is cut out in a flat circle.

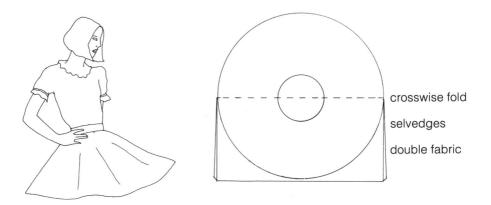

crosswise fold

selvedges

double fabric

Fabric cut in shaped panels can be joined to form a skirt which fits at the waistline, gives enough ease over the hips, and has a wide hem. This is called a **gored** skirt.

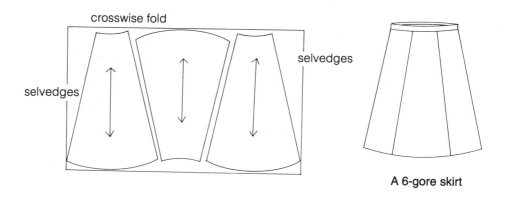

crosswise fold

selvedges

selvedges

A 6-gore skirt

Body shape

Knitted items, or fabrics made from a crimped fibre, stretch to take up the shape of the body. For example, tights fit closely to the legs. A ribbed woollen jumper follows the body shape of the bust and waist. But only certain kinds of material have that amount of 'stretchiness' and in any case skin-tight shapes are not always practical or attractive! Why?

Fabric shape

To give flat fabric shape, and to make it fit, we must have fullness in some areas and remove it from other areas. Fullness can be used attractively to flatter the body shape (see p.101), and to flow into interesting designs or fashions.

The flattest or smoothest appearance is given by making **darts** in a fabric. **Gathers** can give a fuller or more rounded effect (see p. 162).

The fabric weave, thickness, and texture or stiffness play a large part in achieving the right effect. For example, a curtain made from velvet two times the width of the window can be gathered using rufflette tape, and will drape well and look really elegant; but a curtain made with only half that amount of material, or made in calico instead, would be flat, stiff, and unattractive. Similarly a cotton print gathered skirt would flow or drape well, falling in soft folds; but the same design made in denim or crimplene would tend to stick out stiffly and give a clumsy effect as these materials are too thick and stiff for gathering. They would both look better made up in a gored style.

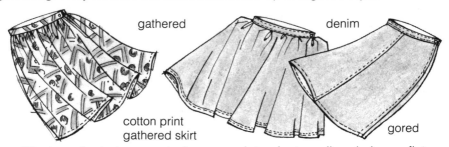

gathered   denim

cotton print gathered skirt   gored

Wool, particularly a worsted, presses into pleats well and gives a flat, smart, tailored finish. Cotton on the other hand tends to drop out of pleats in a more casual style. Thermoplastic materials lend themselves well to pleating as they can be permanently heat-set into a pleated style.

Thus the design of a garment and how a fabric drapes depends upon:
- the amount of material involved;
- the thickness of the fabric – fine or coarse;
- the texture of the fabric – stiff or limp;
- the choice of the most suitable method of disposing of the fullness.

Questions

1 **List the factors that give a garment shape. Explain how and why the methods of treating fullness differ in (a) thick and thin fabrics and (b) men's and women's clothes.**
2 **What is a gored skirt? Explain why the straight grain line is in the centre of each panel.**
3 **Which is the smoothest method of disposing of fullness?**
4 **Which materials will take pleats well and why?**

Tucks

A tuck is a fold in material.
It can be a simple fold
held only by the seam
machining.

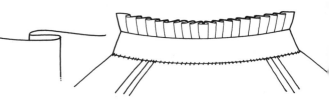

Tucks are used:
At a waistline to give more ease as
the body widens from the waist.

2   In the sleeve where the curved
seam makes the tucks stand out
more to give an effect which is
fashionable from time to time (p.206).

3   On the frill of a loose cover for a settee.

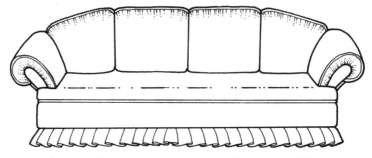

Can you think of other places where simple tucks are used?

Tucks may be held by machining
so that fullness is given lower
down the garment.

They may be machined on the right
side to give a decorative finish.

Pintucks (the width of a pin) can be arranged in a decorative way as a panel on the neckline. This gives the fullness over the bust.

Pattern markings

Tucks are usually indicated on the pattern by lines, sometimes with an arrow to show which way to fold the tuck.

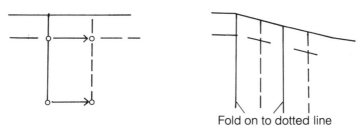

Fold on to dotted line

These lines can be transferred to the material:

1 by tailor's chalk (if sewing is to follow immediately).
2 by tailor's tacks (if sewing a little at a time).
3 by using the iron. This is a quick method. Iron the fold lines on to the fabric with the pattern piece still on the material, doing one half piece at a time, so that the tucks fold the correct way. Then slide the paper pattern out before pinning the tucks down.

As unsecured tucks (those not machined down) are held in position by a seam running at right angles to the tuck, there is no need to remove the pin before machining, as the machine will go over pins at right angles to the line of sewing without difficulty. What might happen if you machine over pins going the same way as the line of sewing?

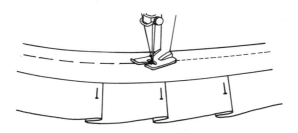

Questions

1 **What is a tuck?**
2 **Draw three different tucks and say where you would use them.**
3 **How are the markings for tucks indicated on a paper pattern?**
4 **How would you transfer the pattern markings on to fabric?**
5 **How are unsecured tucks held in position?**

Pleats

Pleats are very similar to tucks, but they are pressed or machined into position so that they appear as a pleat on the full length of the garment, or from the point of origin right to the hemline.

Knife pleats

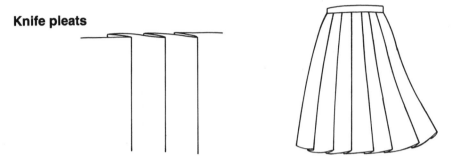

A **knife pleat** is a simple fold in either direction.
Two knife pleats, each folded in opposite directions, form a **box pleat**.

Face the knife pleats towards each other and an inverted box pleat takes shape.

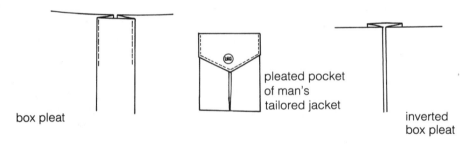

box pleat

pleated pocket of man's tailored jacket

inverted box pleat

A series of knife pleats all facing in the same direction is called **accordion pleating**.

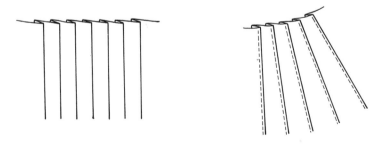

Pleats are pressed into position with an iron, and on fine wool or worsted fibres are often edge-stitched as well, to give a more lasting, sharp, knife-like edge.

On thermoplastic materials (those softened by heat, e.g. polyester), pleats may be heat-set in permanently.

Pleats, like tucks, may be held simply by the machining of the waistband into which they fit; or they can be machined a small part of the way down. This helps them to keep their shape as a pleat all the way down the skirt.

A short pleat at the hem, sometimes known as a **kick pleat**, hangs better if it is folded all the way from the waistline as a pleat, provided this does not make the body of the skirt too bulky. A neat line of machining across the line of the pleat will further hold it in position and prevent the pleat from pulling open. Alternatively small arrowheads are often worked at the top of a pleat to prevent the pleat working undone when walking vigorously, running or taking big steps.

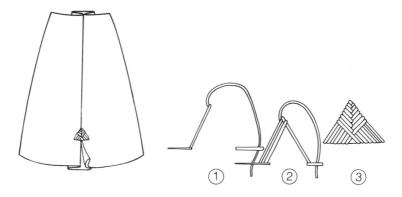

▲ Using the above methods of folding, experiment with fabrics of different composition, weights and textures to investigate how materials lie and drape. Note particularly the effect of temperature, pressure and moisture on, for example, woollens, worsteds, thermoplastics, cottons.
Note the effect of washing the fabric afterwards.
Report on your findings, and draw conclusions which will help you to match a suitable design and method of pleating to particular fabrics.

Questions

1 **How are pleats given a more lasting sharp edge on wool or worsted fabrics?**
2 **Why is this unnecessary on some modern fabrics?**
3 **Explain and draw *two* methods by which a kick pleat can be prevented from pulling open.**

Gathering

A more even form of drawing in fullness is to gather it. This gives a pleasantly rounded effect, for example at the waist line of a dirndl skirt, or at the head and lower edge of a puffed sleeve.

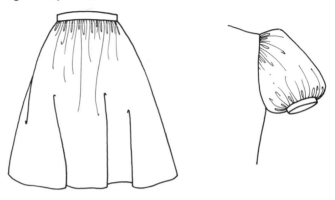

To gather by hand

1   Inside the 1.5 cm fitting line make two lines of running stitches going in opposite directions. Start with a strong knot at one end of each line, and leave a loose thread at the other end.

knot

loose end

fitting line

2   When the threads at opposite ends are pulled at the same time the gathers will draw up evenly.

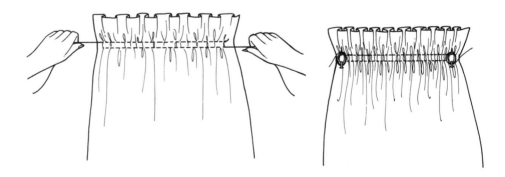

3   Having drawn the gathered material to the correct size, wind the loose ends of cotton round a pin to secure them.

4   Grip the gathers at the top with one hand and the bottom of the material with the other, and pull slightly. This encourages the folds of material to run vertically. The gathers can also be made more even by stroking downwards with a pinhead.

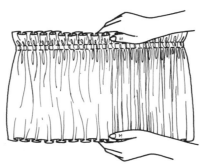

Gathers are held in position by the seam (waist, yoke, or armhole) going across them. The easiest way to make the seam is to leave the gathered section flat on the table after pulling and stroking, and put the flat piece on top, matching any notches that indicate the position of gathers. Insert pins vertically, as shown. Vertical pins (those at right angles to the edge) not only hold the gathers down in a better line, but can also be left in whilst machining to give added security.

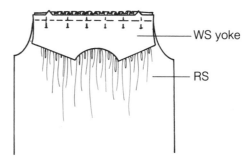

WS yoke

RS

To gather by machine

A gathering line can also be done by machine.

1   Loosen the top tension on the machine (turn the tension disc to a low number or 0) so that the top and bottom threads meet *beneath* the fabric.

top tension

fabric

bottom tension

2   With a loose top tension the thread beneath the fabric (bottom tension) can be used to draw up as a gathering thread.
3   N.B. Remember to reset the tension at normal after use, and to check it using a spare piece of material.

Some machines have a gathering attachment which draws the material up to the required degree. This needs a little practice in setting, but when mastered can prove extremely useful on large items of household furnishings, or when gathers and frills are particularly fashionable.

Gathering using rufflette tape

The making of curtains involves the use of a large quantity of quite heavy fabric. The gathering process is made easier and quicker by using **rufflette tape**. This has two strong threads for drawing up already on it. It also has pockets into which curtain hooks fit when the curtains have been drawn to the required size.

1 Clip selvedges or remove them to prevent puckering when washed.
2 Join seams. Use double stitched method (p.155) to enclose all turnings, or join with an open seam if lining curtains.
3 Fold a single hem at the top of the curtain.
4 Attach the rufflette tape by edge-stitching along both edges of it.
5 Draw the threads up and secure. The curtains will then hang in even folds.
6 Fit the curtain hooks into the pockets and hang on the rail.

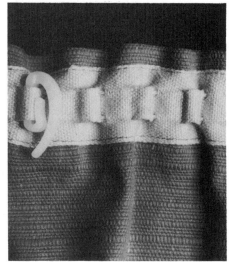

RS curtain

WS curtain   edge stitching

Easing in using a gathering thread

Sometimes a form of gathering is needed when there is not much fullness to be disposed of – where one pattern section is only slightly bigger than the other to give ease or to allow for movement. For example when a waistband is being joined to a straight skirt, the skirt section may need a line of gathers to be drawn up so slightly that the gathers are invisible when the machining is done, yet the required ease is given.

The head of a tailored sleeve (on a blazer or jacket) is not the same shape as the armhole into which it must fit, and so a simple line of gathering, run around the sleeve head between the notches, can be drawn up to fit the armhole. This gives just the required ease for arm movement without the appearance of a gather on the outside.

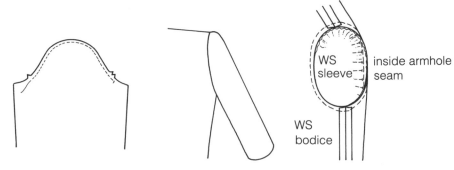

WS
sleeve   inside armhole
seam

WS
bodice

Easing in by pinning

This is another method used on wool or cotton when very little fullness is involved, and it is simply a slight difference between two pattern sections as at the waist join of a dress (see note on synthetics p.136).

1 Put the two sections together matching notches, seams centre front, centre back, and the two ends. This will indicate any section where there is slight fullness.

2 Mark the halfway point on each part by folding. Pin together using a vertical pin and thus halving the difference.
3 Go on halving between the pins until any fullness or difference has disappeared.
4 The seam can then be tacked and machined. However if the seam is straight and regularly pinned, tacking could be omitted because the pins hold the work firmly and the machine will run over pins placed vertically in this way.

Questions

1 **Gathers are an attractive feature on children's clothes. State some places where they are used and draw them.**
2 **How would you gather a long frill to go round the bottom of a skirt?**
3 **Look back at the section on seams. How would you set the gathered section into the yoke of a nightdress?**
4 **Why are gathers necessary on a sleeve head? State the exact position where they begin and end. Explain why no gathers are apparent on the right side of a tailored sleeve.**
5 **What points would you fit together first, when putting a waistband on to a skirt?**
What would indicate to you which was the front and which was the back section of the waistband?

Smocking

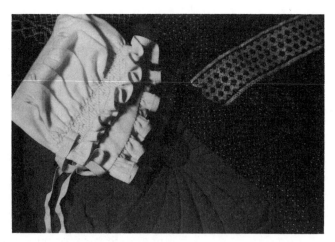

Smocking is a decorative form of gathering used on nightwear and children's and babies' clothes. Regular marking is needed to draw up even folds of material. The check design of gingham lends itself well to this type of decoration, or else a transfer can be used to put smocking dots on to the wrong side of the fabric.

Several gathering threads are done picking up the dots so that when all the threads are drawn up slight folds appear on the right side.

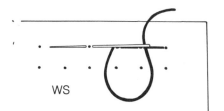

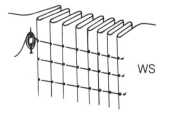

Embroidery stitches are used to sew from fold to fold, making a pattern.

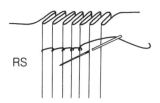

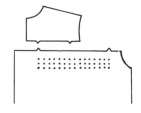

This line of even stem stitch is a good one to give the required size and tension, for a smocked section is usually matched to a yoke or seam. It is important to check that the decorative stitching is not going to pull the embroidered section up too tightly. Therefore check it by matching the notches both when the gathering threads are drawn up, *and* as the first line of stitching is done. Then sew each line of embroidery at the same tension as the first one. Chain stitch, feather stitch, and others found on pp.138–9 look attractive on a smocked panel, but the honeycomb effect is most frequently used and gives a very dainty appearance.

Surface honeycombing

Work from left to right. (A left-handed person would work from right to left.)

1. Draw two folds together with a stem stitch, bringing the needle out between the two folds.

2. Insert the needle right to left (left handers left to right) on the next fold 0.5 cm down, and draw through.

3. Do another stem stitch over the next fold, bringing the needle out between the next two folds above the stem stitch (ready to go upwards on the next stitch).

4. Insert the needle on the next fold 0.5 cm up and draw through.

5. Do another stem stitch over the next fold, bringing the needle out between the two folds ready to come down again. Continue with these four stages across the panel to the end. Repeat this line to form the honeycomb shape.
If the upward and downward thread is taken *inside* the fold leaving only the horizontal stitches, a different effect is given.

Smocked cushions (see photo) are made by honeycombing the inside (wrong side) of velvet or velour cloth with coarser thread to give attractive folds on the right side.

Questions

1 **Suggest where smocking could be used**
   (a) on children's or babies' clothes;
   (b) on adult clothes.
   Using the stitches mentioned on p.166 draw a plan for a panel of smocking on a baby's dress.
2 **Children's clothes are often made more attractive by the use of smocking. Draw a child's dress to illustrate this. Explain:**
   (a) how to estimate the width of fabric needed to smock it;
   (b) how to prepare the fabric;
   (c) how to work *three* different smocking stitches on this garment.
   Give details of the fabric and threads to be used.

Darts

Darts are used to give shape and to fit the curve of the body or the shape of a settee or armchair.

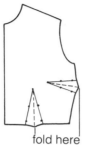  

bustline

fold here

As the dart reduces to a point, more fabric is gradually released to fit the body as it broadens over the bust. This is a more fitting and therefore flatter method of releasing fullness. Darts are marked on a pattern by small dots and these are transferred to the material by tailor tacks or tailor's chalk.

WS fabric

WS fabric

To make a dart

1 Match the dots together by folding the centre of the dart.
2 Pin, tack, and machine to the point. N.B. A fine point gives a flatter result.
3 Reverse machine or knot and sew in the ends to make the point secure.
4 Press vertical darts towards the centre; press horizontal darts downwards. The finished dart should be so well pressed that it is invisible from about two metres distance.

Sometimes a dart has a point at each end. In this style the waistline dart would release fullness for the bust at the upper end and give more ease over the hip at the lower end. To make it lie quite flat, a double-pointed dart can be neatened by machine or hand-buttonholing and snipped.

Questions

1 **Explain why darts are usually worked before seams are done.**
2 **How do you achieve a really flat result when making a dart?**
3 **Which way would you press (a) a shoulder dart; (b) an elbow dart on a sleeve; (c) the waist darts on a skirt?**
4 **Why is it necessary to snip a two-pointed dart at its widest part?**

Elastic

Elastic can be used in several ways to reduce fullness. The type and width and the method of holding it should be chosen to match the weight of the fabric.

Shirring

Shirring elastic makes fine or lightweight fabrics drape well. Lines of machining about 1 cm apart, using shirring elastic on the bottom tension, will draw the fabric up and give an effect rather similar to undecorated smocking. This is useful on the lower edge of puffed sleeves, at the wrist, on a midriff panel, or at the waist.

Another method is to use the swing needle (see p.127): stitch width 3, stitch length 2.

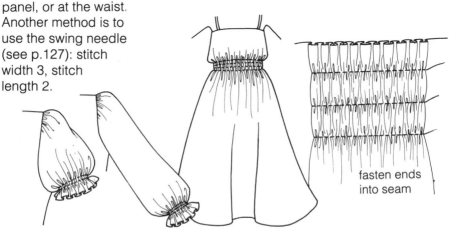

fasten ends into seam

Note: The smocked waistline pictured on the dress or nightdress style on p.166 has a back opening. However, if shirring elastic were used instead, no opening would be needed and that style would be considerably quicker and simpler to make.

Attached by three-step zigzag

This method is used a lot commercially. 0.5 cm or 1 cm elastic can be machined to the wrong side of medium-weight fabric using the three-step zigzag stitch which 'gives' without breaking when stretched. This method is useful for the inside of gloves, for hats, and for children's clothes. The ends of elastic should be turned in neatly and machined down or sewn into a seam to secure them firmly. (Remember the ends are under pressure whilst the elasticated items are being worn.)

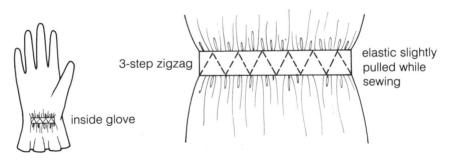

inside glove

3-step zigzag

elastic slightly pulled while sewing

Elastic casing

A neater method is to make a casing through which the elastic may run. This should be the width of the elastic plus 0.5 cm for ease. It can either be a strip of material attached to the inside of a garment as at the waistline or the cuff of a sleeve, or it can be turned up at the edge of a pattern section as on the top of shorts or the lower edge of a full sleeve.

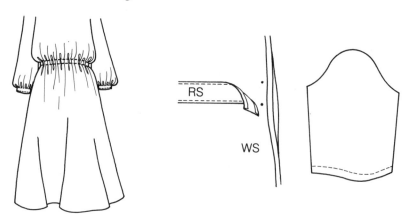

This is a straightforward, speedy process needing only the iron and vertical pinning on crisp material, but slippery fabric should be tacked too before machining.

1 Make and press a 0.5 cm turning.

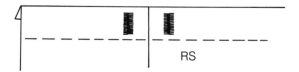

2 On the casing, machine two vertical buttonholes the width of the elastic plus 2 mm, 1 cm either side of the seam (centre back seam of shorts). If working buttonholes by hand, use two round-ended ones to allow the elastic to run through easily.

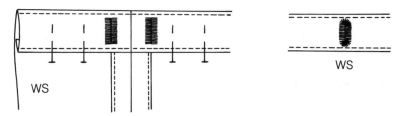

3 Fold the second turning down and press, holding with vertical pins. If the fabric is easy to handle, machine along the folded edge over the pins. If it is slippery or heavy, tack first, then machine.
4 Edge-stitch along the top edge to give a crisp finish and to prevent the elastic rolling.
5 Using a safety pin, thread the elastic through. Draw up to comfortable wear. Join the elastic by oversewing or machining and allow to fall back through the buttonholes so that the join does not show.

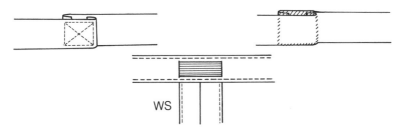

This type of casing, or one made with a strip of material and attached, can be used at the waist or neckline to house a drawstring or tie belt. In these cases the buttonholes would be worked or bound (see p.198) on the right side to allow the tie or drawstring to come through.

Sewn into a waistband

Inside a waistband or belt, wide elastic is useful to achieve a snugly-fitting finish. The elastic may be attached by swing needle or straight stitch to the inside of the waistband in two places at the back, or on each side. As the elastic has slight tension on it, it will stretch whilst being worn. The waistband can be sewn down and finished normally.

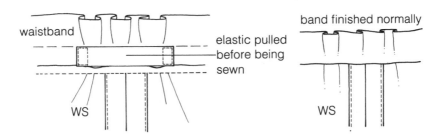

This method is often used on men's trousers, as it removes the need for belt or braces, and on shorts.

Questions

1. **Compare the elastic casing at the lower edge of a full sleeve with the cuff shown on page 193.**
Analyse the needs of young children, and arthritic old people. Give detailed instructions and diagrams for the most suitable sleeve finish for night or day wear.
2. **Why should buttonholes on an elastic casing have two rounded ends? Explain where the buttonholes are positioned and why.**
3. **Explain why both edges of an elastic casing are machined along the edge.**
4. **How is elastic used on young children's clothes? Draw sketches to show examples of three different uses of elastic on them.**
5. **(a) Give *three* examples of where you would use shirring on a garment.**
    (b) What thread would you use in the bobbin?
    (c) What adjustment would you make to the sewing machine?
    (d) How would you keep the stitching parallel? (WJEC)

Further work on Chapter 7

1 Suggest a suitable fabric and name and draw an appropriate seam for the following:
(a) a fine nightdress (b) a pair of ski trousers (c) a child's summer dress (d) the waist join of a gathered dress (e) a man's bathrobe (f) a pair of mens' pyjamas.

2 Stretch fabrics, loose weaves, and bulked textures are in common use. Describe and draw three different ways in which the swing needle can be used in the making and neatening of open seams.

3 Sketch and evaluate the style of dress on page 170, for growing children.

4 With the aid of diagrams show how fullness might be treated on children's clothes made of: (a) fine cotton print gingham or viyella, (b) worsted, (c) denim.
Explain your reasons for your choice of method in each case.

5 A rather plump lady is having a skirt made in grey worsted fabric and has asked your advice on a suitable style. How would you recommend the fullness is disposed of at the waistline, and how would you give freedom of movement at the hem line without making it too wide? Draw a sketch to illustrate the style and explain the reasons for your suggestions.

▲6 Look at the clothes in your family wardrobes. Find examples of as many different methods of treating fullness as you can.
List them under the following headings:

	Types of fullness	Where used	Reason
Example	Tucks	Back neck of jacket lining	To give ease to the lining to prevent pulling

▲7 Look at some men's clothes and see how they are shaped.
  (a) Does the shape come from the pattern (the way the fabric is cut)? Give some examples.
  (b) Is shape given by the body itself when wearing a knitted or crimped fibre?
  (c) Is shape given by any of the methods of disposing of fullness mentioned in the chapter?
      Name as many examples as you can find of the types of fullness used (i) on men's present day clothes and (ii) in the past.

8 (a) What factors might make you decide to use: (i) a French seam, (ii) an open seam, (iii) a double stitched (machine and fell) seam.
  (b) State where and on what garment you might use each seam. At what stage in the plan of work would you make the seams?
  (c) Draw labelled diagrams of the *finished* appearance on the wrong side of an open seam, and a French seam.
  (d) Draw labelled diagrams showing how you would carry out *each* stage of making (a) a French seam and (b) a double-stitched seam.

Chapter 8

Construction processes

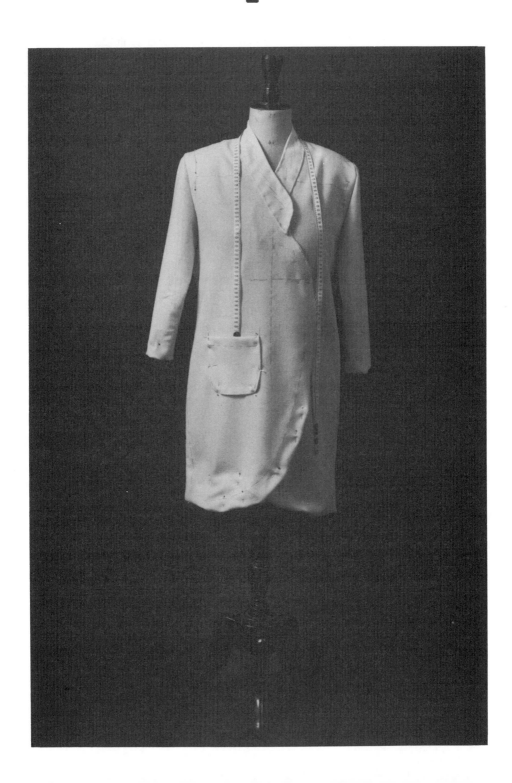

Zips (1)

The most commonly used feature for openings on modern clothes and furniture is the zip. The type of zip should be selected according to the fabric and the job it is required to do, and it must be correctly applied.

As a general rule, use nylon zips on nylon and synthetic fabrics, and metal cotton-backed zips on cottons, other natural fibres, and heavier items. Metal can rust in time, and so metal zips should not be used on things which are likely to remain wet or salty for some time (sailing jackets or beach bags, for example), though metal zips on clothes withstand normal household washing because they are dried well. Dress-weight zips are used on lightweight materials. Heavyweight zips should be used for heavy fabrics, or where there is likely to be a lot of pull. Open-ended zips are extremely useful on jackets.

Always make sure that any zip is amply long enough. If it is not, and it is forced open at the base, this will break the zip by dislodging the teeth. Of course the seam should be secured above the base of the zip, so that it cannot accidentally be forced open at the bottom. Provided it is not exposed to excess pressure it should last more than the lifetime of the garment. If properly selected, applied, and used, it will give good service. So never throw away zips on old clothes; you can take them off carefully and reuse them.

The advantages of using a zip for an opening are that it is quick, invisible when closed, and, provided the fastening at the top is correctly positioned, secure. There are a number of ways of achieving an invisible finish. It is always important to prepare the seam carefully before inserting the zip.

Preparing the seam

1 Pin and tack the seam all the way up, but make a double tacking stitch at the base of where the zip is to go.
2 Machine the seam on the fitting line as far as the double stitch and fasten off securely.

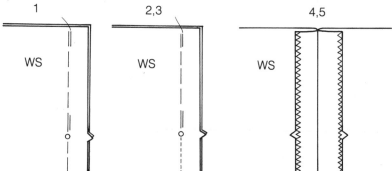

3 Remove the tacking thread from the machined portion. Leave tacking in above the double stitch, as this is where the zip will be.
4 Press the whole seam open. The tacking thread makes the seam appear complete. The correct fold *on the fitting line* is now continuous with the machining so that the zip will become part of the seam.
5 Neaten the whole seam according to the type of fabric. Remove the tacking thread.

Method 1: without a zipper foot

The zip will be invisible when closed in wear, so set it into the seam in the closed position.

1   Working on the right side of the fabric, position the zip head 1.5 cm down the folded edge of the seam to allow for the waistband seam or neck facing. Place the folded edge over the centre of the teeth and pin 0.5 cm in right along the length of the zip. The base of the zip should be below the end of the seam. Check the inside to see that the tapes at the lower end are lying straight and pin to just past the bottom of the zip.

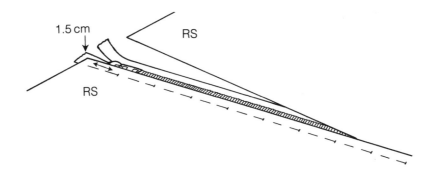

2   Turn the work the other way up and place the other folded edge along the centre of the teeth *overlapping* the folded edges 1 mm. This is to counteract the fact that without a zipper foot the machine will draw the edges slightly apart.
3   Tack along the pin lines, parallel with the opening. This line *must be firm* to hold the zip in position.
4   Cross-tack the opening to draw the two edges together. The closing of the seam ensures that the zip is not seen when finished.

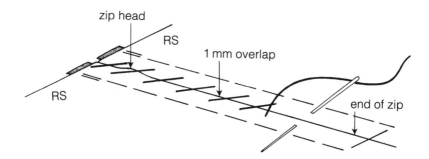

5   A normal straight stitch foot can be used. There is no need to use a zipper foot for this method because no machining is done close to the teeth. It is not possible to machine around the closed ziphead so do not begin at the top. Start to machine 5 cm down the left-hand side and go to just past where the zip ends underneath.

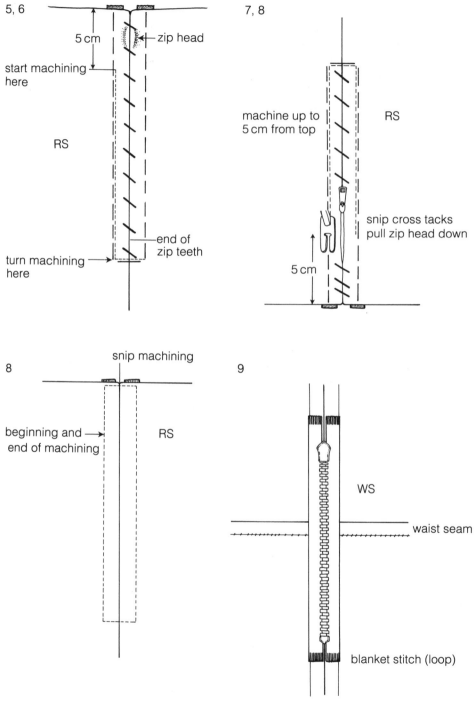

5, 6

5 cm

zip head

start machining here

RS

end of zip teeth

turn machining here

7, 8

machine up to 5 cm from top

RS

snip cross tacks pull zip head down

5 cm

snip machining

8

beginning and end of machining

RS

9

WS

waist seam

blanket stitch (loop)

6 Leaving the needle in the work, lift the presser foot and turn at right angles, then machine across to the other tacking line.

7 Again with the needle in the work turn at right angles and progress up to 2 cm below the zip head. Lift the presser foot.

8   Snip the cross tacks, pull the zip head down to where the zip has already been machined in, lower the presser foot and continue to machine up, across, and down to the start. Fasten off the ends on the wrong side.

9   For a skirt zip or the centre back opening of a dress, snip the machining line at the top, remove tackings, and press. When the waistband or the neck facing is set on, the top tapes will be securely held within it. This method is ideal for the waist opening at the side of a dress as the line of machining across the top holds the top tapes in the same way as the base tapes are held. The raw tape edges can be blanket stitched to the turnings to prevent them curling up and jamming the zip teeth in wear.

Putting a zip in is easiest on flat material. When making up cushion covers or other household items, do the zip seam before joining the rest of the seams. Handling a closed zip presents problems when the article is made up.

Method 2: using a zipper foot

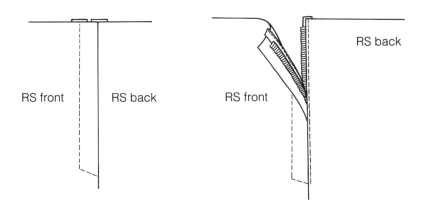

Instead of the zip being sewn with the lines of machining evenly spaced on either side, a side zip method may be used. Here the machining on the back section is very close to the teeth and a zipper foot is used. The machining on the front is at least 1 cm from the fold, giving the impression of an overlap.

Questions

1   **What factors must be considered when buying a zip?**
2   **How can you ensure that a zip will last throughout the life of the garment?**
3   **Name the various types of zips and say what each might be used for.**
4   **What preparation is necessary before putting a zip into a seam?**
5   **Why is it important to tack across a zip as well as tacking both sides of it?**
6   **At what stage in making would you insert a zip into a cushion cover?**
7   **Why is a zipper foot particularly useful?**

Zips (2)

Method 3: with an underlap

Sometimes, on a front opening, a zip is put in with a panel of fabric beneath it as an underlap. Usually the underlap is cut continuously with the panel of the skirt or trouser, but occasionally it needs joining on. In this case one side of the zip can be put into the seam and pressed into position.

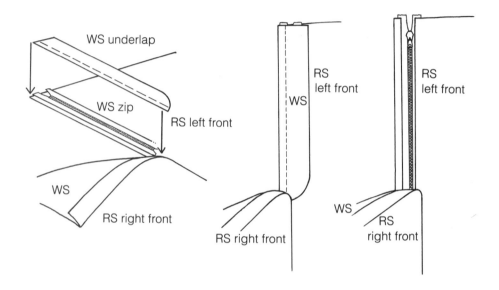

Where no seam has to be made:

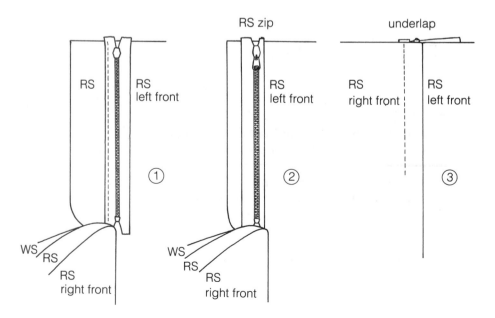

1 Place the zip right sides together with the left panel. Tack and machine just inside the fitting line close to the metal teeth. You will need a zipper foot.
2 Press the zip on to the underlap.
3 Lay the right-hand side over the zip. Fold the underlap out of the way. Pin, tack, and machine the right-hand side.
4 Place the underlap back into position. Machine across the base of the zip. Sew in the ends of machining threads invisibly.
5 Attach the waistband, matching centre front lines and using the underlap to match to the end of the underlap on the left front.

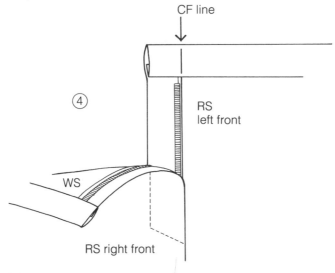

Method 4

With a zipper foot, machining can be done from the right side.

Questions

1 **Why is a zipper foot necessary for the first stage of sewing in a zip with an underlap?**
2 **Why would a zipper foot be helpful to sew the second side?**
3 **Explain why the underlap must be folded out of the way when machining the second side.**
4 **Explain why the machining across the base of the zip is done later with the underlap back in position.**

Continuous strip openings

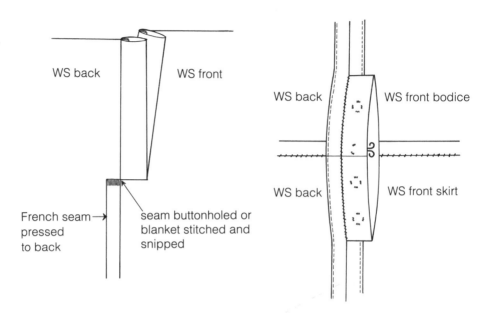

WS back   WS front

French seam→
pressed
to back

seam buttonholed or
blanket stitched and
snipped

WS back   WS front bodice

WS back   WS front skirt

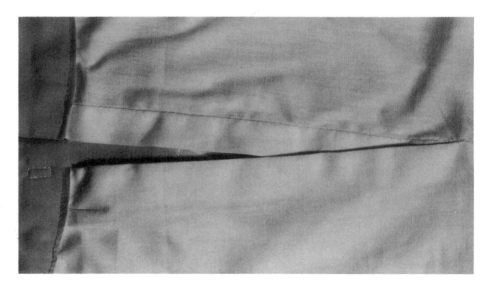

A flat opening may be needed on children's clothes, underwear, and nightwear made from fine fabric. A double continuous strip of fabric can be made and attached as shown in the diagram.

By pressing the strip towards the right when finished, an underlap is formed. Fastenings such as press studs or hooks and eyes can be applied, depending on how much pressure the opening will be subjected to in wear. A hook and eye would be used on the waist join, whilst press studs would be adequate to close and conceal the opening on the rest of the side seam, above and below the waist. For a simple opening below the yoke of a nightgown or child's dress no fastenings would be needed.

To make a continuous strip opening

1 Prepare the seam as far as the opening. Cut across a French seam at the base of the opening and blanket-stitch securely to prevent fraying. An open seam may be neatened and left.

2 Prepare a strip of material 5 cm wide and twice the length of the opening. For a dress opening, allow 2 cm turning for joining.

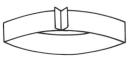

3 Lay the garment out with the unneatened seam turnings on the table. Apply the strip to the garment right sides together. Pin, tack, and machine on the fitting line. N.B. Make sure the seam joins up with the original seam to avoid a weak point.

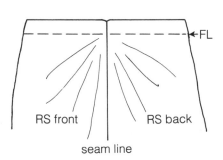
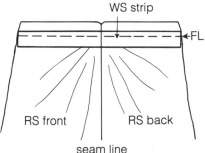

4 Press open. Trim down seam turnings.

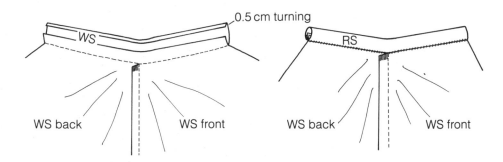

5 Turn under 0.5 cm turning on the strip and fold the strip down to the machining line; pin, tack, and hem into position. Press both sides of the strip towards the right and complete the opening with fastenings if required.

Questions

1 **When is a continuous strip opening used and why?**

2 **What factors would you consider when deciding what type of fastening to use on a continuous strip opening? Say what type of fastening you would choose.**

3 **Where is a possible weak point on a continuous strip opening? How can you avoid this weakness?**

4 **What preparation must be done to the seam before attaching the strip?**

Two-strip and taped openings

Two-strip openings

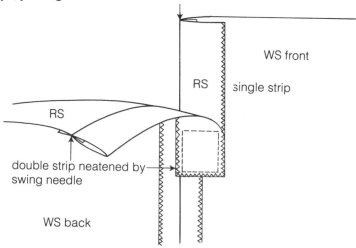

A two-strip skirt placket opening is sometimes used on thicker fabric. It is made with two strips: one single width plus a turning, and one wide enough to be folded double plus a turning for the join. Being thicker, the doubled-over strip is neatened by swing needle and secured to the seam line without a second turning.

Taped openings

The simplest of all openings is the gap left when a seam is only machined part way. Where fastenings are needed, tape is applied to the inside of the turnings. This makes them double and of course stronger. This type of opening can be used on the back neck or across the shoulder of a child's dress.

1 Prepare the seam by machining as far as the gap. Press open all the way up on the fitting line.
2 Cut two pieces of tape the length of the opening plus 0.5 cm.
Press in 0.5 cm raw edge at one end of each tape.
3 Place wrong side of tapes to wrong side of turnings.

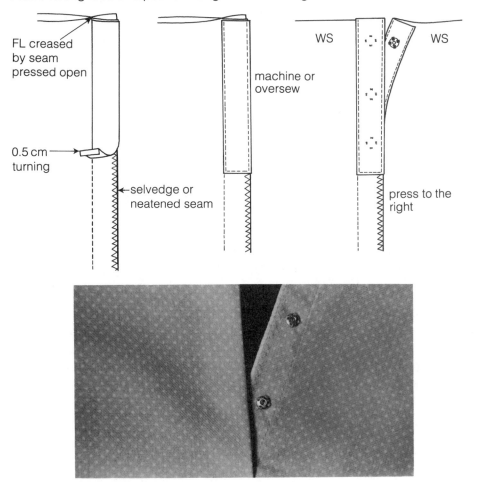

4 Oversew or machine along the tape edges.
5 Machine across the base of the opening, turning both turnings to the right on the wrong side so that an underlap is formed.
6 Attach fastenings.

Questions

1 **Sketch a child's sleeveless dress which opens along the left shoulder seam. It has a plain round neck and ties with ribbons at the left neck point and shoulder point. Give instructions and draw diagrams to illustrate a simple way of making the opening.**
2 **A pleated polyester and worsted skirt is knife-pleated right around as on p.160. What type of opening could be used? Would any fastenings be necessary? Explain your answer. How and at what stage would the top of the opening be finished?**

Wrap and facing openings

Openings are invisible because they continue a seam line and thus become part of a seam. The seam turnings are either incorporated into the opening as for a taped opening, or pressed neatly back as for a two-strip opening.

But what of a double-stitched seam, where there are two lines of stitching on the right side? For this type of seam a wrap and facing opening is used. This method is quite simple if taken in two parts. A double strip is attached to the continuation of the *second* line of machining at the back, and a right side facing is attached to the front, again using the continuation of the fold for the *second* line of seam stitching so that it is flush with the seam edge.

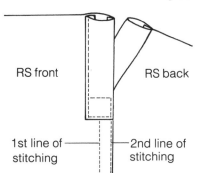

RS front   RS back

1st line of ——   —2nd line of
stitching   stitching

A double-stitched seam is used on clothing which is subjected to tough wear such as overalls, jeans, and boiler suits, and a strong opening is required to match.

To make a wrap and facing opening

Cut the double strip and the facing on the straight grain 2.5 cm longer than the opening to allow for the rectangle of machining to strengthen the base. The width depends upon the item being made and the texture of the fabric. A measurement of 5 cm for the double strip and 3 cm for the facing will give a finished width of 2 cm.

Part 1

1   Join the double-width strip to the back edge using the continuation of the second line of machining on which to tack and machine.

2   Turn through and sew into machining on the wrong side as for a continuous strip opening. With a coarse fabric, neaten by swing needle to reduce bulk instead of making a second turning.

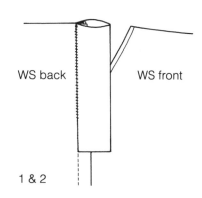

WS back   WS front

1 & 2

Part 2

1 Place right side of facing to wrong side of front. Pin and tack on the crease of the second line of turning. Machine.

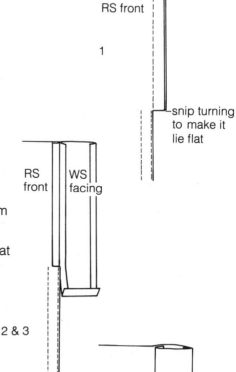

RS front

1

snip turning to make it lie flat

RS front | WS facing

2 Turn through to right side. Press seam open to give crisp edge to facing.

3 Turn in 0.5 cm on each edge except at the waist.

2 & 3

RS front | RS facing

4 Lay the facing over the right side of the garment front. Pin into position. Edge stitch round.

4

Finally:
Position the base rectangle from the double strip neatly beneath on the wrong side. Tack and machine across the base of the opening to strengthen.

Questions

1 **Study the first diagram which shows the finished wrap and facing opening. Copy it and with arrows mark on your drawing the following: (a) the *fitting line* on the double-stitched seam; (b) the line on which the double strip is attached by machining. Explain which it is a continuation of; (c) the line on which the right side facing is machined.**

2 **The base of an opening could be a weak point. How is the base of this one made very strong and secure?**

3 **Why is this type of opening often used on boiler suits? Why is it sometimes used at the waist of pyjamas?**

Front band openings

On the front of a dress or man's sports shirt, two separate double strips are used to form the centre front bands. These have vertical buttonholes on the centre front line. When making this opening remember that women's clothes button right side over left side, but men's clothes left over right.

To make a front band opening

1 Apply interfacing to each band on WS. This is usually half the width of the strip and can be ironed on or basted.
2 To strengthen what might be weak points, stay-stitch by machine where the snips will be made later.

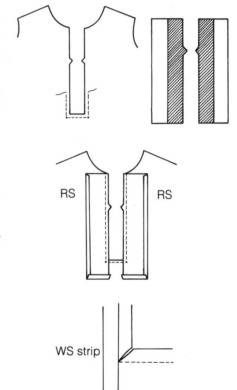

3 Matching the notches, apply RS strip to RS of front on each side.
  Pin, tack, and machine on FL as far as the tailor tack. Fasten off securely.
  Press seams open to give a flat finish, then turn both turnings towards the CF line and trim.

4 Snip diagonally down to the dot.
5 Press in turnings on the free edges and the base of the strips.
  Turn work to the wrong side.

Enlargement of snip

6 On the left-hand side (right-hand side for men's clothes) fold the strip in half and bring through to the wrong side using the snip to draw the base section through to lie flat on the wrong side.
  Trim turnings down and pin folded edge to machining line.
  Pin, tack, and secure by hemming.

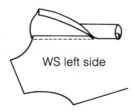

7   On right-hand side (left for men's clothes), fold the strip in half and put the folded edge to the machining line, using the snip to leave the base rectangle on the outside of the front. Pin, tack, and hem.

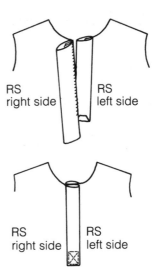

8   Place the right-hand side band over the left-hand band (left over right for men) and machine a rectangle through all thicknesses enclosing the raw edge.

To avoid bulkiness

1   The raw edge of thicker fabrics may be trimmed to 0.5 cm and neatened with zigzag or overlock stitch.
2   The inner fold of both strips can be cut away at the base before machining the rectangle.
3   An alternative method used commercially is to dispense with the base rectangle altogether. Making the strips only a turning's depth longer than the opening, place the bottom turning of both strips and the snipped piece together. On the wrong side, machine across and overlock them.

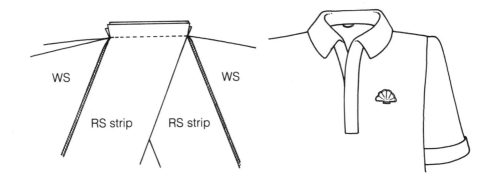

Questions

1   **Where are the possible weak points on a front band opening, and how can they be strengthened?**
2   **Describe the steps which differ in the treatment of a front band opening on the following pairs of similar garments:**
    (a)   a man's sports shirt and a woman's sports shirt.
    (b)   a polyester and a woollen dress.

Faced slit openings

Sometimes an opening is needed where there is no seam and a slit has to be made. This has to be neatened on the wrong side with a facing and is called a faced slit opening. It can be used at the wrist edge of a long sleeve where a cuff is to be attached, for the sleeve seam does not fall where the opening is needed. No fastening is used on this opening for it barely meets and is held together by the buttoning of the cuff.

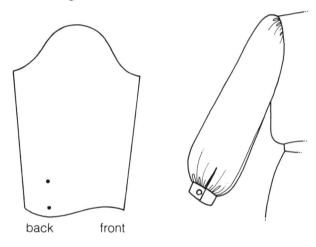

back   front

To make a faced slit opening

1 For the facing, cut a rectangle of fabric on the straight grain, 5 cm longer than the opening, and 7.5 cm wide.
2 Neaten the two longer edges and one end by edge-stitching or by swing needle, according to the thickness of the fabric.
3 Mark the centre line with chalk or a tacking stitch.

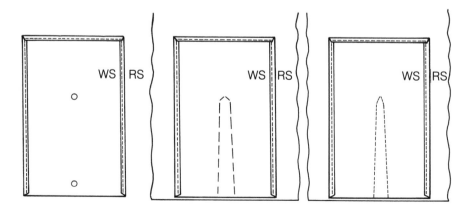

4 Apply the fabric to the garment, putting right sides together and the centre line over the mark for the opening.
   Pin and tack from 0.5 cm on one side of the centre line to 0.5 cm on the other side via the marked end of the opening.

5 Machine making a *blunt* point at the end. (If the point were to be too fine the cut would be too close to the machining, causing the raw edge to fray through the seam.)

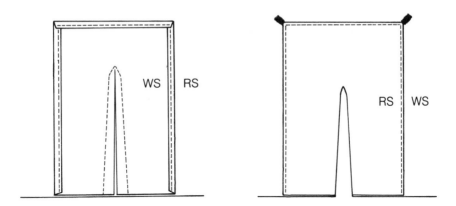

6 Cut the slit.
7 Using the iron, turn the facing through to the wrong side. Press flat.
8 Bar tack corners.

blanket (loop) stitch over threads

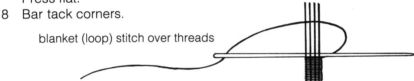

Sometimes a faced slit is used as a decorative feature on a sleeve hem, pocket, or neckline facing.

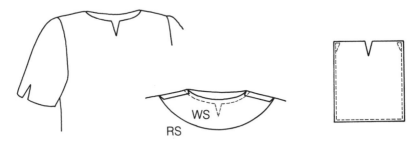

Questions

1 **Why is a faced slit opening machined to a blunt point?**
2 **What is the main difference between a faced slit and all other openings? Say where it is used and why this particular method is chosen.**

Shaped facings

A facing is one piece of fabric applied to another to back it and neaten the edge, for example on a faced slit or wrap, and facing opening, armholes, necklines and pockets. Because it takes the shape of the piece to be faced it is called a shaped facing. It may be slightly stiffened with ironed or basted interfacing where extra body is required. Correct cutting and good pressing are vital.

     Two ways of achieving a good finish are described in 4 a) and b).

▲ Try out both methods on a pair of shaped patch pockets for trousers. Evaluate each for the type of fabric you use, and draw conclusions on their merits.

To make and attach a shaped facing

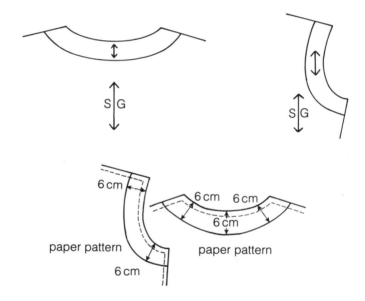

Cutting Cut the facing on the same grain as the piece to which it will fit, so that it lays quite flat. (Remember the straight grain goes from top to toe.) Make a direct copy of the edge to be faced to the depth of a line drawn exactly parallel 6 cm inwards.

1 Join facing sections. (In the diagram these are at shoulder and underarm seams.) Press seam open and trim to 0.5 cm.

2 Neaten the outer edge of the facing by edge-stitching, zig-zag or overlock according to fabric. (It is easier to neaten facings before they are attached to the garment.)

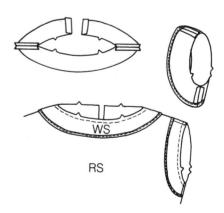

3 Matching seams and notches, place RS facing to RS garment. Pin, tack, and machine on fitting line. (Vertical pinning removes the need to tack.)

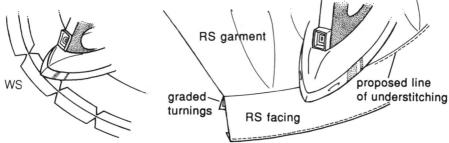

4   Snip on corners and at 1 cm intervals on curves. Press seam open carefully and trim turnings to approx. 0.5 cm, grading them to lose bulk. Then follow a) **or** b):

a) Fold exactly on the seam line, turning the facing in to the wrong side. Press well to give a crisp join not visible on either right or wrong side.

b) Press the turnings towards the facing. With facing uppermost, and leaving the garment free, machine close to the join on the facing and turnings only (understitching). This keeps the facing inside.

Both methods may be edge-stitched to give a crisper edge. Bar tack at seams to secure into position.

5   When a facing meets a zip, turn the edge of the facing in and hem it on to the stitching line of the zip.

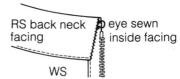

Decorative facings

A shaped facing is usually applied right sides to the garment and then turned on to the wrong side, but a contrasting right side facing can make a decorative feature. To do this apply the right side of the facing to the wrong side of the garment, so that when turned through the facing is on the outside. Finish by edge-stitching to the garment on R.S.

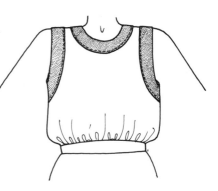

Crossway facings

The only exception to the rule about cutting on the same grain is when a crossway facing is used. This is either to make a decorative feature on a gingham pocket or as a narrow crossway facing to neaten a curved edge. In the latter case it lacks the body, crispness, and finish of a shaped facing cut on the correct grain.

Questions

1   **Describe how you would cut out a shaped facing for the armhole of a sleeveless top. Why is grain particularly important?**
2   **How can the edge of a shaped facing be made crisp and neat?**
3   **Give clear instructions for preparing and attaching a right-side facing at the lower edge of a short sleeve.**

Waistbands

The waistband is the part of the item that fits close to the body and it therefore needs to be strong. For this reason waistbands are often cut on the warp thread (parallel to the selvedge). A correctly stiffened and applied waistband is an integral part of a well-made garment. As the band fits the body, whatever fastenings are used will be exposed to some pressure, and so the choice of fastening must be carefully made, and they must be properly applied. A common fault with cheap mass-produced goods is that the fasteners tend to come off. When buying low-priced ready-made clothes it is always a good idea to reinforce the sewing of buttons, hooks, and poppers, and to fasten the ends off properly.

The width of a waistband is governed by the style of the garment, the fabric, and the figure. A wide waistband emphasizes a narrow waist on a slim figure. On a plump figure with a 'spare tyre', a wide waistband would be forced to bend or crease over, as well as being rather uncomfortable to wear, and so a narrower width is usually selected.

It is usual to put some form of interfacing or stiffening in a waistband to give it strength. With a light fabric, vilene can be used to give extra body to the waistband. Where more strength and stiffness are required, petersham or belt backing are used.

Petersham is perhaps the most common stiffening. It is sold in 25 mm and 38 mm widths, and can be boned or unboned. As petersham is often used to back the waistband, it is sold in a limited range of colours including black and white. Petersham with a rubber surface bonding holds a shirt or blouse in position in wear. This is often applied to ready-made shorts, trousers, and skirts.

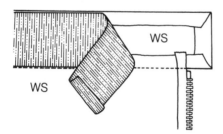 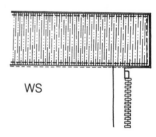

If you are setting petersham or vilene inside a waistband, it is important to secure it at both the top and bottom with a line of machining to prevent it curling up inside when washed.

Belt backing is very stiff and is used for separate belts for dresses as well as waistbands.

Whichever type of stiffening is used, a piece the length and width of the finished waistband is needed. If it is to back a band, allow 0.5 cm at each end in addition.

To stiffen and attach a waistband

1 Fold the waistband in half lengthwise and position the stiffening to the centre line.
2 Press up the turning beneath it on the seam line.

3   Shaped ends can be machined and turned through before attaching the waistband.

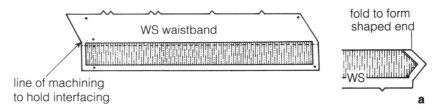

4   Using notches and tailor tacks to match the skirt, place right sides together. Pin, tack, and machine on the fitting line.

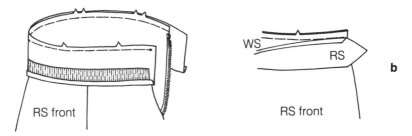

5   Press the seam open to flatten it; then trim turnings down (trimming them separately layers the fabric). Press both turnings upwards.
6   Fold the waistband in half. Bring the folded edge to the line of machining. Pin, tack, and hem.

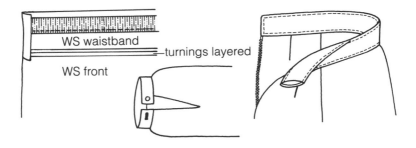

The small right-hand diagrams **a** and **b** show an alternative method for putting on a waistband, which could also be used for attaching a cuff to a long sleeve. On a cuff the usual interfacing is vilene, and buttons, press studs, or hooks and eyes may be used to fasten it.

Questions

1   **(a)   For which figure type would you consider a wide belt most suitable?**
    (b)   State *two* effects of wearing a wide contrasting belt.   (NWREB)
2   **You are making a blouse which has long sleeves gathered into a cuff.**
    (a)   Name and sketch a suitable opening for the sleeve.
    (b)   Using clearly labelled diagrams, explain how to gather the lower
          edge of the sleeve and make and attach the cuff.   (AEB, 1982)

Fastenings

Hooks and eyes

The underlap on the back of a waistband is important as it enables fastenings to hold the waistband together without themselves being seen or the skirt popping open. The eyes or bars are attached to the back section so that the hooks on the front hook on to them.

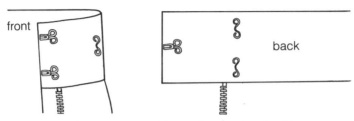

If the underlap is long a second fastening is attached in reverse on the inside, that is, with the eye on the overlap and the hook on the underlap.

Hooks and eyes are sewn on with buttonhole stitch for security in wear and in addition at the hook end the hook is sewn with several over-stitches to prevent it moving and becoming loose.

A **skirt hook** or **bar** the width of the waistband can be sewn into the seam.

Press studs

Press studs or poppers are used to keep something in place rather than to resist any pull. They are used on children's clothes, underwear, and household items, and are a quick and convenient method of fastening. Silver and black metal are both available in varying sizes. Size 00 is the finest press stud: size 4 is 1 cm in diameter and is used for furnishings and heavy-weight items.

Press studs are fastened on securely with buttonhole stitch or oversewing. The knob presses into the hole, so the knob is always on the overlap (the part that laps over), and the hole on the underlap.

Velcro

Velcro works on the principle of the burrs that we pick up on our clothes as we brush past burdock in the country. It is two layers of nylon, placed face to face. One consists of tiny hooks as on burrs, and the other has a more furry surface. When pressed together the two layers stick. This is ideal for closing openings where there is no pressure, for example pockets, cuffs, and plackets, and for attaching different badges to sports clothes to suit each occasion. Stage costumes can be changed very quickly using velcro. A wrapover skirt or kilt can be adjusted for several sizes with a strip of velcro along the waistband, and the end secured with a tie. A buckle and strap or a skirt bar is used on a kilt.

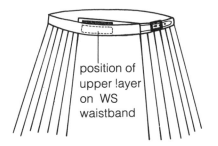

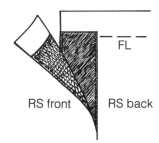

FL

RS front   RS back

Buttons

Button with shank
Used on thick fabrics for coats, blazers, and jackets to give room for two thicknesses beneath the button when fastened (see also p.130).

Covered button
Stroke fabric on to points with a pin. Then clip on the lower portion.

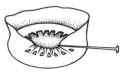

Buttons can have two or four holes: those with four are usually used on shirts. Choose the colour of button to match or contrast with the garment.
Choose the size of button to be in proportion with the item; for example, use small, neat buttons on small items such as babywear and fine fabrics. Heavier fabrics require a heavier button to secure them.

A button can be used to fasten two overlapping sections of an item, and itself form a decorative feature. Because those sections are usually double thicknesses of fabric, the button should not be sewn tightly into position. The thickness of two pins crossed under the button is usually enough to make a shank by winding cotton around it. This gives room for the thickness of the second section when the button is done up. Whip or blanket stitch the threads together on the inside.

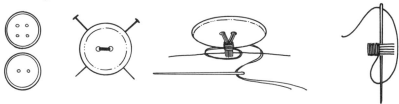

Questions

1 **Explain how you would attach hooks and eyes to fasten a long underlap on the waistband of a skirt.**
2 **Give several examples of where press studs could be used satisfactorily.**
3 **Why is velcro particularly useful for (a) sports team shirts, (b) handicapped people, (c) stage costumes?**

Worked buttonholes

All buttonholes are the diameter of the button plus the width of two fabric threads for ease. The raw edge is finished either with buttonhole stitch, or on thick fabrics, bound as a bound buttonhole (see p.198).

Buttonhole stitch is worked with the knot at the top, and so forms a very firm protective edge which withstands the button's rubbing as it is constantly fastened and unfastened.

Very close swing needle machining called **satin stitch** is used to work a buttonhole by machine (see p.197).

Vertical buttonholes are usually put on a band, and horizontal buttonholes used where two sections overlap.

On a **horizontal** buttonhole the button sits at the end nearest the edge, on the centre front line. That end is therefore made as a round end, by using an odd number of overcasting stitches (so that the one in the middle follows the line of the cut). Overcasting keeps the end smooth and neat, yet firmly shaped. What would happen if buttonhole stitch were used around the end?

The end housing the button is on the centre line, so that the button sits in the middle of the garment and it looks symmetrical. It is always at least half a button's width from the edge.

A **vertical** buttonhole is worked on the centre line and the button sits in the centre of it. Therefore the buttonhole is finished with a bar at either end.

Buttonholes are used to thread elastic through an elastic casing (see p.170). One is worked either side of the centre back seam. This is the only occasion when a buttonhole is made on single fabric. The size of the buttonhole is made to equal the width of the elastic plus two threads, and as the elastic will rub on both ends, a rounded finish is given to each end.

centre
front
line

Hand-worked buttonholes

1 A buttonhole is usually worked on fabric backed by a facing, or where a band makes the fabric double thickness. To keep the fabric together whilst working the buttonhole, machine a box the length of the buttonhole about 0.25 cm on either side of where the cut is to be. The box

should end on the centre line. A vertical buttonhole would be machined 0.25 cm either side of the centre line.

2 Cut along the centre thread of the buttonhole, folding in half to start the cut. Each buttonhole should be worked immediately it is cut.

3 Starting at the end furthest from centre front, buttonhole stitch along to the corner, working from left to right.

4 Overcast round the corner, making an odd number of stitches. Pass the needle through to the raw edge.

5 Buttonhole stitch along the remaining side of the buttonhole.

6 Make a bar at the end and loop stitch along it without sewing into the material. Whip the bar on the wrong side. Press.

A vertical buttonhole is worked in the same way, with buttonhole stitch along the two sides, but with a loop-stitched bar at each end.

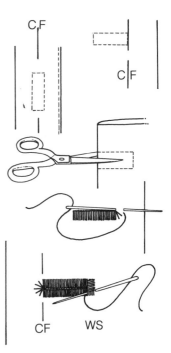

Machine-worked buttonholes

You will need a buttonhole foot.
Turn the machine to zigzag or swing needle, and turn the tension to $2\frac{1}{2}$.
Put the needle in the left-hand position.
Set the stitch length at 0.3. Stitch width 2 or 4 and length 0.3 gives a good satin stitch.

1 Turn stitch width to 4; lock, then turn to 2.
Sew down one side of the buttonhole. Finish with the needle *in* the material on R.H. side. Lift presser foot.

2 Turn material round. Put presser foot down.
Take needle out. Alter stitch width to 4.
Hold material towards you and make a bar tack using 3 or 4 stitches.
Finish with the needle *out*.

3 Turn width to 2. Stitch along second side.
Stop with the needle out.

4 Bar tack on 4.
Finish with needle *out*. Unlock width catch.

5 Turn to 0. Fasten off.

The needle would break if it were left in the material when altering stitches.

Questions

1 **Investigate and explain the size and position of buttonholes for the front fastening of a cotton shirt.**

2 **What is the purpose of a shank?**
For what fabric or garment might a button with a shank be used?

3 **Evaluate the handworking of a buttonhole with one done by machine.**

Bound buttonholes

These are used on thick fabrics, mainly on outer garments.

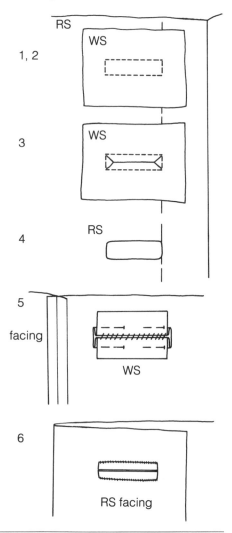

1   Cut a piece of fabric for each buttonhole.
    Width: the button diameter plus 3 cm.
    Depth: 5 cm approximately.
    Mark the position of the buttonholes.
2   Leaving the facing hanging free, place the piece RS together with the single fabric of the garment. Tack along the buttonhole.
    Machine a box 0.5 cm deep and the diameter of the button plus two threads.
3   Cut along the buttonhole, snipping out towards each corner.
4   Using the iron and a damp cloth to press well, post the facing through the 'post box'.
5   Turn to the inside of the garment and fold a pleat to the centre line of the buttonhole.
    Pin and oversew with tacks to hold in position.
6   Place the facing in position.
    Carefully snip the buttonhole along the line of the cut and out towards the corners.
    Turn this under, and tack along the buttonhole facing.
    Closely hem the facing into position.
    Press well.
    Undo the tackings.

Questions

1   **In what circumstances would you make a bound buttonhole in preference to a worked one? Suggest garments and fabrics on which you would use bound buttonholes.**
2   **Explain carefully how to snip and press the buttonhole when the facing has been attached. Why is it important to tack the buttonhole closed after it has been turned through?**
3   **What faults might cause a bound buttonhole to fray at the corners? How can this be prevented?**

Pockets

Bound pockets

A bound pocket opening is made in exactly the same way as steps 2 to 5 for the bound buttonhole (p.198). Sometimes the piece is used as the inside of the pocket (see diagram) and a further pocket-shaped piece is then attached to make the pocket complete.

RS inside of pocket

WS pocket facing

Patch pockets

A patch pocket can be both practical and decorative. Above all it must be sewn on securely, as use of the pocket and the weight of its contents can force it away from the garment. One line of machining is not strong enough to stand the strain of regular use. Therefore a safety triangle should be machined across the top or a double line of stitching used.

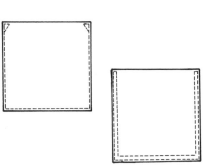

Patch pockets are easy to construct. Right-angled corners should be mitred, and curved turnings clipped to reduce bulk.

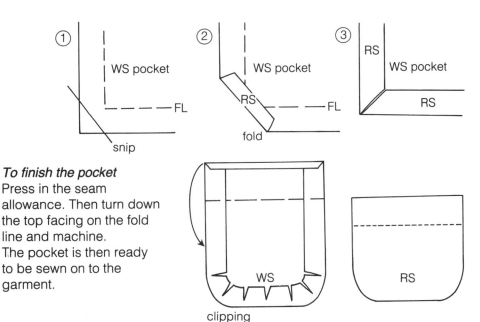

① WS pocket — FL — snip

② WS pocket RS — FL — fold

③ RS WS pocket RS

To finish the pocket
Press in the seam allowance. Then turn down the top facing on the fold line and machine.
The pocket is then ready to be sewn on to the garment.

WS — clipping

RS

Seam pockets

A pocket sewn into a seam can be both practical and invisible. It can be cut as part of the pattern or may be joined on after cutting out.

    When the two side seams are joined together the pocket is pressed towards the front, and so a snip has to be made and neatened to allow the side seam to be pressed open. For this reason, and because it is more economical to cut out, the pocket pieces are sometimes cut separately and joined.

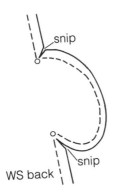

Hip pockets

A hip pocket can be made with a facing to neaten the curved edge. The pocket back is then joined RS together with the facing, along the notched edges. The free edge of the pocket back then completes the side seam.

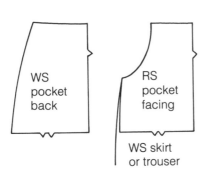

Questions

1 **Why do the tops of patch pockets need to be strengthened?**
2 **(a)** **Briefly describe _two_ ways of strengthening the tops of patch pockets.**
  (b) **Draw a diagram of the finished appearance of _each_ method described.** (WJEC)
3 **(a)** **Name _four_ types of pockets.**
  (b) **Draw and label one.** (SEREB)
▲ 4 **Using paper make a 1.5 cm turning on two adjacent sides and mitre the corner.**

Necklines

A shaped facing can be used to finish a number of interesting necklines.

Before buying the dress or pattern, ask yourself:
Have you got a long, medium, or short neck, or sloping shoulders?
Which figure features do you want to emphasize or conceal?

A **V-neckline** can be used to make the neck look longer. The **bateau** (boat) shape tends to make the eye travel across. It can be quite a low neckline.

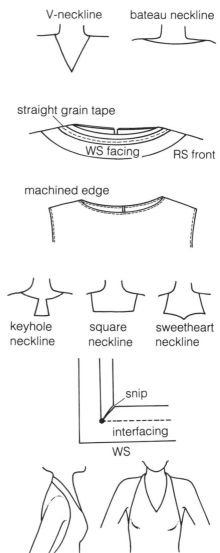

V-neckline   bateau neckline

Notice that the seam with the facing will be on the cross or bias grain in both these cases, so it could stretch during machining or in wear. To avoid this stretching put prussian binding or tape on the wrong side on the seam when machining. This is cut on the straight grain and therefore will not allow stretching to occur. Another way to avoid cross-cut seams stretching is to machine over the finished edge of the facing.

straight grain tape

WS facing   RS front

machined edge

Necklines change with fashion. All three of these neckline styles have sharp corners which need care.

keyhole neckline   square neckline   sweetheart neckline

To produce a neat corner
1   Machine into the corner, leave the needle in the work. Lift the presser foot and turn the work round to make the correct angle. Then continue.
2   Snip into the corner. Press the seam open and turn through.
3   Fold exactly on the machining line and press down.

snip

interfacing

WS

A **halter neckline** looks good on some people, but very fat arms, sloping shoulders, or a bony neck are better concealed by attractive fabrics.

Questions

1   **A corner of a neckline is often a weak point. Draw three examples of necklines which have corners and say how you would deal with them.**
2   **Draw collarless necklines which disguise the following figure faults: (a) a long, thin neck   (b) a very short neck.**

Collars

A facing is cut the same shape as the neckline and lies flat on it. A **Peter Pan collar** is similar in that it is double fabric following the neckline curve. It therefore sits flat on the dress. The centre back and centre front are rounded fully so that the collar does not pull away from the centre, even though it has come over the shoulder.

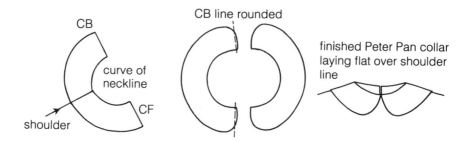

But usually a collar has 'stand'. This is achieved because it is not cut to the same shape as the neckline. It therefore does not lie flat.

A **shirt collar** is cut straight and joined on to the neckline curve.

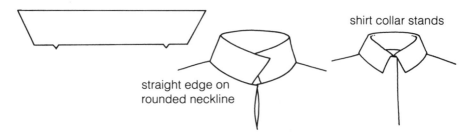

A **mandarin collar** (Chinese style) may be straight or may have a slight curve to fit more closely into the neck.

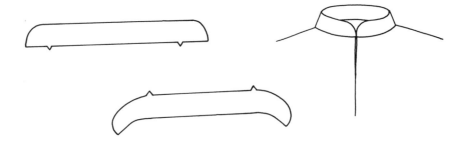

The collar is cut double. To give more stand it is stiffened with interfacing. This is attached to the wrong side of one piece. 'Iron-on' vilene is quick and useful here. 'Sew-in' vilene is tacked on. The weight is selected according to the fabric.

To make up the collar

1 Cut out the collar pieces, marking the notches on the neck edge carefully. Place the vilene on WS of one piece. Tack or iron on.
2 Machine along the fitting line. Trim 'sew-in' vilene to 3 mm.
3 Press the collar seams open. Trim turnings to 0.5 cm. Cutting separately is important as it layers the fabric (grading) and prevents a ridge showing on the right side. Snip the corner off.

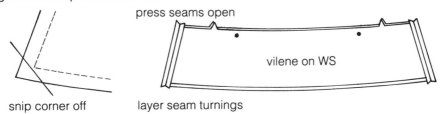

snip corner off   layer seam turnings

4 Turn through and press well on the right side. The join must not show on either side. It must be right on the edge.

To attach a collar with facings

1 Prepare the facings. Join the front and back facings at the shoulder seams. Press and neaten the outer edge of the facing.

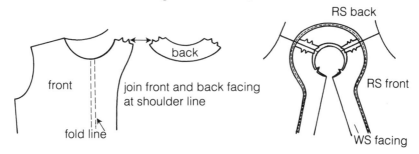

2 Place the double collar between the RS neckline and RS facing. Match the end of the collar to the centre front line. Match notches, seams, and centre back line.

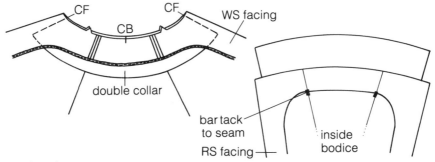

3 Pin and tack.
4 Machine round.
5 Trim, by layering. Snip the curved seam. Snip the CF corner diagonally.
6 Make a neat corner at centre front by pressing.
7 Press on right side.
8 Bar tack on shoulder seams (see p.138).

To attach a collar where there is no back facing

1 Make up the collar as before.
2 On the fitting line, machine from the fold line to centre front line. Snip on CF line.
3 Turn through to right side.
4 Pin, tack, and machine *one* side of the collar on to the neck line. Press and trim turnings.
5 Turn in the turning on the upper layer of the collar. Pin, tack, and hem into position.

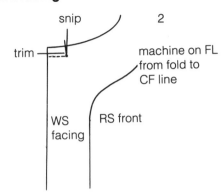

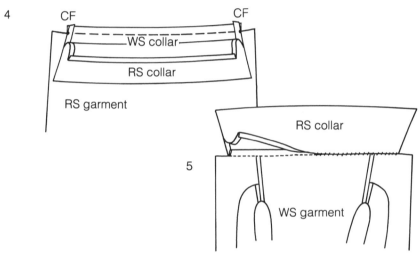

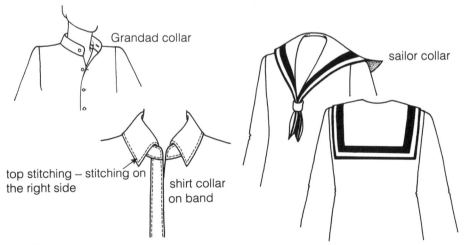

Collar fitting up to the fold line
A **grandad collar** or a collar band overlaps and fastens at the centre front with a button and horizontal buttonhole.

A **sailor collar** can be attached by either method, depending on whether or not there are facings. No snip is required as the collar meets at the centre front.

Roll collars

This method of collar attachment is used where the fabric is thick. The upper collar has further to go to bend over the under collar, so it cannot be attached to it at the neckline. That would make it poke out at the back. To make it fit snugly round the neck, attach the *under* collar to the garment and the upper collar to the facing.

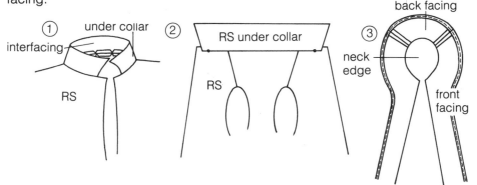

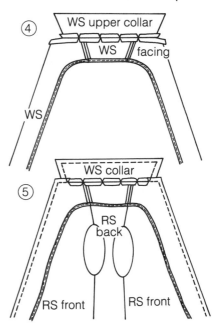

1   Interface the undercollar piece. Join it to the neckline RS together matching the notches. Snip, trim, and press the curved edge.

2   Lay collar and bodice out flat.

3   Join front and back facings at shoulder seams. Trim and press, neaten outer edge of facing.

4   Join upper collar to neck edge of facing.

5   Join upper collar and facing, right sides together with lower collar and bodice. Sew a continuous line from the left lower edge to the right lower edge. Press all seams open. Snip any curved edges if the collar is rounded. Trim off points to reduce bulk. Turn through. Press. Secure with bar tacks.

Questions

1   **Draw and name six different styles of collar.**
2   **Say how you would attach one of them when using cotton fabric.**
3   **Which method of attaching a collar would you choose when making a blazer or jacket? Why?**
4   **Why are facings so important when attaching a collar?**
5   **Why should the neck seam be trimmed and snipped well?**

Sleeves

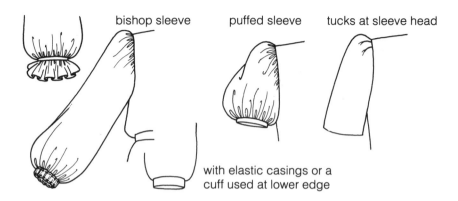

bishop sleeve

puffed sleeve

tucks at sleeve head

with elastic casings or a
cuff used at lower edge

A sleeve head is larger than an armhole. This enables the arm to move freely. The difference in the amount of fabric is dispersed by making a gathering thread and 'easing in' a tailored sleeve. Full gathers are a feature on a puffed sleeve. From time to time tucks at a sleeve head are fashionable.

Prepare the sleeve by doing as much construction as possible before it is attached to the bodice. Finish the casing, cuff, or hem at the lower edge of the sleeve.

Tailored jacket sleeves are often cut in two parts, and/or may have an elbow dart for a good fit. All this construction, and even the attachment of the lining at the cuff, is easiest whilst the sleeve is separate.

When using fabric which is the same on both sides label the right side of the sleeve front of each sleeve *before* taking it off the paper pattern. You do not want to end up with two left sleeves!

Prepare the armhole by fitting the bodice. The armhole seam line should pass over the sharp bone at the top of the arm. Adjust the seam line if necessary by marking with chalk. This avoids the sleeve hanging below the shoulder line.

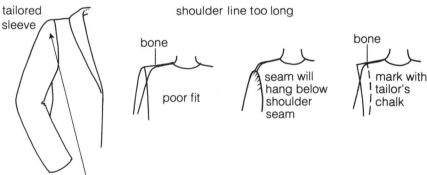

tailored
sleeve

shoulder line too long

bone

poor fit

seam will
hang below
shoulder
seam

bone

mark with
tailor's
chalk

no sign of fullness – difference between armhole and sleeve head eased in

To insert the sleeve

1   Turn the bodice inside out. Put the sleeve inside the armhole with right sides together. Match seams, tailor tacks, and notches. Pin around the lower armhole using vertical pins.

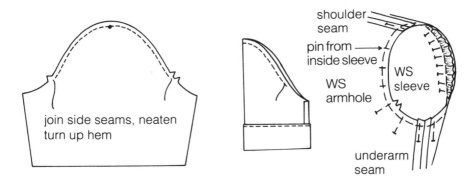

join side seams, neaten turn up hem

shoulder seam
pin from — inside sleeve
WS sleeve
WS armhole
underarm seam

2 Draw up the gathering thread around the sleeve head evenly and wind around a pin at both ends. Pin the gathers down evenly. Tack. Try on the item to check the fit. Each shoulder is slightly different. Too long a shoulder line is illustrated opposite. Too much taken off the shoulder line makes the sleeve too tight in the armhole.
3 Machine on the fitting line. A tailored sleeve should be smooth and have no gathers or puckers on the right side.
4 Neaten the armhole seam by trimming and swing needle, by binding or by self neatening.

Raglan sleeves

A raglan sleeve joins right up to the neck line, has a dart on the shoulder line, and sloping seams with the bodice back and front. The corner seam requires strengthening with tape.

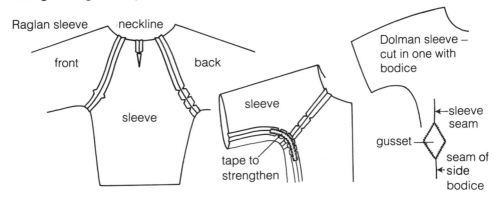

Raglan sleeve   neckline
front   back
sleeve
tape to strengthen

Dolman sleeve – cut in one with bodice
sleeve
←sleeve seam
gusset
seam of ←side bodice

Dolman sleeves

A dolman sleeve is cut in one piece with the bodice. The underarm seam and sleeve seam are continuous. The corner needs strengthening with tape. Knitted fabrics are elastic enough to stretch to allow free arm movement, but woven fabrics require a gusset in the seam under the arm.

Questions

1 **Why is the sleeve head bigger than an armhole? How can the fullness be disposed of?**
2 **Name three different types of sleeve. How do they differ?**

Hems

A hem is one of the last processes to be done on a garment. To give a complete line, facings on slits and pleats have to be folded *after* the hem has been completed, but apart from these, construction is usually complete when the hem is reached.

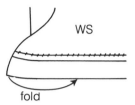

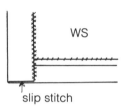

The garment hangs from the waistband, shoulder, or yoke. Where fabric is hanging on the cross it may drop. Hang flared, gored, or circular skirts for at least 24 hours before measuring the hem up. This allows the fabric to drop before wearing it. Then use a skirt marker to get a level line, or get a friend to help, or fit the dress on a body model.

How much fabric should be turned up?

1 The hem allowance given on a pattern should be just right if you *checked* and adjusted the length *beforehand*. Consider the total look of the garment when fitting the pattern *before* cutting out.
   Adjust the length at the pattern alteration lines – not by chopping off the lower section of the skirt. To do that would alter the shape and width of the skirt. You chose the style as it looked on the picture, so keep it that way!

2 On children's clothes it is usual and useful to have a deep hem. The item will last longer as the child grows.

3 Adult fashions in hem length change, so there are times when we may want to lengthen or shorten an existing hem.

4 A deep hem gives a skirt weight and improves the hang.

Hang a skirt on the cross – it will drop

Don't shorten by chopping the bottom off...

It's a different skirt!

Where the skirt or trouser is straight, this presents no problems, but such items as a gored skirt, a circular skirt, or flared trousers increase in width towards the lower edge.

On trousers this is often put right by the pattern being shaped inwards below the hem edge – another reason for checking the length *before* cutting out. However as the hem is turned up, the fullness can be dealt with in two ways:

1 For curved woollen hems. Hang for two days for fabric to drop. Mark hemline. Run a gathering thread 0.5 cm from raw edges between the seams. Pin at seams. Draw up threads to make the hem lie flat. Remove pins from seams. Shrink away fullness with a damp cloth. (This is not a satisfactory method on synthetics. Why? (p.136). Attach bias binding and slip hem.

2 Match the seams and centres of panels carefully, and make small tucks in the hem to remove the fullness. This can be done neatly on light and medium-weight fabrics. It looks clumsy, and shows through on heavier materials. Remember the deeper the hem, the greater the difference will be between the hem line width and edge of fabric width. Therefore, where a style increases in width towards the hem, avoid a deep hem.

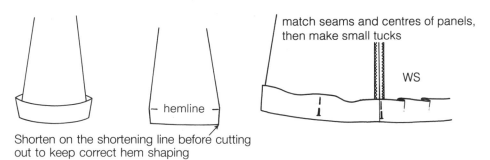

Shorten on the shortening line before cutting out to keep correct hem shaping

When turning up a hem consider these factors, and place them in order of importance:

growth   style of skirt
fashion   fabric/fabric weight

Then decide on the appropriate method and depth of hem to use.

How to turn up a hem

A hem on a straight skirt is not going to drop. If you check the length before cutting out, the hem allowance can be measured and pinned up using the iron and ironing board. Simply match the seams carefully and the hem will hang well.

A curved hem requires more attention. First hang it for at least 24 hours. Then try the garment on and use a skirt marker to give a level hem line. Lay the skirt out. Unless growth is a vital factor, allow a maximum of 5 cm for a curved hem, and carefully trim the excess away, so that an even turning is left.

Two simple methods of securing a hem have already been dealt with elsewhere:

1 Wundaweb on p.146.
2 Blind-hemming by machine on p.129.

There are three other methods. In every case the aim is the same: to achieve a smooth invisible finish on the right side.

3   On *fine cotton fabrics* make a small turning of 0.5 cm or 1 cm. Press and edge stitch. Slip hem to secure.

4   On *wools, medium or heavyweight fabrics*:

a   For straight hems, overlock or swing needle, or attach **Paris binding** (mercerized cotton on straight grain) to neaten the edge. (A second turning would be too bulky.) Herringbone or slip hem to secure.

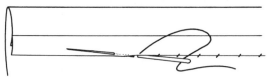

b   On curved hems, overlock or swing needle or attach bias binding. More elasticity is needed on the curve. Slip hem into position.

To achieve a smooth invisible finish

As usual, select thread which has the same elasticity as the fabric. Use polyester on knitteds. Use a matching colour and small stitches, and never pull hemming stitches too tightly. Hand-sewing should be invisible on the right side. Do not give a final press over the line of stitching as this would create a visible edge on the right side.

A very long narrow hem such as on a frill or circular skirt should be secured by machine. It is unlikely to have to be altered. Machining is time-saving and neat.

Lengthening a hem

When altering hems, unpick and wash to remove the original hem line. When dealing with a garment that cannot be washed, use wet string with the iron to remove the unwanted line. The dampness pressed along the old fold line removes the crease.

A **false hem** is often used on children's clothes. It is fabric added on the same grain as the original. The join can form the hem line and therefore be invisible, or even more length can be added by concealing the join with ricrac braid and making it a decorative feature.

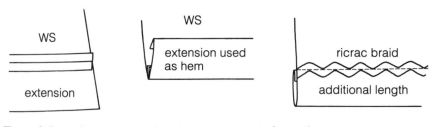

A **French hem** is one turned to the right side for decoration. It may be a false hem or may simply be used to reveal an interesting effect of the 'other side' of a fabric.

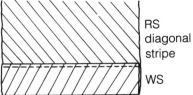

Hems with lace

Lace forms a delicate edging to underwear. In this method of attaching → it no turning is necessary (see p.127). Why is this method particularly suitable for underwear?

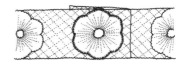

Machine stitch: width 2
length 0.3

Alternatively a narrow double turning can be made and gathered lace attached with one line of machining. This method is used on sleeve edges and handkerchieves.

Cotton lace has a gathering thread which may be drawn up to the correct size and the **lace join** made before attaching the trimming to the garment. A lace join is quite a skilled and interesting job. Match the lace pattern exactly by laying the two pieces to be joined, one over the other. Oversew right across the lace from one side to the other and back, following exactly the pattern line. Trim the remaining edges off with sharp embroidery scissors.

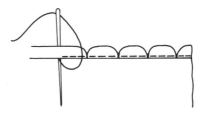

Lace may be cotton or synthetic. Choose lace to match the fabric, so that it sits well on the garment and will withstand the washing and ironing the fabric receives. Do not put nylon lace on cotton fabric.

Shell edging is a decorative feature used on underwear, nightwear, and dainty silk blouses. Turn (or roll between the fingers) a very narrow double turning. Secure the hem with three running stitches, then one (or two) at right angles over the edge. This can also be done by machine.

Questions

1 **Why should a flared or circular skirt be hung up for 24 hours before the hem line is levelled?** (SEREB)
2 **State *four* points to remember when making a hem in order to make a good finish.** (SEREB)
3 **How would you secure the hem of:**
   (a) a thick woollen skirt
   (b) a lightweight cotton dress
   (c) the frill round the bottom of a nylon satin nightdress? (EMREB)
4 **(a) Name *two* instances when the attaching of a 'false hem' might be useful.**
   (b) Using labelled diagrams, show how a 'false hem' can be attached to a garment. (EMREB)

Renovations

Giving new life (renovating)

1 Clothes and fabrics are rather expensive to discard when fashions change.
2 Fabrics bought because they are serviceable can outlive their appeal.
3 Though you tire of them some fabrics may be too attractive to throw away. Their appeal re-asserts itself when used for something different. There are endless possibilities for all forms of creative work, from the textiles in your home.

▲ Find an exciting use for some discarded textile.
Investigate the properties of the fabric and match them to a use in leisure, household items or clothes.

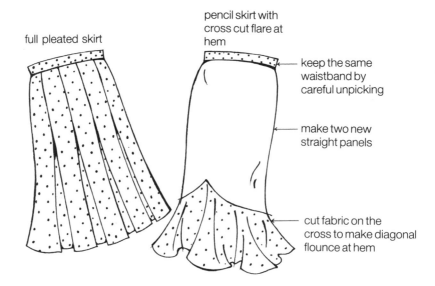

full pleated skirt

pencil skirt with cross cut flare at hem

— keep the same waistband by careful unpicking

— make two new straight panels

— cut fabric on the cross to make diagonal flounce at hem

- introducing a matching or contrasting colour
- changing the colour: dyeing, tie-dyeing, or using fabric paint.

General points

1 Make a smaller item. For example, use coat fabric for a new skirt; make a dress into children's wear.
2 Incorporate some of the existing features into the renovation. Coat pockets can be used in the style of the skirt. This uses fabric wisely and saves unpicking.
3 Take out only what is really necessary. Undoing is a daunting task. Streamline the process by cutting off a waistband to release the pleats. The hem is easy to let down by snipping the slip hemming at intervals.

4 Pleats, gathers, and full sleeves give a lot of fabric.
5 Wash the fabric to remove hem or pleat marks and seam lines, and to shrink it.
6 When using a paper pattern, watch the straight grain line of the fabric. Place the largest pattern pieces on the biggest sections first. Then fit the others in.
7 Incorporate other discarded matching or contrasting fabric. This gives a novel effect and increases the amount of fabric available.
8 Decorate plain fabrics with machine embroidery, piping, lace or paint. Use your inventive powers and initiative in creating new items from old.

open pleats to give fabric or use again

coat fabric

add new fabric

child's hat, coat, trousers

waistband removed for sundress

▲ Look around your wardrobe. You will find something which you haven't worn for years.
Think of as many ideas as you can using that garment to make:
(a) a new fashion item for yourself,
(b) something attractive for the house,
(c) a child's garment.
Carry out one of your ideas and cost it.
Compare it with the price of a ready-made product.

Questions

1 **You are helping with the infant school Nativity play. What old household items could you use to make the costumes? Sketch your ideas, and say how you would make the clothes for the Nativity characters and the angels.**
2 **Patterned and plain fabrics team well together. Suggest how you might make a discarded dress (perhaps your school dress when you leave) into an attractive wearable garment by teaming it with some fresh material.**
3 **Investigate possibilities for renovating an old blazer or pullover.**

Repairs

From time to time fabrics are damaged or worn and need repair. The repair must restore strength and be as invisible as possible. Therefore:

1 Make the repair extend on to strong material around the damaged area.
2 Use matching type and colour of thread and fabric.
3 Follow the grain of the fabric. Cut a patch straight by a thread, or darn following the knitting line.
   Simple repairs by bonding have been dealt with on p.146. Other methods are given here.

On a **printed woven fabric** the repair may be made invisible by using the pattern to conceal it.

1 Select a spare piece of fabric with identical markings to the damaged part. This can be cut from an inside facing and replaced by plain fabric, or left-over fabric can be used.
2 Cut the patch so that it will cover the hole completely *and* reach to strong fabric on each side. Also allow for a 0.5 cm turning all round. Cut the patch straight by a thread.
3 Press in the turnings to the wrong side.

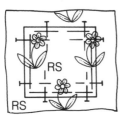

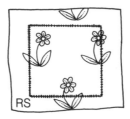

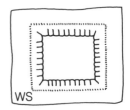

4 Pin and tack to right side, matching pattern carefully.

5 Oversew.

6 On wrong side, cut away the worn section and loop stitch or swing needle the edges.

On a **plain fabric** the patch cannot be concealed by the pattern of the fabric so a **household or calico patch** is used. This makes the patch as small as possible on the right side.

1 Cut the patch on the straight grain as before, but press the turnings on to the right side.

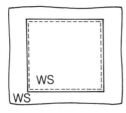

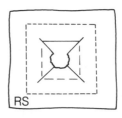

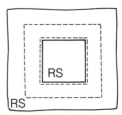

2 Pin, tack, and machine or hem on wrong side.

3 Turn to right side. Cut away worn fabric to leave small turnings. Snip corners.

4 Turn under, making square corners. Pin, tack, and machine or hem down.

A worn linen or cotton sheet can be turned 'sides to middle', cutting out the worn middle area and joining the two sides with a double stitched seam. This makes a narrower strong sheet. The side edges can be turned as hems and machined.

Flannel patch

Some fabrics are too thick to allow turnings to be taken. To repair a hole in blanket, tweed, or other heavyweight fabrics, three-step zigzag or swing needle may be used to neaten the edges of the patch cut on the straight grain. This prevents fraying. This method of patching is shown on p.128.

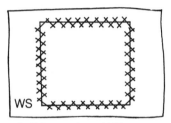
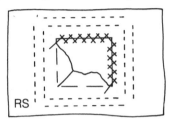

1   Attach RS patch to WS garment. Pin, tack, and herringbone stitch, turning corners neatly.

2   Turn to RS. Cut the fabric away from the edge of the patch. Herringbone stitch into position.

Darning

A protruding nail can pull fabric and tear it in a right angle along the warp and weft. A hedgetear darn is needed. This can be done by hand or machine.

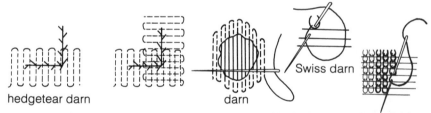

hedgetear darn   darn   Swiss darn

Knitted items can be darned following the line of knit. To allow for washing, leave a small loop at each end. Work the darn up and down. Then weave across the threads.

A more invisible darn called a **Swiss darn** can be made. This resembles the appearance of the knitted stitches more closely and is used on special items. For machine darning, see page 130.

Questions

1   **Choose a suitable method and make an illustrated plan of action to:**
    (a)   strengthen a thinning area at the elbow of a hand-knitted jumper
    (b)   camouflage the original fold line of the hem of a sundress which has been lengthened. Justify your solutions over other methods.
2   **How would you repair a scorch mark burned right out of a new calico ironing-board cover?**
3   **Describe with the aid of a diagram how you would mend a hole in your sock, explaining how you would ensure that the darn did not show, pull, or form another hole later.**

Linings

Interlining

An under- or interlining is cut exactly as the main fabric of a garment and sewn with it. An interlining may be used to give support and strength; to add body; or simply to show through an open fabric like lace, giving an opaque quality or an attractive background colour.

Interlining may be non-woven, woven, or knitted. A **non-woven** interlining is cheaper to produce and can be cut very economically because there is no grain. Further details about **vilene**, a non-woven interlining, can be found on p.28 (construction) and p.146 (use).

The term **interfacing** is used when only part of a garment, for example a shaped or front facing, is stiffened.

Woven or **knitted** interlinings must be cut on the same grain as the garment. Suitable woven interlinings for lightweight fabrics are organza, which gives stiffness; or mull, muslin, or lawn. These latter three add body, but give a softer handle. All four are used on lightweight dresses, blouses, and evening wear.

Coat canvas is used for medium and heavier weight fabrics, particularly in tailoring. There are a number of weights and qualities from which to choose. Linen, cotton, wool, and the man-made fibres are all used to make this fabric nowadays. It is important when selecting interlining fabric to choose one which will have similar properties to the main fabric. Otherwise it will hang and behave differently, causing pulling and puckering, particularly when the garment is laundered or cleaned.

Lining

A lining is made separately from the garment. Its purpose is:

1. To keep a garment in good shape. Loosely woven or knitted fabrics are likely to 'seat' or bag out of shape. Unsightly wrinkles may form as the fabric is stretched in wear. A lining provides a firm base and prevents this happening.
2. To neaten and finish the inside of jackets, coats, and skirts.
3. To add a decorative touch. The colour and pattern of attractive fabric enhances the inside of a workbox, beach bag, or jewel box.

Suitable fabrics
Fine silky-type woven fabrics are suitable. Acetate; viscose, satin, or taffeta are reasonably priced, smooth, and add no bulk. Polyester, tricel, and nylon may be used.

Construction

The lining may be cut using the garment pattern minus facings, and with a shorter hem line. French seams are used for smoothness.

To line a skirt
A skirt can be lined halfway down, fully lined, or lined across the back only. The lining is attached to the skirt at the waist, before the band is put on.

1. Make up the lining using French seams. Leave an opening for the zip. Take care! A side opening is on the left-hand side, with the *right side of the*

lining facing inwards. The hem may be turned up and machined approximately 4 cm shorter than the skirt length. It is *not* sewn to the skirt.

2 Lay the lining over the skirt *wrong sides together* and pin at the waist edge. Make sure the lining fits easily, or it will pull the skirt on the right side.

3 Pin the folded opening edge along the zip, and oversew or make running stitches to prevent the raw edge catching in the zip.

4 Attach the skirt waistband. The lining may be attached to the skirt at the seams by 2 cm bar tacks. It can then still move freely from the skirt.

To line a jacket

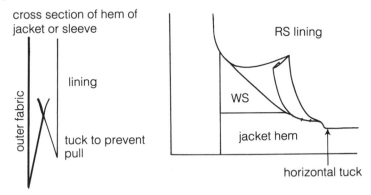

Position the lining at the neckline, making a centre back tuck to prevent pulling the outer fabric. Match the folded edge of the lining to approximately 1 cm from the inner edge of the facing, spreading the lining flat inside the garment. Match shoulder seams and darts before pinning. To avoid pulling the main fabric, make a horizontal tuck along the hemline. Attach the lining by slip hemming.

To line a sleeve

A made-up sleeve lining can be machined to the sleeve at the wrist edge. Press a horizontal tuck along the wrist. Draw the lining up the armhole leaving the tuck to prevent the lining pulling the sleeve in wear. Using a gathering thread on the sleeve head, secure the sleeve lining to the bodice lining at the armhole seam by oversewing.

Questions

1 **Suggest some interesting examples of how a fabric could be changed in colour and texture by an interlining. Think of some decorative uses of interlinings on beach bags, household items, or disco clothes.**

2 **Name some different types of interlining and say with what fabrics you would use each of them.**

3 **(a) Give the names of *three* fabrics suitable for use as linings.**
 (b) What are the purposes of linings?
 (c) During the construction of a skirt how would you:
   (i) attach a lining
   (ii) finish the hem of a lining
   (iii) neaten the lining at the zip-closure opening
   (iv) attach the lining to the skirt at the seams?

Efficiency in textile work

Short cuts

Electric scissors, fabric markers, tailor's chalk, iron-on interfacing, the iron, the swing-needle machine, the overlock, and modern fabrics can reduce what would once have been several evenings' work into a few hours.

1 Understand your machine and how it can save time.
2 Understand your fabrics, what they will do, and how they will drape. Fraying or slippery fabrics are more time-consuming than firm, closely woven or knitted ones.
3 Easy-to-sew patterns are those with few sections and therefore fewer seams and processes. (Use these on suede and leather too.)
4 Tailor's chalk and vertical pinning reduce time in preparatory work.
5 Do all similar processes together, for example all darts on both top and skirt sections, all gathering features, and so on.
6 Keep the iron handy and *use* it.
7 Sew as many processes as possible while the fabric is flat, as this makes for easier, quicker work. That is the way it is done in industry. You can go ahead with confidence if you have checked the pattern measurements and made appropriate alterations *beforehand*. Inserting the zip or putting on a collar are simplified when handled flat.

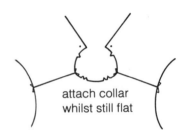

attach collar whilst still flat

Further adventures in textile work

Spend time looking at fashion and clothes in shops. Then design and decorate your own. You can put your own stamp of originality on the clothes you make. Piping, ricrac braid, ribbon, other trimmings, and machine embroidery can alter the appearance of a basic pattern.

A **multi-size pattern** gives several sizes in one. It is therefore possible to have a more personal fit.

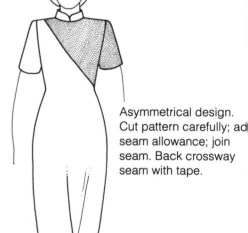

Asymmetrical design. Cut pattern carefully; add seam allowance; join seam. Back crossway seam with tape.

Altering style

Patterns are too expensive to use once only. When you have a pattern that fits well, make a template of it in thin card to use as a basic block. Then draw out a paper pattern in greaseproof paper, alter the style, and use it again and again.

To draw a shaped neckline

1 Cut out a greaseproof paper pattern folded on the centre front line. (This removes the button extension or front opening from the original pattern.)
2 Draw in a new neckline. Cut it. Open the paper out and try it against the body to find a satisfactory shape.
3 Add 1.5 cm turning.
4 Cut a facing pattern 6 cm wide by drawing a line 6 cm from the edge parallel to the new neckline. Mark turnings on the facing too.

Sleeves can be replaced by facings.
Pleats can be added by increasing the pattern width for a box pleat.
Cut new features on the same grain as the original.
To change the style of the skirt or the bodice, use one from another dress, or draft your own.

To draw a circular skirt pattern

1 Decide on the finished length you want, say 60 cm.
Take a large sheet of brown paper or newspaper. Draw a quarter circle 11 cm radius in one corner.
2 Measure 62 cm from the line all around the $\frac{1}{4}$ circle.
Join the dots carefully. This is now one quarter of a circular skirt. Cut four.
A half-circle skirt is made similarly, beginning with a 22 cm radius to make a half circle pattern. Cut two.

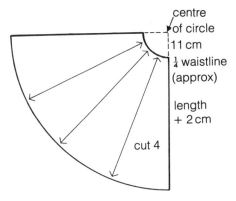

new necklines   make facing pattern

CF   CF

10–12 cm extension

back

join at centre back seam
fold to form pleat ⟶

centre
of circle
11 cm
$\frac{1}{4}$ waistline
(approx)

length
+ 2 cm

cut 4

Questions

1 **Fashions change quickly. Give illustrated notes of your plan of action to solve these problems:**
   (a) Convert a straight skirt with a front slit into a straight skirt with a 10 cm (4″) inverted pleat.
   (b) Make a neck facing for a round-necked dress with no collar.
   (c) Shorten a flared skirt by 5 cm (2″). (London)
2 **Asymmetrical styles (that is, styles where right and left sides are different) add interest and originality to clothes.**
   Sketch an asymmetrical styled dress. Name the fabric chosen and give the width. State the occasion for which the dress would be worn. Give your reasons. With the aid of a diagram, indicate the points to be considered when laying out the pattern for this dress. (AEB, 1982)

Working to a brief

Brief: Design and make a textile item for your room

Analysis	Answers to identify human needs and material factors.
Who?	Self. Use of room? Sleeping, studying, hobbies. What is needed?
Why?	To complement decor of room? Functional? Decorative?
Where?	Aspect of room (e.g. facing north)? Existing decor?
When?	Complete item in time available. Room in continual use – evening, night, morning.
How used?	Could be functional e.g. shoe rack or curtain. Could be decorative e.g. wall hanging.
What?	Decide on priority of human need: a new duvet cover and valance will have the greatest effect on the room. It may be cheaper to make than buy. It can be completed in the time available.

Specification

Warm cheerful colour, attractive design, to complement decor.
Fabric: resilient, preshrunk, easy care, hardwearing.

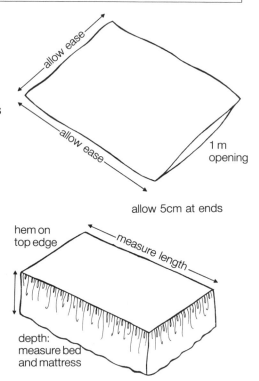

allow ease

allow ease

1 m opening

allow 5cm at ends

hem on top edge

measure length

depth: measure bed and mattress

1   **Investigations** Take measurements of duvet (with ease) and bed (with mattress).
Sketch preliminary design. Calculate fabric required.
Duvet cover: width × twice length + 5 cm + turnings.
Valance: Base = width × length of mattress + turnings.
Gathered frill = depth required + hem + turnings.

2   **Research** Read catalogues and visit shops to look at fabrics and ready made items to compare costs.

3   **Experiments** Design experiments to test fabrics for safety, wear, durability, etc. Consider cost as well.

4   **Use the evidence to make your choice** Think about safety while weighing up the evidence. You might decide on polyester cotton.

5   Check widths available and costs. Plan layout of fabric using scale paper 1 mm to 1 cm. Estimate quantity of fabric and cost.

6   The next stage is to develop the design. Investigate: cost, position, and type of fastenings e.g. velcro or popper tape and the size and position of openings.

Formulate a plan of action

List equipment and processes.

Possibilities

(a) French seams.
(b) Plain seam neatened by zigzag.
(c) Plain, turn through and top stitch.

List the decorative as well as the construction processes.
Decorative piping – consider your ability and your time.
Gathering – can be unwieldy so think about working in sections.
Valance hem – very long and straight so should be done before gathering.

Order of processes

1 Cut out both items.

Duvet cover

2 Seam RS together leaving an opening of 1m at one end.
3 Press in 5 cm seam allowance on opening.
4 Turn through to RS and press.
5 Attach velcro or popper tape to inside of each edge by machine.
6 Topstitch to encase raw edges.

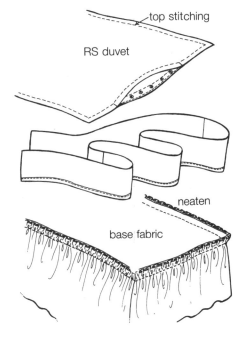

Valance

2 Seam valance pieces into one length.
3 Work hem (easier whilst flat).
4 Gather top edge in three sections using the machine (difficult to handle large amount).
5 Draw up. Space gathers evenly.
6 Place RS together with base. Pin and tack.
7 Machine. Neaten raw edges with swing needle.
   Finish hem on top end of base.

Preliminary evaluation

Consider any pressure or strain in use: strengthen ends of opening.

Realization

Note any difficulties e.g. gathering lines would be easier divided into four parts.

Evaluation

Does it fit the specification? Does it complement the decor?
If you were starting again would you make any changes?
Was it completed in the time available?
Compare cost with ready-made item (if available).
What have you learned?

Further work on Chapter 8

▲1 Research and experiment to find openings suitable for use on (a) a viyella dress (b) the front of a polyester cotton shirt. Mount your attempts. State what problems you found with the methods you rejected.

▲2 Necklines change continually with fashion (p.201).
    (a) Use the scale patterns on page 113 to show how to make a pattern for a neckline of your choice. (First, remove the front facing by cutting down the centre line to make half a front. Label it 'place to fold'.)
    (b) Draw labelled diagrams to show how you would prepare, neaten, and attach a shaped facing to the neckline.
    (c) Suggest suitable interfacings to give body, and to prevent stretching.

▲3 What are the human needs involved in the choice of fastenings? Investigate where you might position and how you might apply fastenings to: (a) help a toddler learn (b) a cyclist's rain cape (c) a disabled woman's dress.

▲4 Carry out a piece of investigative work to find a suitable design for the pocket in a waiter's apron; the back pocket of hipster trousers; a seam pocket in a full skirt.
Explain the needs on which you base your design in each case.
Explain in detail how you would work one pocket.

▲5 Devise a series of experiments to find the most suitable type of button hole for a shirt-blouse in slippery polyester jersey fabric. Make an illustrated plan of work to show how you would carry out your chosen method. Justify your choice over those methods you rejected.

▲6 Sketch and develop a design for a leisurewear shirt incorporating a collar without a band. Investigate and suggest suitable fabrics. Name appropriate interfacings and thread for each possibility.
Select the most suitable way to attach the collar. Work out a plan of action. Give precise details of the method you have chosen for making and attaching the collar.

▲7 The hem on a garment helps it to look attractive and hang well. Select a suitable method and explain how you would work the following hems:
(a) on a child's cotton dress (b) on a pencil skirt in trevira (c) on a nylon satin circular skirt (d) on denim jeans.

8 What factors must be considered when choosing fabric and haberdashery for nightwear? Sketch sleepwear for your younger sister who likes lace.

▲ Experiment to find the best method for making a lace join.
Make a brief plan of action for making the sleepwear. Explain in detail the best method of attaching the lace trimming to your design.

9 Name five ways in which physical ability changes with age.
Give an example of a design feature in clothing which suits a person's ability in each case.

Crossway strips (p. 111)

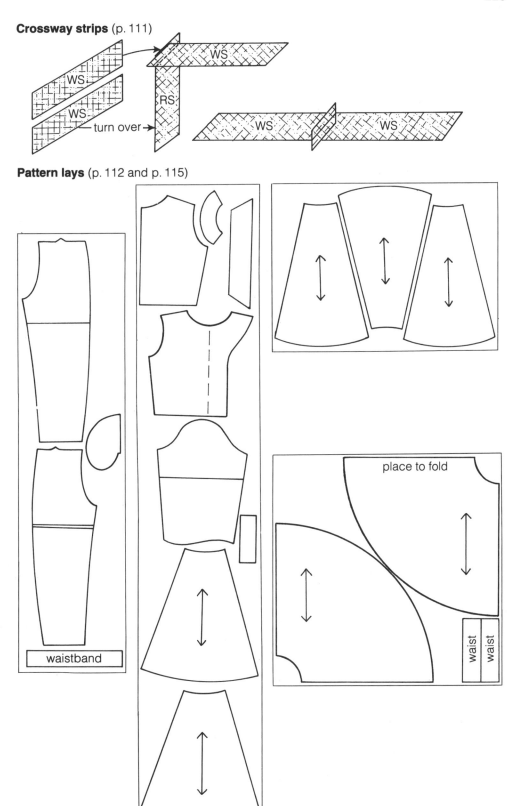

Pattern lays (p. 112 and p. 115)

Index